EXERCISES, CASES, AND READINGS

MANAGEMENT
APPLICATIONS

John T. Samaras

PRENTICE HALL

Englewood Cliffs, New Jersey 07632

Prentice-Hall International (UK) Limited, *London*
Prentice-Hall of Australia Pty. Limited, *Sydney*
Prentice-Hall Canada Inc., *Toronto*
Prentice-Hall Hispanoamericana, S.A., *Mexico*
Prentice-Hall of India Private Limited, *New Delhi*
Prentice-Hall of Japan, Inc., *Tokyo*
Simon & Schuster Asia Pte. Ltd., *Singapore*
Editora Prentice-Hall do Brasil, Ltda., *Rio de Janeiro*

Dedicated
to
Management Students
Wherever They Are

MANAGEMENT APPLICATIONS: EXERCISES, CASES, AND READINGS

John T. Samaras
Central State University

TABLE OF CONTENTS

PREFACE

PART ONE: INTRODUCTION TO MANAGEMENT

Exercises

Cases

Readings

PART TWO: PLANNING AND DECISION MAKING

Exercises

Cases

Readings

PART THREE: ORGANIZING FOR STABILITY AND CHANGE

Exercises

Cases

Readings

PART SIX: ENTREPRENEURSHIP, CAREERS, GLOBAL ECONOMY

PREFACE

MANAGEMENT APPLICATIONS: Exercises, Cases, and Readings is a book that stands alone or can be utilized with any standard management text.

It is designed to give students a "hands-on" experience in dealing with realistic situations to reinforce lecture material in any principles or fundamentals of management classes.

There are 24 exercises with each one constructed for individual use. Although group exercises are beneficial, I have found that most professors prefer individual work, inasmuch as this gives them an indication of the progress of the individual student. Each exercise page is perforated for easy tear-out purposes with a designated space for the student's name, class, and time/section in the upper right corner.

A total of 24 cases are in this book. Each case is derived from actual business experiences of either managers or employees.

Both the cases and the exercises are selected with the objective of presenting a wide range of problems and incidents crucial to the development of future managers.

There are also 24 readings taken from established management scholars, such as: Frederick Herzberg, George Odiorne and B. Joseph White who is the Associate Dean of the School of Business Administration at the University of Michigan; and management practitioners such as Jerry Wilkenfield, a corporate director for Occidental Petroleum Corporation and Joseph Izzo, President of JIA Management Group.

The readings, not unlike the exercises and cases, were selected to present established and new concepts to support the exercises and cases. Most of the readings are recent publications from well known journals, many of which are refereed. Journals represented are: *Academy of Management Review, Business Horizons, Executive Female, Sloan Management Review, Journal of Business Strategy, Black Enterprise, Industry Week, Central State Business Review* and many others.

Some readings are classics and are expected to be included in any management compilation, like Mary Parker Follett's, *Management as a Profession*, or *The Four Faces of Social Responsibility*, by Dan R. Dalton and Richard A. Cosier.

Acknowledgements are extended to a number of people who, in some measure, have made the publication of this book possible; Alison Reeves, Ed Fortenberry, Joe Kinzer, Elaine Lorentzen, Myrtle Christian, Pam Beveridge, Jackie Taylor, and Jack Hill.

PART ONE
INTRODUCTION TO MANAGEMENT

EXERCISE 1.1 THE MANAGEMENT PROCESS INTO THE "REAL WORLD"

Management is the process of involving four basic activities or functions; planning, organizing, leading, and controlling. Let's see if a small research project would verify this statement.

Select two local companies representing two different industries. Ask to speak to a manager at the supervisor level, the middle level, and a top manager. Ask each one what percent of his/her time annually is spent on the management activities or functions. Categorize your answers below.

Managerial Levels

Firm # 1: Industry:				Firm # 2: Industry:			
	Supervisory Level	Middle Level	Top Management		Supervisory Level	Middle Level	Top Management
Planning:	%	%	%	Planning:	%	%	%
Organizing:	%	%	%	Organizing:	%	%	%
Leading:	%	%	%	Leading:	%	%	%
Controlling:	%	%	%	Controlling:	%	%	%

1.   What is the pattern between the two companies regarding the four functions among the managerial levels?

2.   What is the relationship, if any, between the two industries?

EXERCISE 1.2 MANAGEMENT THEORY AND EXECUTIVE PRACTICE

Management theory has evolved, over the years, through a number of stages from scientific management to the contingency approach. Each stage made its contribution with many of its principles, concepts and ideas very much in practice today by managers everywhere.

By studying a person's background we should get an idea of what they have contributed to management.

Select an executive from the list below, research his/her background and business practices and fill in each of the five categories.

1. Henry Ford,   Ford Motor Company
2. Lee Iaccoca,   Chrysler Motor Company
3. Mary Kay Ash,   Mary Kay Cosmetics
4. James F. Lincoln,   Lincoln Electric Company
5. David Packard,   Hewlett Packard Company
6. John D. Rockefeller, Standard Oil Company
7. Alfred P. Sloan, Jr., General Motors Corporation
8. Eiji Toyota,   Toyota Motors Sales
9. Sam Walton,   Wal-Mart Stores
10. Thomas Watson,   I.B.M.

1: Personal background:

2: Business/professional background:

3: *Contributions to management, such as: creative or ideas, innovative practices:*

4: *His/her greatest single accomplishment:*

5: *Present status of this executive:*

EXERCISE 1.3   INFLUENCE OF STAKEHOLDERS

All companies must interact with external and internal stakeholders. To do otherwise could result in business failure.

Listed below are three external and three internal stakeholders. Briefly, discuss the impact each stakeholder has at General Motors.

External Stakeholders

1.   *Customers:*

2.   *Competitors:*

3.   *Labor Unions:*

Internal Stakeholders:

1.   Employees:

2.   Shareholders:

3.   Management:

EXERCISE 1.4   THE IRAN-CONTRA AFFAIR

The Iran-Contra arms deal is an intriguing study involving the military, government, and private business.

The issue is ethical behavior on the one hand and a moral issue on the other.

Research two articles detailing the most recent events that led to the congressional hearings and answer the following questions.

Article:	
Author:	
Issue:	Publication:

Article:	
Author:	
Issue:	Publication:

1.   What was the intent of Congress in prohibiting the sale of arms to the Contras?

2.   What was Colonel North's position at the Department of Defense?

3. Was Colonel North exceeding his authority in the diversion of funds to the Contra?

4. What is the moral and ethical issue in this affair?

5. What was President Reagan's stand on this?

6. Do you think other countries acted in a socially responsible manner by donating funds to buy arms for the Contras?

7. Did you find the arms dealers performing in an ethical manner?

Jack Wilborn, a college sophomore at Tech, came home for the Thanksgiving Holidays. During the course of the meal Thursday afternoon, Jack's mom asked, "Jack, have you decided your major yet?"

"Yes, I have, Mom. Management."

His mother frowned and questioned, "Management? You're going to learn to be a manager?" Before Jack could reply, his fourteen year old brother laughed, "Yeah, Jack, what are you going to be, a big shot executive?" Jack narrowed his eyes and with his mouth full of turkey dressing blurted, "You bet and you'd be the first guy I'd fire if you were working for me!"

"That's enough boys!" said Jack's father. "Jack, why don't you explain to all of us just what management is. Being an engineer, I'm kinda curious, too."

"Well," said Jack, "management covers a lot of territory. As a matter of fact, Dad, you're a manager yourself."

"Whadda ya' mean?" asked his dad. "You know I'm an engineer for Sunset Electronics."

"Yeah, I know," Jack retorted, "but do you ever plan your work? By that I mean, don't you plan a schedule of work?" Jack's dad laid his fork down and reached for a glass of iced tea. "Of course I do. If I didn't I'd never get anything done. I have to be organized."

Jack looked up quickly and laughed, "Dad, you just mentioned one of the most important functions of management—organizing! See, you plan and organize and I bet you perform other management functions, not to mention roles and different skills."

"Well," answered his dad. "You're probably right. But why don't you explain what a manager does."

1. Assume you are Jack Wilborn. Explain, in detail, the functions of management and give an example for each function.

2. Discuss (keep in mind your brother and mom are also interested) how interpersonal, informational, and decisional roles contribute towards successful management practices.

3. Explain how management, today, is considered as more of an art than a science.

CASE 1.2 TO LEAD OR NOT TO LEAD

The supervisors were a downcast lot as they left their meeting with Jud Blackburn, the production superintendent of Ajax Manufacturing Company.

The supervisors had been told that since the plant opened six months ago, production has steadily declined, absenteeism has increased, and last month there was a 20 percent employee turnover.

Jud had opened the meeting by announcing that "heads were going to roll" unless things turned around. Shirley Margiolleti, a supervisor, laid the blame on the personnel department's ineffective recruitment and selection process. Jud had retorted, "Bull, that won't wash! They were all skilled workers with good work records. You guys don't know how to motivate and get out productivity. We have the highest pay in town and a good bonus system! The engine boys and personnel have done a great job in setting up work standards and incentives. It's you guys. You're falling down on the job. Solve it or get out!" With that Jud stormed out of the meeting.

As he walked back to the welding shop, Jackson Langley wondered what to do. "What Jud had said was true enough," he mumbled, "but what can I do?" His men were well paid, the work was not any more difficult than other industrial jobs, "So where is the problem?" he wondered.

1. Which management approach or theory would be most applicable in solving this problem?
2. After identifying your approach or theory, explain why this is applicable and how should Jackson Langley utilize this with his welders?

CASE 1.3 AS THE ENVIRONMENT TURNS

Jack Whitener was mildly upset when he looked at last month's sales and next quarter's forecast. He began to worry how he was going to explain this at the stockholders meeting scheduled in two weeks. The thought that slowly crept into his mind was that computer manufacturing, as an industry, was in the growth stage and some stockholders would certainly ask if the company was going to survive.

Adding to Jack's woes, as sales manager, was the visit this morning from Victoria Small, the personnel director. She had received resignations from two engineers in research and she had heard rumors for the past week that two of the best sales representatives were going to quit. After Victoria left, Jack mumbled, "Why am I the last one to hear these things?" Jack turned his attention back to the sales figures analyzing sales division and product break downs. He noticed the state-of-the-art designs were not moving and three sales divisions were down this quarter from last year. He wondered how the competition was doing.

1. Why do you think sales have declined?
2. If Jack had monitored the external environment, identify the specific variables which may have warned him of potential problems.

Tom Sims had worked hard to receive this promotion and now he felt rewarded. He had recently moved his wife and three daughters to Midville, enrolled the girls in schools, and now Joan was busy putting the house in order. He had checked out his new office and his administrative personnel and he was quite pleased. He liked what he had seen of Midville, but he knew he would miss Chicago and the many friends he had left behind, but the challenges were ahead of him.

Tom pulled out of his driveway and started for work when he realized he was low on gas. He pulled in at the first service station, got out and filled his tank, went to the attendant's booth and handed over his credit card. "Looks like rain," said Tom. "Sure does," replied the attendant, "say, aren't you the new big shot chemical feller whose picture is in the paper?"

"Well, I'm not a big shot," answered Tom modestly, "But, yes, I am the new manager here for Northern-United Chemical Company."

"Humpf," grunted the attendant, "I guess we need the industry, but I wouldn't work there with all those chemicals and poison."

Tom signed his credit slip and said, "To each his own. The company has been good to me."

"Yeah," answered the attendant, "but for the rest of us, we can't fish or swim in any of the lakes or rivers, not to mention having to breathe those damn fumes."

Tom got into his car and drove off. He parked his car and began his three-block walk to the office, stopping at a newsstand to buy a morning paper. Before Tom could find the change for the paper, huge raindrops began to fall. He ducked under the newsstand canopy, then paid for the paper and started to read the headlines when someone nudged his elbow and asked, "Hey, ain't you that new chemical feller down from Chicago?"

"Yes, I am," answered Tom, looking at an elderly man with a Cub baseball cap.

"Saw your picture in the paper. Guess your PR people put it in."

Tom smiled, "Well, I guess I have to say they are on the ball. Thanks for noticing."

"Yeah, well," drawled the old man, "That's about all that's on the ball with your company. You people have poisoned our fish, stunk up our water, and you get a free tax ride on top of that!"

"Wait a minute," Tom retorted as the downpour stopped, as suddenly as it had begun.

"No, you wait just a minute," the old man said. "You just take your chemicals and git the hell out of here. Your payroll ain't nothin' when you add all that up." With that, the old man trudged off as Tom stared after him.

He put the newspaper in his briefcase and went to his office. He sat down and thought, "I've got one terrible image problem here. I know we've had fish kills and air pollution, but that's being take care of, but we need to do more, I guess."

In 500 words, draw-up a social action plan hopefully designed to change Northern-United's image. The plan should involve all personnel.

MANAGEMENT AS A PROFESSION

Mary Parker Follett[1]

The word *profession* connotes for most people a foundation of *science* and a motive of *service*. That is, a profession is said to rest on the basis of a proved body of knowledge, and such knowledge is supposed to be used in the service of others rather than merely for one's own purposes. Let us tonight ask ourselves two questions: (1) How far does business management rest of scientific foundations? (2) What are the next steps to be taken in order than business management shall become more scientific?

PRESENT SIGNS OF A SCIENTIFIC BASIS FOR BUSINESS MANAGMENT

We have many indications that scientific method is being more and more applied to business management. First, of course, is the development of so-called "scientific management" which, after its early stages, began to concern itself with the technique of management as well as with the technique to operating.

Secondly, there is the increasing tendency toward specialized, or what is being called functionalized, management. Functionalized management has, indeed, not yet been carried far. In some cases the only sign we see of it, beyond the recognition that different departments require different kinds of knowledge, different kinds of ability, is the employing of experts for special problems. In other cases a further step is taken and a planning department is created; but the powers given to planning departments vary greatly from plant to plant—some take up only occasional problems as they are asked, some are only advisory bodies. Yet in most plants the functionalization of management is a process which in one way or another has gained a good deal of ground recently. That is, the fact is very generally accepted that different types of problems require different bodies of knowledge.

In the third place, arbitrary authority is diminishing, surely an indication that more value is being put on scientific method. The tendency today is to vest authority in the person who has most knowledge of the matter in question and most skill in applying that knowledge. Hiring, for instance, is now based on certain principles and special knowledge. The job of hiring is given to those who have that knowledge. It is not assumed by someone by virtue of a certain position.

Perhaps nowhere do we see more clearly the advance of business management toward becoming a profession that in our conception of the requirements of the administrative head. It would be interesting to take some firm and note how one duty after another has in recent years passed from the president to various experts, down to that most recent addition to many businesses, the economic advisor. One president, of whom I inquired what he thought exactly his job to be, said to me: I can't define my job in terms of specific duties because I can't tell what special duty which I have today may be given at any moment to someone better able than I to handle it." One of the interesting things about that remark (there are several) is that he recognized that someone might handle some of his duties better than he could; and yet his is an exceedingly

---

[1] Reprinted from Chapter IV of *Business Management as a Profession*, edited by Henry C. Metcalf (A. W. Shaw Company, Chicago, 1927), pp. 73-87, by permission of McGraw-Hill Book Company.

able man. He saw that some particular task might develop a special technique and that men might be trained as experts in that technique.

The stereotype of the successful businessman is indeed changing. The image of the masterful man carrying all before him by the sheer force of his personality has largely disappeared. One good result of this is that we now consider that executive leadership can in part (remember, I say only "in part") be learned. Sheldon calls executive leadership "an intangible capacity." I do not wholly agree. Someone else says it is "beyond human calculation." There are many things, we hope, which have not yet been calculated which are not beyond calculation. I think that one of the hopes for business management lies in the fact that executive leadership is capable of analysis and that men can be trained to occupy such positions. I do not, of course, mean every man; but not every man can become a doctor or an architect. I mean that for business management, exactly as for other professions, training is gaining in importance over mere personality. I know a man who told me ten to fifteen years ago that he relied on his personality in business dealings. He has not made a success of his business. It was once thought that the executive's work rested largely on "hunch," and his subordinates' on obeying—no science in either case. The administrative head who relies first on the magic shortcut of "hunch," and secondly on his adroitness or masterfulness in getting others to accept his "hunch," is, I believe, about to be superseded by a man of different type.

Can you not remember the picture we used to have of the man in the swivel chair? A trembling subordinate enters, states his problem; snap goes the decision from the chair. This man disappears only for another to enter. And so it goes. The massive brain in the swivel chair all day communicates to his followers his special knowledge. An excellent plan if—there seem to be too many if's in the way! And so we resort to the humbler method of scientific research, the method of all the professions.

But with this agreed to, there is another misconception in regard to the administrative head. Many writers speak as if he were only the glue to hold together all these departments and functions of our big modern plants. As the need of coordination is daily and hourly felt in these vast, complex organizations, it is said that the president must do the coordinating. True; but I think that coordination is very different from matching up the pieces of a picture puzzle, to change our metaphor. Later, I am going to say just what I think it is; but let me say now that those of us who think of the administrative head as more than a mere coordinator and those of us who think that administrative decisions should rest on more than "hunch" (although "hunch," too, is important) are thinking of scientific foundations for business management.

A significant indication of the different type of management required today is the fact that managers are somewhat less inclined to justify their behavior by a claim of abstract "rights." An employer used to say, "I have a right to treat my men so and so." Or, "My behavior in this matter is perfectly reasonable." Today there are many who are more inclined to say: "If I treat my men so and so, how will they behave? *Why* will they behave in that way?" It takes far more science to understand human beings—and their "rights"—than to proclaim loudly our own rights and reasonableness.

We have a very interesting indication of the new demand made upon management in the fact that the idea, which is everywhere gaining ground, that we may have greater conscious control of our lives is seen in the business world most significantly. For example, those fatalistic rhythms, business cycles, are now considered susceptible to study, not as mysteries wholly beyond the comprehension of man. Again, take unemployment. Consider the steel industry. There you have an imperishable commodity. Moreover, you can calculate pretty well the demand. And you have rather permanently located firms and mills. There seems no reason, therefore, why the steel industry should not eventually be stabilized. Every time we take a problem out of the unsolvable class and put it into the solvable, and work at it as such, we are helping to put business management on a scientific basis. Mr. John Maynard Keynes, in an address last summer, spoke of the three great epochs of history described by Dr. John R. Commons,[1] and stated his belief that we are on the threshold of the third of these epochs. The first of these was the era of scarcity, which came to an end in about the fifteenth century. Next came the era of abundance, the dominating idea of which was the doctrine of laissez faire. Finally, there has come the era of stabilization upon which we are now entering and in which the doctrine of laissez faire must be abandoned in favor of deliberate, conscious control of economic forces for the sake of the general social good.

Many people today think of business not as a game of chance, not as a speculative enterprise depending on rising and falling markets, but as largely controllable. The mysteriousness of business is in fact disappearing as knowledge in regard to business methods steadily increases.

This is seen in the increased sense of responsibility for failure. You know the old excuses if a business failed or was not getting on well: the hard terms of bankers, the unscrupulousness of competitors, the abominable behavior of trade unions. I think that today there is less inclination of take refuge in such excuses; that there is a tendency to seek the difficulty in the running of the business. There is greater frankness in facing difficulties and a keener zest in overcoming them. You know, perhaps the story of little Mary who was naughty and was told by her mother to go into the next room and ask God to forgive her. When she came back her mother said, "Did you do what I told you to?" And received the reply, "Yes, I did; and God said, 'Mercy me, little Mary, I know heaps worse'n you.'" Many an employer takes this attitude, but their numbers are diminishing.

Moreover, many of the points disputed with trade unions, many points which both sides have thought to be legitimate fighting issues, are now considered problems which we should try to solve. To increase wages without increasing price is sometimes a solvable problem. Wherever thinking takes the place of fighting, we have a striking indication that management is coming to rest on scientific foundations. In international relations—but I have only to mention that term for you to see the analogy, for you to see the barbarous stage we are yet in, in international relations. Business men have the chance to lead the world in substituting thinking for fighting. And businessmen are thinking. One of the things I have been most struck with in the last four or five years has been the vitality of the thinking of businessmen. I said last winter to a professor of philosophy, "Do you realize that you philosophers have got to look to your laurels, that businessmen are doing some very valuable thinking and may get ahead of you?" And he acknowledged this fully and generously, which I thought was a significant concession.

Finally, management, not bankers nor stockholders, is now seen to be the fundamental element in industry. It is good management that draws credit, that draws workers, that draws customers. Moreover, whatever changes come, whether industry is owned by individual capitalists or by the state or by the workers, it will always have to be managed. Management is a permanent function of business.

There are many circumstances, let us note in concluding the first part of this talk, which are impelling us toward a truly scientific management: (1) efficient management has to take the place of that exploitation of our national resources whose day is now nearly over; (2) keener competition; (3) scarcity of labor; (4) a broader conception of the ethics of human relations; (5) the growing idea of business as a public service which carries with it a sense of responsibility for its efficient conduct.

WHAT ARE THE NEXT STEPS TOWARD MAKING BUSINESS MANAGEMENT MORE SCIENTIFIC?

Recognizing that business management is every day coming more to rest on scientific foundations, what has it yet to do? First, the scientific standard must be applied to the whole of business management; it is now often applied to only one part. Business management includes: (1) on the technical side, as it is usually called, a knowledge of production and distribution, and (2) on the personnel side, a knowledge of how to deal fairly and fruitfully with one's fellows. While the first has been recognized as a matter capable of being taught, the latter has been often thought to be a gift which some men possess and some do not. That is, one part of business management rested on science; the other part, it was thought, never could. Oliver Sheldon says:

"Broadly, management is concerned with two primary elements—things and men. The former element is susceptible to scientific treatment, the latter is not."[2] And again, "Where human beings are concerned, scientific principles may be so much waste paper."[3] If we believed that, we should not be here tonight in a Bureau of Personnel Administration. Let us take that statement—that human relations are not susceptible of scientific treatment—and ask what scientific treatment is . Science has been defined as "knowledge gained by systematic observation, experiment, and reasoning; knowledge coordinated, arranged, and systematized." Can we not accumulate in regard to human relations knowledge gained by systematic observation, experiment, and reasoning? Can we not coordinate, arrange, and systematize that knowledge? I think we can.

Sheldon says further: "There may be a science of costing, of transportation, of operation, but there can be no science of cooperation."[4] The reason we are here studying human relations in industry is that we believe there can be a science of cooperation. By this I mean that cooperation is not, and this I insist on, merely a matter of good intentions, of kindly feeling. It must be based on these, but you cannot have successful cooperation until you have worked out the methods of cooperation—by experiment after experiment, by a comparing of experiments, by a pooling of results....It is my plea above everything else that we learn *how* to cooperate. Of course, one may have have a special aptitude for dealing with men as others may have for dealing with machines, but there is as much to learn in the one case as in the other.

In all our study of personnel work, however, we should remember that we can never wholly separate the human and the mechanical problems. This would seem too obvious to mention if we did not so often see that separation made. Go back to that sentence of Sheldon's: "There may be a science of costing, of transportation, of operation, but there can be no science of cooperation." But take Sheldon's own illustration, that of transportation. The engineering part of transportation is not the larger part. Please note that I do not say it is a smaller part. It is a large part, and it is the dramatic part, and it is the part we have done well, and yet the chief part of transportation is the personal thing. Everyone knows that the main difficulty about transportation is that there have not always been sensible working arrangements between the men concerned. But you all see every day that the study of human relations in business and the study of technique of operating are bound up together. You know that the way the worker is treated affects output. You know that the routing of materials and the maintenance of machines is a matter partly of human relations. You know, I hope, that there is danger in "putting in" personnel work if it is superadded instead of being woven through the plant. You remember the man who wanted to know something about Chinese metaphysics and so looked up China in the encyclopedia and then metaphysics, and put them together. We shall not have much better success is we try merely to add personnel work. Even although there is, as I certainly believe there should be, a special personnel department run by a trained expert, yet it seems to me that every executive should make some study of personnel work a part of that broad foundation which is today increasingly felt to be necessary for the businessman.

If, then, one of the first things to be done to make business management more scientific is to apply scientific methods to those problems of management which involve human relations, another requirement is that we should make an analysis of managers' jobs somewhat corresponding to the analysis of workers' jobs in the Taylor system. We need to get away from tradition, prejudice, stereotypes, guesswork, and find the factual basis for managerial jobs. We know, for instance, what has been accomplished in elimination of waste by scientific methods of research and experiment applied to operating, to probable demand for commodities, and so on. I believe that this has to be carried further, and that managerial waste, administrative waste, should be given the same research and experiment. How this can be done, I shall take up later.

The next step business management should take is to organize the body of knowledge on which it should rest. We have defined science as an organized body of exact knowledge. That is, scientific method consists of two parts: (1) research, and (2) the organization of the knowledge obtained by research. The importance of research, of continued research, receives every year fuller and fuller appreciation from businessmen; but methods of organizing the results of such research have not kept pace with this appreciation. While business management is collecting more and more exact knowledge, while it is observing more keenly, experimenting more widely, it has not yet gone far in organizing this knowledge. We have drawn a good many conclusions, have thought out certain principles, but have not always seen the relation between these conclusions or these principles.

I have not time to speak here of more than one way of organizing in industrial plants our accumulating knowledge in regard to executive technique. There should be, I think, in every plant, an official, one of whose duties should be to classify and interpret managerial experience with the aid of the carefully kept records which should be required of every executive. For such classification and interpretation of experience—this experience which in essentials repeats itself so often from time to time, from department to department, from plant to plant—it would be possible to draw useful conclusions. The importance of this procedure becomes more obvious when we remember that having experience and profiting by experience are two different matters. Experience may leave us with mistaken notions, with prejudice or suspicion.

A serious drawback to a fuller understanding of an utilization of executive experience is that we have at present (1) no systematic follow-up of decisions, of new methods, of experiments in managing; and (2) no carefully worked out system of recording. Poorly kept records, or the absence of any systematic recording, are partly responsible for what seems in some plants like a stagnant management, and in all plants for certain leaks in management. For instance, the fact that we have no follow-up for executive decisions with a comparing of results—a procedure necessary before business management can be considered fully on a scientific basis—is partly a deficiency in recording. The fact that an executive, if he wished to introduce a certain method (not in operating but in management itself), cannot find in any records whether that method has been tried before or anything like it, and what the results have been, is a serious deficiency in recording. If an executive is facing a certain problem, he should be able to find out: (1) whether other executives have had to meet similar problems, (2) how they met them, (3) what the results were. It seems to me very unfortunate that it is possible for one man to say to another, as I heard someone say at the suggestion of a new method, "I believe our department tried that a few years ago, but I've forgotten what we thought of it."

I have heard it said that the Harvard football team was put on its feet when Percy Haughton introduced the system of recording football experience. After that, if someone thought he had a brilliant idea that such and such a play could be tried on Yale, the first thing done was to examine the records; and it might be found that that play had been tried two years before and failed. It might even be discovered why it had failed. This system of recording—I believe it already existed at Yale—was Mr. Haughton's great contribution to Harvard football. Because of it, the team could not, at any rate, go on making the *same* mistakes.

The recording of executive experience, which will probably need a technique somewhat different from that used for the rest of business recording, should have, I think, our immediate attention. The system of both recording and reporting should be such that records and reports can be quickly mastered, and thus be practically useful to all, instead of buried underneath their own verbiage, length, and lack of systematization. And there should be required, from every executive, training in the technique of keeping records and making reports.

But we need more than records. We need a new journal, or a new department in some present journal; we need sifted bibliographies of reports; ways of getting information from other parts of the country, from other counties; above all, we need executive conferences with carefully worked out methods for comparing experience which has been scientifically recorded, analyzed, and organized. When many different plants are willing to share with one another the results of their experience, then we shall have business policies based on wider data than those of present.

The Graduate School of Business Administration and the Bureau of Business Research of Harvard University are now collecting cases of business policy, thus opening the way for classifying and cross-indexing. Harvard has, of course, been able to get hold of a very small number of cases, but this seems to be a valuable and significant undertaking.

I have been interested also in what a certain recent committee, with representatives from various firms, deliberately stated as its object: "the comparison of experience." I should like to know how frank and full their exchange of experience was; but any attempt of this kind is interesting, indicating, as it does, the attitude on the part of those participating that they expect to gain more by working together than they will lose (the old idea) by allowing other firms to gain any intimate knowledge of their affairs.

Moreover, not only should we analyze and compare our experience, but we should deliberately experiment. We should make experiments, observe experiments, compare and discuss these with each other, and see what consensus we can come to in our conclusions. For this we should be wholly frank with one another. If we have the scientific attitude toward our work, we shall be willing to tell our failures. I heard of a man who made an ice machine which did not work, and the following conversation took place between him and a friend he met:

Friend: "I was sorry to hear your experiment was a failure!"

Man: "Who told you it was a failure?"

Friend: "Why, I heard your ice machine wouldn't work."

Man: "Oh, that was true enough, but it was a great success as an experiment. You can learn as much from your failures as from your successes."

From such experimenting and from the comparison of experience, I think certain standards would emerge. But we should remember that, as no Taylorite thinks there is anything final in "standardization," so we should not aim at a static standardization of managerial method, executive technique. We should make use of all available present experience, knowing that experience and our learning from it should be equally continuous matters.

If science gives us research and experimentation as its two chief methods, it at the same time shows us that nothing is too small to claim our attention. There is nothing unimportant in business procedure. For instance, I spoke above of record keeping. I know a firm where they tell me that they are not getting nearly so much advantage as they should from their records because they have not yet worked out a system of cross-indexing. Yet to some, cross-indexing may not seem to be of great importance. I know a man who says frequently about this detail or that, "Oh, that doesn't matter." Everything matters to the scientist. The following incident seems to me to have some significance. I told a man that I was working at the technique of the business interview, at which he seemed rather amused and said, "I guess most businessmen know how to conduct interviews." It was evident that he though he did—but he is a man who has never risen above a small position. Later, I said the same thing to a clever man in a good position, a New York man, by the way. I said it a little hesitatingly, for I thought he too might consider it beneath his notice, but he was much interested and asked if he might see my paper when finished.

I have spoken of the classification of experience, the organizing of knowledge, as one of the necessary preliminaries to putting business management on a scientific basis. This organized body of knowledge tends at first to remain in the hands of a few. Measures should be taken to make it accessible to the whole managerial force. There should be opportunities for the training of executives through talks, suggested readings (including journals on management), through wisely led discussion groups and conferences, through managers' associations, foremen's associations, and the like. The organized knowledge of managerial methods which many of the higher officials possess should spread to the lower executives. In some cases, the higher official does not even think of this as part of his responsibility. He will say to a subordinate, "Here is what I want done; I don't care how you do it, that's up to you." Indeed, many an official has prided himself on this way of dealing with subordinates. But this is changing. It is part of the Taylor system that standards and methods for each worker's job are made accessible to the worker; also knowledge of the quality or work expected, which is shown him by specifications or drawings. Some such system should be developed for management. To develop it might be made part of that analysis of managerial jobs which I spoke of a few moments ago. Indeed, more and more of the higher executives are seeing now that managers' jobs as well as workers' jobs are capable of carrying with them accepted standards and methods.

Of course, it is recognized that many of these standards and methods need the sanction of custom rather than of authority, that they should be indicated rather than prescribed, also that much more elasticity should be allowed than in the detailed instructions of the Taylor system—but this is all part of that large subject, the method of training executives. Possibly in time, as business organization develops, we shall have an official for executives corresponding to the functional foreman who is sometimes known as the "methods instructor," an official whose duty it will be to see that certain managerial methods are understood and followed, as it is the duty of the functional foreman to see that certain operating methods are understood and followed. But I should not advocate this unless the executives were allowed fullest opportunity for contributing to such prescribed methods. The development of managerial technique has been thought by some to involve the risk of crushing originality, the danger of taking away initiative. I think that, rightly managed, it should give executives increased opportunity for the fruitful exercise of initiative and originality, for it is they themselves who must develop this technique even if helped by experts. The choice here presented is not that between originality and a mechanical system, but between a haphazard, hit-or-miss way of performing executive duties and a scientifically determined procedure.

Yet when business management has gained something of an accepted technique, there still remains, as part of the training of executives, the acquiring of skill in its application. Managerial skill cannot be painted on the outside of executives; it has to go deeper than that. Like manual workers, managerial workers have to acquire certain habits and attitudes. And just as in the case of manual workers, for the acquisition of these habits and attitudes three conditions must be given: (1) detailed information in regard to a new method; (2) the stimulus to adopt this method; and (3) the opportunity to practice it so that it may become a habit.

A businessman tells me that I should emphasize the last point particularly. He says that his firm has been weak just here; that they have done more preaching than giving opportunity for practice. he says; "We've given them a lecture on piano playing and then put them on the concert stage. This winter we are going to try to invent ways of giving real practice to foremen so that a set of habits can be formed." No subject is more important than the training of executives, but as it is a subject which would require an evening for the most superficial consideration, we cannot speak further of it tonight. Let me just say, however, as a hint of what I shall elaborate later, that if you wish to train yourself for higher executive positions, the first thing for you to decide is what you are training for. Ability to dominate or manipulate others? That ought to be easy enough, since most of the magazines advertise sure ways of developing something they call "personality." But I am convinced that the first essential of business success is the capacity for organized thinking.

In conclusion: What does all this imply in regard to the profession of business management? It means that men must prepare themselves as seriously for this profession as for any other. They must realize that they, as all professional men, are assuming grave responsibilities, that they are to take a creative part in one of the large functions of society, a part which, I believe, only trained and disciplined men can in the future hope to take with success.

NOTES AND REFERENCES

1. John Rogers Commons, 1862-1945. American economist, educator, and author. Also had considerable influence in labor legislation.—Editor

2. Oliver Sheldon, *Bulletin of Taylor Society*, Vol. 8, No. 6 (December, 1913), p. 211.

3. Oliver Sheldon, *The Philosophy of Management* (London: Sir Isaac Pitman & Sons, Ltd., 1923), p. 36.

4. Ibid., p. 35.

IS MANAGEMENT A SCIENCE?

Ronald E. Gribbins
and
Shelby D. Hunt[1]

> Within perhaps five years—certainly not more than ten years hence—a general theory of management will be evolved, stated, and generally accepted in management circles.
>
> William Fredrick, 1963

The rapid development of management thought over the past 70 years has produced a fundamental question that remains unresolved: is management a science? (4,11,15,16, 31, 34,35).

The fact that (a) the question receives significant attention in the literature and (b) reasonable people continue to disagree on many dimensions of the issue makes the proposed resolution worthy of consideration on scholarly grounds alone. Other practical implications have also spurred the development of this note. For those who purport to both study and teach management: if management is not a science, what then is the nature and purpose of research in the area and what is the nature of the material being conveyed in the classroom? If management is not a science, it may be that future managers should learn in the "school of hard knocks" or at least take an apprenticeship under someone who has a proven ability to manage in the real world. The issue of whether management is a science has substantial consequences for the *discipline* and *practice* of management as well as the *training* of managers.

Is management a science? There are numerous strongly held perspectives. Drucker suggests:

> ...management, in other words, is a practice rather than a science or profession, though containing elements of both. No greater damage could be done to our economy or to our society than to attempt to "professionalize" management by "licensing" managers for instance, or by limiting access to management to people with a special academic degree (11).

The question elicits equally strong opinion from those who argue that management is definitely a science. Gulick believes:

> Where a field a knowledge has been defined, made "public," pursued for some time, organized into a an elaborate system of explicit primary and secondary theories, which have been or are being tested by logic and the realities of the universe, so that past and current changes in the system can be explained and future changes predicted or produced, we call that ball of knowledge (management, in this case) a science (15).

---

[1] Reprinted by permission of the *Academy of Management Review*, Vol. 23, No. 1, January, 1978, pp. 139-144.

Others advocate a middle position and suggest that while we may proceed to expand our knowledge of management through scientific procedures, management still remains an art (16, 31). To attempt to resolve the issue, we must turn our attention to the nature of science.

THE NATURE OF SCIENCE

Science is a concept having a systematic ambiguity often referred to by philosophers of language as the *process-product* ambiguity (29, p. 7). Like the terms "harvest" and "vote," the term *science* refers both to an end-product (a body of knowledge) and to a process (the activities and procedures employed by scientists). This is consistent with the static versus dynamic perspectives of science proposed by Kerlinger (19). The static view holds science to be a body of facts which represent the current state of knowledge. The dynamic view perceives science as an *activity*, focusing on the procedures employed by scientists rather than on the output of those procedures.

The problem with the static view of science is that some writers choose to withhold the designation "science" from any *discipline* that does not have a general, unifying theory. Thus Buzzell suggests that all sciences are "organized around one or more central theories" (8, p 37). The "general theory" criterion confuses the *successful culmination* of scientific effort with *science* itself, and is an unnecessarily harsh criterion that would exclude management, and conceivably all social science, from being designated sciences.

Focusing on science as a *process* seems more reasonable. Braithwaite notes:

...the function of science...is to establish general laws covering the behaviors of empirical events or objects with which the science in question is concerned, and thereby to enable us to connect together our knowledge of the separately known events, and to make reliable predictions of events as yet unknown (5).

In this broader view, science has as its main purpose the discovery of laws and theories to explain and predict phenomena. The result of this effort is an aspect of science, but not science in its entirety.

This point has implications for management in particular because there is disagreement concerning whether or not management will ever produce a general, unifying theory (2, 13, 14, 20, 24, 33). Consider the "approaches to" or "schools of" management theory listed by Koontz (20). The various "schools" are: management process, empirical, human behavior, social system, decision theory, and mathematical. Can these schools be joined together in a unified theory of management or are they fundamentally irreconcilable?

Many writers are openly pessimistic. Behling typifies their views by asserting:

...that fundamental and inescapable substantive differences do exist among the various approaches to the study of management, that these differences are practically unresolvable, and thus, that a unified theory of management is an impossibility (2, p. 4).

Others, like Laufer (23) and Suojanen (33), adopt a more optimistic perspective. Laufer draws a striking parallel between the *present* problems of management and the *past* problems of biology. Biologists were able to resolve their discipline-definitional problems only after they successfully reached general agreement on a taxonomy for biological phenomena. *That is, biologists reached a consensus on the nature of their discipline by first reaching a consensus on its scope.* Perhaps the same process would succeed in management.

Laufer further suggests that management theory is amenable to rigorous classification, although the results are likely to be a polythetic arrangement (32). With polythetic classifications, the phenomena in any given class will share many characteristics in common; but no individual phenomenon need possess *all* characteristics of the class. Laufer's own taxonomical effort utilizes the pattern followed in the Periodic Table with the functions of management (planning, organization, directing, staffing, control) as a basis. The result is a first step, open to further elaboration and refinement. While the actual taxonomy proposed may be questionable, the proposed procedure remains reasonable and we are well advised to heed his final point: "One purpose of a science is to synthesize the parts...into an organized conception of its field of study)" (23).

Granting that the *pursuit* of empirically testable laws and theories constitutes scientific activity, three other observations should help clarify the nature of science. First, for a discipline to be characterized as a science in its own right, separate from other sciences, it must have a distinct subject matter drawn from the real world serving as the focal point of investigation. "Distinct" does not imply that other disciplines have no interest in the subject matter. Rather, each science has its own *point of focus*. For example, the science of chemistry focuses on *substances* and attempts to understand the predict phenomena related to them. Physics is also interested in substances but does not *focus on* them. Hence chemistry and physics (though related) are appropriately referred to as separate sciences.

Consider the following recent definitions of management. Management is:

the process by which the elements of a group are integrated, coordinated, and/or utilized so as to effectively and efficiently achieve organizational objectives (9).

a process or form of work that involves the guidance or direction of a group of people toward organizational goals or objectives (30).

the work of creating and maintaining environments in which people can accomplish goals efficiently and effectively (1).

Distilling these definitions, one finds the *primary* subject matter to be *coordination for goal accomplishment*. Some may limit management to coordination within a distinct organization while others may expand the domain to include coordination activities across organizations and/or cultures, but all recognize coordination of the interdependent parts of organizational systems as essential to management. Other disciplines will overlap with the subject matter of management, for example psychology, social psychology, organizational behavior and sociology. But only in management is *coordination* the focal point. The first distinguishing characteristic of a science is that it has its own subject matter (some more distinct than others). With coordination activity as its primary focus, management would seem to fulfill this requirement.

The second characteristic of science rests in that attempt to develop "general laws" which govern the behavior of empirical events. A major assumption of any scientific endeavor is that there are underlying uniformities or regularities may not be initially evident, but their eventual discovery produces empirical regularities, law-like generalizations, and laws. The underlying regularities are necessary because (a) the primary goal of science is to find general explanation of empirical events, and (b) regularities are a necessary component for theory development since "theories are systematically related sets of statements, including some law-like generalizations, that are empirically testable" (29, p. 10).

The question becomes: are there underlying uniformities or regularities interrelating the phenomena comprising the subject matter of management? The answer can be affirmatively based on the following arguments. First, the coordination of activities is one small part of human behavior. Since numerous uniformities and regularities have been observed in other sciences involving human behavior, (3) there is no a priori reason to believe the same will not be found in behavior focusing on coordination for the purpose of goal accomplishment. The second argument rests in a review of any journal reporting scholarly research in management. While the literature makes one aware of how much has yet to be done, progress has been made in identifying some uniformities. Leadership, motivation and organizational design are but three of the areas in which significant progress has been made in the last decade.

The final characteristic of science is its method. Management may have a distinct subject matter and there may exist underlying regularities, but we still must decide if the scientific method (the activities and *process* of science) is applicable to management, for as Bunge (somewhat tautologically) suggests, "No scientific method, no science" (7, p. 12).

Detailed explication of the scientific method is beyond the scope of this note (18), but the cornerstone requirement of the method of science must be mentioned. The word science has its origins in the Latin verb *scire*, meaning "to know". There are many ways to know things. The methods of tenacity, authority, faith, intuition and science are often cited (10, p. 183). The characteristic which separates scientific knowledge from other ways to "know" things is the notion of *intersubjective certification.*

Scientific knowledge, in which theories, laws, and explanations are primal, must be objective in the sense that its truth content must be empirically testable. This ensures that its theories, laws, and explanations will be intersubjectively certifiable since different (but competent) investigators with differing attitudes, opinions, and beliefs will be able to make observations and conduct experiments to ascertain their truth content. As Pierce notes:

To satisfy our doubts,...therefore, it is necessary that a method should be found by which our beliefs may be determined by nothing human, but by some external permanency—by something upon which our thinking has no effect...The method must be such that the ultimate conclusion of every man shall be the same. Such is the method of science (6, p. 18).

Berelson and Steiner (3) have also discussed the scientific method. They propose six distinguishing characteristics:

1. The procedures are public,
2. The definitions are precise,
3. The data-collecting is objective,
4. The findings must be replicable,
5. The approach is systematic and cumulative,
6. The purposes are explanation, understanding, and prediction.

The first five of their characteristics are all subsumable under the *intersubjectively certifiable* criterion.

Can the scientific method be applied to management phenomena? One approach is to suggest that there is no reason to presume that it cannot. Another approach is to recognize that the practice of management is embedded in observable behavior, that this behavior is measurable through public and replicable procedures, and that one can proceed in a systematic fashion for the purpose of understanding and predicting managerial behavior. This is not to say that in every instance the method is appropriately applied. The quality of application depends on the research scholars applying the method. While difficulties abound (measurement being a prime example), it is heartening to note the scientific quality of much recent scholarship in the area.

One further point deserves consideration. We are not suggesting that science lacks any artistic characteristics. Kuhn (21) speaks of the development of scientific knowledge through revolution. While a vast amount of scientific endeavor is considered "normal science," there comes a time when the old "paradigm" no longer suffices and revolutions occur. Rudner (29) labels this process the "logic of discovery." In either case, the process or procedure which generated the new insight may have substantial artistic content. But the testing of whether or not an insight is correct remains in the realm of "science."

To summarize, each science: (a) has a distinct subject matter drawn from the real world; (b) presumes underlying uniformities or regularities that specify relationships among the phenomena studies; and (c) applies inter-subjectively certifiable methods to the study of subject matter. This perspective can be described as a consensus summation of views on science. For example, Wartofsky suggests that a science is:

> ...an organized or systematic body of knowledge, using general laws or principles, that it is knowledge about the world; and that it is that kind of knowledge concerning which universal agreement can be reached by scientists sharing a common language (or languages) and common criteria for the justification of knowledge claims and beliefs (36, p. 23).

CONCLUSION

It is our conclusion that management is a science. Some may disagree. For example, Carlisle (9) asserts that for a discipline to be a science, it must have a systematized body of knowledge and that management presently lacks a generally accepted knowledge base. Without this, management remains an art and experience continues to be the best teacher. Implicit in this argument is the process-product ambiguity noted earlier. Carlisle assumes a narrow definition of science while we argue for a broader view that includes process activities.

Having analyzed three other dimensions of science (existence of a distinct subject matter, presumption of underlying regularities, and application of the scientific method), in each instance we conclude that the discipline of management satisfies these criteria and can therefore appropriately be labeled a science. If disagreement is to continue, this paper provides criteria for focusing the debate. These dimensions will lead to more effective discussion and resolution of the issue.

REFERENCES

1. Albanese, Robert. *Management: Toward Accountability for Performance* (Homewood, Ill.: Richard D. Irwin, 1975).

2. Behling, Orlando. "Unification of Management Theory: A Pessimistic View," *Business Perspectives*, Vol. 3, No. 4 (Summer 1967), 4-9.

3. Berlson, Bernard, and Gary A. Steiner. *Human Behavior: An Inventory of Scientific Findings* (New York: Harcourt, Brace and World, 1964), 16-18.

4. Boettinger, Henry. "Is Management Really an Art"? *Harvard Business Review* (January-February 1975), 54-65.

5. Braithwaite, R. *Scientific Explanation* (Cambridge: Cambridge University Press, 1955), 1.

6. Buchler, J. (Ed.). *Philosophical Writing of Pierce* (New York: Dover, 1955).

7. Bunge, Mario. *Scientific Research I: The Search for System* (New York: Springer-Verlag, 1967).

8. Buzzell, Robert. "Is Marketing a Science," *Harvard Business Review*, Vol. 41 (January-February 1963), 32+.

9. Carlisle, Howard M. *Management: Concepts and Situations* (Chicago: Science Research Associates, 1976).

10. Cohen, Morris R., and Ernest Nagel. *Logic and the Scientific Method* (New York: Harcourt, Brace and World, 1934).

11. Drucker, Peter. *The Practice of Management* (New York: Harper & Row, 1954).

12. Dubin, Robert. *Theory Building* (New York: Free Press, 1969).

13. Frederick, William C. "The Next Development for Management Science: A General Theory," *Journal of the Academy of Management*, Vol. 6, No. 3 (September 1963), 212-219.

14. Greenwood, William T. "Future Management Theory: A Comparative Evolution to a General Theory," *Academy of Management Journal*, Vol. 17, No. 3 (September, 1974), 503-513.

15. Gulick, Luther. "Management is a Science," *Academy of Management Journal*, Vol 8, No. 1 (March 1965), 7-13.

16. Haimann, Theo, and William G. Scott. *Management in the Modern Organization*, 2nd ed. (Boston: Houghton Mifflin, 1974).

17. Hempel, Carl G. "The Theoretician's Dilemma," in *Aspects of Scientific Explanation* (New York: The Free Press, 1965).

18. Hunt, Shelby D. Marketing Theory: *Conceptual Foundation of Research in Marketing* (Columbus, Ohio: Grid Publishing Co., 1976).

19. Kerlinger, Fred N. *Foundations of Behavioral Research* (New York: Holt, Rinehart and Winston, 1964).

20. Koontz, Harold. "The Management Theory Jungle," *Journal of the Academy of Management*, Vol. 4, No. 3 (December 1961), 174-188.

21. Kuhn, Thomas S. *The Structure of Scientific Revolutions*, 2nd ed. (Chicago: University of Chicago Press, 1970).

22. Kyburg, Henry E. *Philosophy of Science* (New York: Macmillan, 1968).

23. Laufer, Arthur C. "A Taxonomy of Management Theory: A Preliminary Framework," *Academy of Management Journal*, Vol. 11, No. 4 (December 1968), 435-442.

24. Litchfield, Edward H. "Notes on a General Theory of Administration," *Administrative Science Quarterly*, Vol. 1, No. 1 (June 1956), 3-29.

25. Luthans, Fred. "The Contingency Theory of Management," *Business Horizons*, Vol. 16, No. 3 (June 1973), 67-72.

26. Nagel, Ernest. *The Structure of Science* (New York: Harcourt, Brace and World, 1961).

27. Popper, Karl R. *The Logic of Scientific Discovery* (New York: Harper & Row, 1959).

28. Rescher, Nicholas. *Scientific Explanation* (New York: The Free Press, 1970).

29. Rudner, Richard S. *The Philosophy of Social Science* (Englewood Cliffs, N.J.: Prentice-Hall, 1966).

30. Rue, Leslie W., and Lloyd L. Byars. *Management: Theory and Application* (Homewood, Ill.: Richard D. Irwin, 1977).

31. Simonds, Rollin. "Toward a Science of Business Administration," *Journal of the Academy of Management*, Vol.2, No. 2 (August 1959), 135-138.

32. Sokal, Robert R., and Peter H. A Sneath. *Principles of Numerical Taxonomy* (San Francisco: W. H. Freeman, 1963).

33. Suojanen, Waino. "Management Theory: Functional and Evolutionary," *Academy of Management Journal*, Vol. 6, No. 1 (March 1963), 7-17.

34. Urwick, Lyndall F. "Papers in the Science of Administration, " *Academy of Management Journal*, Vol. 13, No. 4 (December 1970), 361-371.

35. Walker, J. M. "Paper of the Science of Administration: Comment," *Academy of Management Journal*, Vol. 14, No. 2 (June 1971), 259-265.

36. Wartofsky, Marx W. *Conceptual Foundations of Scientific Thought* (New York: Macmillan, 1968).

MANAGER, MANAGE THYSELF!

Sumer C. Aggarwal[1]

Politicians, journalists, academicians, and corporate managers all give their particular prescriptions for reversing economic decline, but few of their ideas address managerial causes for losses in productivity. In my various contacts with government and corporate managers, I have found repeatedly that these managers know pretty well what causes such losses in their respective organizations. But they are not willing to tell publicly what they know because it concerns them and their colleagues.

I shall explain that (1) the selfish attitudes and greed of the managers are the main roadblocks to economic recovery, and (2) the large number of overhead managers and their support staffs represent the largest single cause of economic decline.

UNREALISTIC EXPECTATIONS AND GREED

During the early fifties, a middle manager in a U.S. corporation was getting a salary of $6,000-$7,000; a mechanic made about $2.00 per hour; an office worker $1.00 per hour; and a construction worker nearly $2.50 per hour. In comparison to that, during 1981 a middle manager made $50,000 to $60,000, whereas a mechanic made about $10 per hour, an office worker $5 per hour, and a construction worker $18 per hour. This means that during the last thirty years managerial salaries have gone up by about eight times, whereas the workers' wages have increased by about five times. In addition the benefits and perquisites now available to managers have increased by a much higher proportion than the benefits available to lower-level employees. The rate of these increases has been much higher for top corporate managers. During these thirty years, as professional managers gained more and more control of corporations, they rewarded themselves with a larger and larger share of the profits. As the percentage share of profits going to managers increased, the share going to investors and employees decreased. This is nothing but the sheer greed of managerial class.

As managers were expanding their share, the unions, office employees, service workers, and retailers also expected larger rewards. Expectations rose constantly during these three decades of prosperity. The increases in salaries and wages were reasonable as long as productivity gains could support these extra costs. However, with rising expectations, work content and output of most groups in the work force was decreasing because technological advances were constantly transferring work from humans to machinery. This resulted in a decreasing workload and a decreasing commitment to work output.

These opposing trends began causing noticeable problems in 1979 when steel companies, auto manufacturers, electronic appliance producers, and others started losing money, layoffs became common, and some plants had to be shut down. Companies blamed excessive government regulations, excessive demands by labor unions, and unfair foreign competition. But little was said about the inertia of managers, their excessive support staffs, or their self-indulgence in personal and political cliques with their suppliers, customers, and colleagues. Corporate staffs

[1] *Business Horizons:* Copyright, 1983, by the Foundation for the School of Business at Indiana University. Reprinted by permission.

have been growing like amoebas in a warm pool. A hundred are doing what was once done by ten, and it seems as if one thousand will soon take the place of the hundred. Exploding staff populations required modern buildings, fancy limousines, jet aircraft, yachts, antiques, and paintings. A sea of paper, corporate meetings, extensive travel, and unnecessary surveys generated by managers filled the need to keep everyone busy. Hardly anybody cared about costs; everybody was having too much fun. The spectacle bolstered managerial reputations and individual egos.

Let me illustrate this type of climate by describing the confusing but comfortable situation in a large plant in central Pennsylvania where I was invited to help with a productivity problem. The plant employs nearly 3,000 persons. Nearly 1,000 are direct-production employees; another 500 look after materials, maintenance, tooling, and so on. The remaining 1,500 are analysts, supervisors, and managers. The plant makes an excellent profit of nearly 23 percent before taxes. The majority of the middle-level and senior managers made from $50,000 to $100,000. Most employees are receiving an average wage or salary which is about $100 per week more than the salaries of employees of any other company within a 50-mile radius of the plant. The managers told me that the employees and management staff expect even higher salaries because they are aware of the higher profit level of the plant. I questioned the managers about the value of several large support staffs (forecasting, scheduling, planning, data processing, and so on). They were not at all sure about what these support services added, but they all thought it was nice to have such extensive staffs.

Regarding productivity, we discussed the plant's recent installation of a huge complex of machinery of producing a specific group of items, at a cost of $15 million. The new complex has replaced an old group of machines. This new complex required only seven persons for operation, compared to thirty-six persons for the old equipment. However, the new complex required eleven additional white-collar workers: planners, data processing personnel, and so on. The net savings in payroll was about $20,000 per month, but the monthly cost of invested capital and capital consumption was estimated to be $324,500. The managers sincerely believed they had increased productivity; in reality, they were spending about $304,5000 per month more on the same level of production with no increase in profits. However, the managers were quite comfortable because they though they could write off the entire $15 million cost during the next three years under President Reagan's Investment Tax Credit Incentive programs. However, discussions revealed that the new complex may not be used at full capacity during the coming years because the demand for its product group is decreasing.

Further, the plant manager recognized that during the last twenty years of his career at this plant, each time some high technology group of machines was added for improving productivity, the demand of the related products/components fell considerably between the time the machines were ordered and the time they became operational. Each time, only the costs went up, both the production efficiency and the profit contribution went down. Each time, management had only the satisfaction of having decreased the output/direct man hours ratio. At this stage, I told the management that they did not have any desire or motivation for increased productivity; during day-long discussions, they had rejected all my suggestions about reductions in overhead and other indirect costs. Just before my departure from the plant, the plant manager and I agreed that only when the Japanese or German competition moved in would managers think seriously about improving productivity. Now the situation is too comfortable for anyone in the plant to accept any changes, let alone cuts in the operating budgets or overheads.

INTOLERABLE OVERHEADS

Gradually, 90 percent of the U.S. working population has moved into nonproductive status. Only the remaining 10 percent made goods, grow food, or dig out minerals. Most people agree that the fast-growing numbers of attorneys, accountants, analysts, supervisors, managers, and a host of other "non-productive" professionals add little to national productivity. Most organizations allocate anywhere between 30 percent to 70 percent of their total expenditures to overhead functions. The most common types of overheads may be grouped under the three categories in the accompanying Table.

Most of these overhead costs are not kept in check because these are the favorites of managers. During normal as well as prosperous times, overhead costs keep growing with the help of managers' exotic justifications. It is not uncommon to find that several sections within the same organization are engaged in the same type of nearly equivalent overhead activity. A large portion of the overhead costs results from the irrelevance of the overhead services and their inefficient use.

Underutilization of overhead services or the waste of overhead services is promoted by the kingdom-building practices of various departments or sections of the organizations.

Any time an organization conducts value analysis of its overhead services, it is sure to find that the majority of these services add little to the products/services being generated by it. A few services may have marginal value and often may not be available when needed. For example, the controller's department of a Pennsylvania company was providing certain cost control reports to manufacturing about two months after the completion of each order. The purpose was to educate manufacturing sections about high-cost items. Because these reports were received two months after the fact, the supervisors an foremen did not bother to look at them. By this time, many factors had changed, and they were busy with problems at hand.

THE MOST COMMON OVERHEADS

Necessary and Required Overhead Services	Services Whose Tangible Value is Questionable	Popular Overhead Services
Accounting and auditing Personnel R & D (focused) Planning and forecasting Plant engineering Sales and brand management Corporate offices and general managers Depreciation of capital facilities	Public relations office Corporate lawyers Advertisements In-house newspaper Counseling Productivity office/efficiency improvement office Training Elaborate audio-visual services Superfluous data processing services	Photocopying Telephones Entertainment Travel Luxury offices and personal conference rooms Personal secretaries Corporate jets Expensive paintings Antiques

Normally, each large corporation wants to employ the best specialist in the scientific fields related to their products and services. In reality, the company's needs may best be served by specialists of average ability because the best specialists are usually more concerned with their professional excellence rather than with adding value to the products and services of their employer. For example, the market researchers of a company in Maryland were planning during August 1980 to promote a declining product, at the same time that the top executive committee was debating about whether to continue with this product at all.

The focus of some of the overhead services is often to please their superiors rather than to serve the goals of the organization. In such an organizational climate, section heads often ignore cost-savings considerations. For example, the manager of the general services section of a company in upstate New York wanted a promotion and a higher salary. He concentrated on pleasing each of the company vice-presidents. He succeeded in expanding his section's budget so that he could provide modern furniture, fancy rugs, paintings, expensive decorations, and a variety of telephone and audio-visual gadgets to each of the vice-presidents. He did get his targeted promotion and a big raise, but about a year later, expenditures on the luxury items were strongly criticized by the comptroller's office in an overall performance review meeting. At this time, most of the vice-presidents agreed that they were misguided by the general services manager. The manager was fired but a large sum of money had already been wasted.

Contrary to all the logic and principles of scientific management, managerial promotions in private companies and government departments alike are dependent upon (1) the number of persons the candidate supervises and (2) the size of the operating budget he or she controls. In normal times, both these factors motivate the managers to add more personnel to their departments and to push for a larger operating budget each year. If some manager attempts to realize substantial savings from his or her budget, the supervisor may suspect either that the manager has been inefficient in the past or has been neglecting certain important functions such as preventive maintenance, training, and R&D.

A large portion of the overhead expenditure may be attributed to the personal preferences of managers and is of a discretionary nature; hence managers are responsible for most of the non-value-adding overheads. A cost-conscious manager should be able to eliminate all such brightwork.

VALUE ANALYSIS FOR SLASHING OVERHEADS

In a great many cases, a sincere and focused value analysis of overhead[1] can result in decreasing overhead costs by 30 to 50 percent. However, thousands of small and unrelated activities constitute overheads, and arbitrary cuts in overhead expenditures can be damaging to the integrated goals of the company. Therefore, much care should be taken in distinguishing between wasteful and valuable overheads. The value analysis of overheads must be jointly conducted by the user-managers and supplier-managers of overhead services. The final cost control decisions must be made by the top management. The estimates of several corporations indicate that the overhead value analysis of an organization employing about 2,000 persons can be completed in about four months.

The value analysis of overheads requires going through four stages in a definite sequence. These are:

Stage 1: Chief executive officer appoints a high-level task force consisting of the most efficient and creative departmental managers. This task force appoints value analysis challenge teams for each of the major overhead functions. Each team includes the section head of the overhead service, the heads of its major user sections, and one or two experts, such as an industrial engineer, a value specialist, a cost accountant, and others. The task force sets the goals in terms of cost reduction percentages for each of the challenge teams. However, no special targets are singled out and no specific overhead services are pin-pointed as possible culprits.

Stage 2: Each challenge team identifies the demand for overhead services and asks the users to put a dollar value on the services they receive. The team then challenges the concerned head to justify the value of services supplied by his or her section.

Stage 3: Each challenge team attempts to develop options for cutting or reducing the overhead services under consideration. The team holds server meetings and investigates thoroughly each of the major overhead services under its purview. The team can make use of a typical Options Form (see the accompanying Figure) to facilitate their analysis. The Options Form forces the team members (section heads) to consider all possible means for reducing or reorganizing overhead services by requiring them to list all the possible options on the form no matter how radical or crazy they may seem. The receivers, who may become quite value conscious if they are made to pay for the services they receive, may put forth the most imaginative and creative options.

Stage 4: The possible cost reductions from individual options proposed by challenge teams may look small, but when hundreds of them are added together, they become significant. The challenge teams can assign rankings or priorities for each of the proposed options. This can be of considerable help to the task force and the top management. Next, all options are reviewed by the task force, which chooses some options from those proposed by all the challenge teams. Then the task force assigns its ranking to the chosen options. Finally, the shortened and combined list of options reaches the top management executive committee, and they decide on cuts, reductions, eliminations, or substitutions. Thus, the final decisions become the shared responsibility of suppliers, receivers, and managers of overhead services. The overhead cuts may involve elimination of some jobs, but any tough and objective management can handle it. The difficulties and risks involved in implementing reductions and cuts are not as great as they often look.

OPTIONS FORM

Overhead Section

Overhead Service	Eliminate	Defer	Reduce Quality	Reduce Amount	Reduce Frequency	Substitute
Reports						
1					●	
2			●			
3	●					
4				●		
Analyses						
1						●
2		●				
3	●					
Decisions						
1	●					
2						●
Plans						
1	●				●	
2						●
3				●		
4		●				
5			●			
Recommendations						
1						
2				●		
3	●					
4						
5						
Additional Suggestions						
1						
2						
3						
4						
5						

To illustrate how value analysis of overhead works, I give a brief account of three successful cases:

• Value analysis of the purchase function of a manufacturing company indicated that personnel were spending too much time on expediting the 10 percent of the requisitions which allowed less than adequate lead time. Top management decided that the purchasing department would bill the requisitioning department for expediting such rush acquisitions; the requisitioners were to pay out of their operating budgets. Soon afterward, the purchasing department was able to release three of its staff members to other sections.

• Value analysis of the check processing section of a bank showed that the interest money available from the flat of the checking accounts was not sufficient to pay for free checking services to the customers. The bank management quickly changed its policy of no minimum balance to a minimum balance of $300 during each calendar month. Otherwise, each customer would have to pay a $2 monthly service charge. The new policy generated enough float that the interest earnings could more than pay for the free checking services.

• In one wholesale distribution center, the workers who filled orders had almost nothing to do on Mondays but worked overtime every Friday because the standing policy was to fill every order by noon Friday. This situation created unnecessary idle time costs and overtime costs. After a value analysis study, the management of the distribution center introduced a system of workload forecasts and flexible scheduling of order fillers. Further, they changed their Friday noon deadline to one that allowed an order to be filled within 24 hours after it was received. This way, all the orders received on Fridays could be filled on Mondays, and the problem of drastic fluctuations in workload disappeared.

• • •

Suffice it to say that managers' attitudes, intentions, and motivations are the prime movers that drive the economic health and vigor of a company. Managers need to be objective and conscientious about their personal gains and comforts. They must be able to isolate and eliminate wasteful and non-value-adding overhead functions that provide prestige, power, and ego satisfaction only to them. Given such managers, a company will be more able to avoid its economic decline, low productivity, dwindling profits, and low morale among its employees.

REFERENCES

1. John L. Neuman, "Make Overhead Cuts That Last," *Harvard Business Review.* May-June 1975: 116-126.

SHOULD YOU MANAGE LIKE A MAN?
The Great Debate: Experts lead the way out of the Patton-or-Pollyanna Trap

Nancy Arnott[1]

When women began moving into middle management in the mid-'70s, the career-planning gurus who turned out in force to guide them all tended to sound like graduates of the Frankie Valli School of Business. To his directives, "Walk like a man, talk like a man, think like a man and act like a man."

That amounted to following the hierarchical, military model that men had established long before women joined their ranks. It meant wearing a uniform (a "dress-for-success" suit), issuing orders like a drill sergeant and engaging in cutthroat competition for promotions.

In the last couple of years, though, some of those advisors have been singing a different tune, one that sounds more like "I've Gotta Be Me." Consider the chorus from these voices:

• In her 1985 book, *Feminine Leadership, or How to Succeed in Business Without Being One of the Boys*, consultant Marilyn Loden identifies and advocates a style of management that embraces "exactly the skills women were advised to leave behind when they entered the world of business," a non-traditional approach she christened "feminine leadership." According to Loden, feminine leaders are characterized by a greater awareness of, and regard for, people's feelings; a greater concern for maintaining close personal relationships at work; a preference for win-win solutions; and a tendency to place the long-term health of their organization before their own short-term personal gain. She contrasted these values with the traditional, "masculine" management characteristics of competitiveness, aggressiveness and a preference for an analytic, strategic approach.

• Peter Dubno, Ph.D., professor emeritus of New York University's Graduate School of Business Administration, says "Based on what we know today, the answer to the question, 'Should women manage like men?' is a resounding 'no.' A lot of men who are authoritarian and issue orders ar not very good managers. They fail in the long run. If women feel they have to act like men, they are rushing into failure."

• In their book, *The Feminization of America,* Elinor Lenz and Barbara Myerhoff claim that "the morale-boosting, performance-improving impact of the feminine presence has not escaped the notice of corporate personnel managers. Jane Evans [then executive vice president of General Mills, now president and general partner of Montgomery Consumer Fund, Montgomery Securities] reports that corporations are searching for women who know how to help men open up and [learn people skills]."

• Based on his survey of 2,191 private- and public-sector executives, Weston Agor, Ph.D., author of *Intuitive Management*, reports: "Women consistently scored higher on the right-brain

---

[1] Reprinted by permission, *Executive Female,* March/April, 1988, pp. 20-24.

scale for intuition than men in every group sampled...What may be most significant about this pattern of scores is the fact that women's overall management style appears to approximate that of the *top* managers tests more closely than men's style does."

BETTER THAN BRAND X?

Call this *nouvelle* management intuitive, feminine, androgynous; call it Japanese (you wouldn't be the first). Whatever you call it, the true test is not how many books it sells, but how effective and productive it makes the people being managed. Carol D. Watson, Ph.D., an assistant professor at the Graduate School of Management, Rutgers University, in Newark, New Jersey, tested subordinates' reactions to women using different leadership styles. She found that, under all circumstances, the "feminine-considerate" style worked at least as well as the "masculine-dominant" style, and when the subordinates were all men, it worked far better.

"To me," says Dr. Watson, "the answer is very clearly that what we think of as a male management style doesn't work for men *or* women, but it works less well for women." Managerial women, she says, "are already assertive enough, and it may be a strike against them to be *too* assertive. It doesn't make sense to tell women to act more like men. It makes sense to tell them to use the skills we assume they already have."

It doesn't make sense to everyone. "When people say, 'Bring feminine leadership into the workplace,' I say, 'Hooey! Bring an *effective* style of leadership—not male, not female—into the workplace," says Paula Bern, Ph.D., author of *How to Work for a Woman Boss (Even is You'd Rather Not)*. I am opposed to that type of thinking because it will keep women in middle management forever. Women who use a 'feminine' style of leadership will protest, "But look how far I've gotten—I'm a manager with six people under me.' I say, 'Great—but you're always going to have six people under you. If you ever want *200* people under you, you will have to act more like your male boss!

"Bella Abzug told me, 'If women don't want to change the workplace, they shouldn't be in power, '" Dr. Bern relates. "I disagree. Men who are successful have developed, over the years, a way of operating: They're tough, aggressive and willing to take risks. As long as we have a male-dominated workplace, we have to emulate male role models and incorporate our own strengths." She adds, "You still can't look at the president at AT&T or any major corporation and say, 'I want to be just like *her*.'"

PLAYING BALL

The male-dominated system of the marketplace rewards individuals who perform to its standards" concurs Pauline Lyttle, president of GenderCorp, a Scottsdale, Arizona-based consulting firm specializing in gender-based differences, and coauthor of *Why Jenny Can't Lead*. "We are on male turf, forced to learn male politics, not because we want to imitate their behaviors—but because competent men know how to get what they want from their turf, and we don't."

Lyttle names some of the strategies she feels women must learn to do battle on male turf: refraining from making constant moral judgements; changing people's behavior without attacking their entire value systems; and creating relationships of mutual reliance and protection with others in the corporation.

"Women test others against their own values and principles," she says. "If we decide we can't be friends with certain people, we make them enemies and feel justified in working against their interests, even if they work for our company." Men, Lyttle adds, "have morals and values, but keep them to themselves. They assume that the company pays them to play ball with anybody who can help them achieve the company's goals.

"Women spend a lot of time and energy trying to convert people to the side of truth and justice," she says. "Savvy men don't try to change other people. They say, 'You and I disagree.

What will it take to change your behavior?' [This tactic] allows them to get things done with people of different persuasions, without compromising their own values."

Critics of the "feminine leadership" approach see practical, as well as philosophical, differences between the sexes. Dr. Bern describes some typical weaknesses of female managers:

"Women can't give crisp, efficient orders. They go into a long song and dance, saying, 'Would you mind doing this? I would appreciate it. I prefer to have it by 3, but if you can't finish it until 6, it's OK.'" When it comes to negotiating, she says, "women either get embarrassed and back down or panic and push the other person to the wall and lose." And on a day-to-day basis, "we don't look at the broad picture, but at little nitty-gritty things," says Dr. Bern. "When men break into senior management, they see the big picture and don't worry about whether their secretary took 10 extra minutes for lunch."

NO BIG DEAL?

Is all of this ado about nothing? The current consensus of academic opinion, as expressed by the New York City-based business research and advisory organization Catalyst, is that "gender differences in managerial style may be mainly in the eye of the beholder. In fact, there are more similarities than there are differences between men's and women's managerial styles."

"I don't believe management qualities are necessarily gender-related; it's mainly our conditioning," says Dr. Bern. "Little girls are brought up to take, not to give, orders, so when women get into management positions, they have problems delegating. Women have to learn how to take risks, how to delegate and how to negotiate, otherwise they are not going to make it. Those are not masculine traits, but they have been typed as masculine."

What about the supposed advantages women's conditioning gives them? "I think most women, because they've traditionally been caretakers, tend to be more empathetic, more nurturing, than the average man," Dr. Bern says. Their emotional reinforcement pays off when employees who feel well-cared-for reciprocate with increased loyalty and productivity.

Women managers themselves see some clear differences between their own style and that of their male counterparts. "I'm the kind of manager who like to explain things inside and out," says Grace Lozito, circulation director for seven consumer publications at Murdoch Magazines in New York City. "Women tend to do that more than men. With men, you have to figure out the who, what, where, when and why." Another difference she sees is that "women tend to listen better and be more responsive to people's needs."

Dale Venturini, general manager at Rochester Midland Corporation, a chemicals manufacturer in Providence, Rhode Island, expresses a similar sentiment: "We [women] are looked at differently, so I think, 'How can I use that to my benefit?' I use it in dealing with people's feeling, and I have excellent listening skills that men don't have."

"Generally speaking, women managers tend to be more emotional—not in their decision-making, but in their style of presentation," says Jan Rock, director of marketing for the diagnostics division of Tambrands, Inc. in Lake Success, New York. "When people argue for something they believe in strongly, I see women make more passionate pleas. Women are *not* over-reactors," she says firmly, "but they feel more comfortable expressing exhilaration as well as anger." Like many psychologists and sociologists studying gender-related style differences, Rock attributes this one to cultural messages. "It has to be that little girls are taught it's OK to express their emotions," she reasons.

As for being "softer" managers, Rock says, "Anyone who's too concerned about being liked may have a problem getting tough. It's not that women can't be tough when they have to be."

LEADING THE WAY

All managers, whether they fit the masculine or the feminine mold, try to get the best from their people by using the methods they believe will make them effective leaders. What is a good leader? To get to the root of that question, Barry Z. Posner, director of graduate education for the Leavey School of Business and Administration at Santa Clara University in California, and his colleague, James R. Kouzes, director of the university's Executive Education Center, spent five years studying the factors that are at work when people achieve their "personal best" as leaders. By analyzing 500 case studies, 50 in-depth interviews and 6,500 questionnaires filled out by the managers' bosses and subordinates, the researchers found a pattern of leadership that was the same for male and female managers in five key ways: innovating; communicating goals; sharing information; demonstrating commitment; and breaking the plan down into a series of small "wins," to motivate people to keep trying.

The only significant difference showed up in the sixth characteristic. "Subordinates see women as 'encouraging the heart' more—building a team, recognizing individual achievements and celebrating them in a public way," reports Posner. "That jibes with other research that says women are more comfortable showing appreciation and cheerleading.'"

When it came to difference in style, Posner notes, "the female executives in our sample were more willing to listen in order to develop a consensus, to gather and integrate alternative viewpoints and to build a team." These characteristics, he says, add up to "a successful style that works for both men and women."

THE BEST OF BOTH WORLDS

There's no prescription for the perfect, all-purpose management style, but these are some common traits of successful managers that combine the best elements of the "masculine" and "feminine" approaches:

1. Listen—for the hard facts *and* the emotional undertones—but guide the discussion to keep people's thoughts on track.
2. Gather information from all sources, weigh all sides, then make firm decisions.
3. Stay flexible. Be democratic enough to get the best from your people, but authoritative enough to give orders when necessary.
4. Accept that most gains require risk. Learn to manage risk, rather than avoid it.
5. Look for mentors of both sexes, and incorporate their strengths into your own style.
6. Don't get bogged down in picayune details; focus on the big picture.
7. Don't be afraid to show your feelings, but keep your emotions under control in crises and back up your arguments with facts, not feelings.
8. Put aside personal differences with colleagues and collaborate on common goals.

MAKING A GAME PLAN

Venturini, like many successful senior-level managers, has worked out a style of her own that incorporates elements of both kinds of leadership. "You have to be intuitive and caring, but you also have to be a team player and have political skills to be a great manager." She characterizes her own style as "forthright and very decisive," but with a "win-win" approach typical of feminine, or participative, management.

No matter how "feminine" their instincts, seasoned managerial women acknowledge the real-world necessity of learning the games men play and of sometimes playing along. Venturini, the supervisor of 17 men and three women, observes, "If two men can't stand one another, they'll still throw their arms around each other if they have a common business goal. But I've seen two women who don't like each other go into a board meeting and sit at opposite ends of the room so they don't have to speak to one anther." She says, "I consciously play the game, whether I agree with all the rules or not. You make that decision the day you decide to make more than $40,000 a year."

"Some women say they don't like a cutthroat. You have to have a tough, aggressive streak within you. You can't come to work and say, 'I baked some cookies and we're all going to sit around eating them and drinking tea.' That's not how business operates."

Even "feminine" management may not be as soft as it seems on the surface. "Both men and women need to be participative managers, but most people feel that means being 'nice,' and not being assertive," says Dr. Watson. "In fact, it is possible to be concerned for your subordinates and still be very assertive. You give people a lot of freedom, but decide which areas to give them that freedom in."

SUPERWOMAN LIVES

For some women, the current message that they should combine all the best qualities of male and female managers sounds like another impossible-to-live-up-to Superwoman image in the making. "We're like the mother who is expected to 'do it all,'" complains Lozito. "We're expected to be gentle, sensitive, emotional, rational, sensible and bottom-lined oriented. I don't think there's that much of a burden placed on men. Women are not allowed to have a bad day; they don't have the luxury of flying off the handle once in a while, the way men do."

Another troubling aspect of having women managers widely advertised as "nurturing" and "supportive" may be that it shortens the distance from their subordinates that all managers need to function effectively. "People complain about my being unavailable," says Lozito. "I think they expect a woman manager to be totally accessible and to respond to their every need."

In addition, Dr. Bern says that, often, a female subordinate "expects a woman boss to be her confidante, to be understanding if she can't come in because she's taking Johnny to the pediatrician. And she resents it when the boss says, 'You'd better get your husband or a sitter to do it, because we have a deadline to meet.' A woman boss can be understanding, but not always responsive, because she can't afford to be—and the higher she goes, the less she can afford to be."

"People's different expectations of women create conflict [for them]," Dr. Watson confirms. "Women are not supposed to be aggressive, strong, dominant—yet society says that's the way to act if you're going to be a leader." She says, "Women managers have to walk a tightrope: They have to be strong enough to inspire confidence, but not aggressive enough to scare people off."

THE COMPANY OF MEN

When all other factors are equal, does the gender of subordinates affect the way women manage them? The managers interviewed said that it does not, but research suggests that gender may affect the way the subordinates *react* to a particular style or supervision. A study of 40 male and female managers conducted by Professor Anne Statham of the University of Wisconsin revealed that the "hands-on" style of close supervision favored by many female managers is misinterpreted by male workers as a lack of faith in their abilities. These men are more comfortable with the typical male management style of stepping back and leaving subordinates to work out the details on their own. Meanwhile, Dr. Watson's laboratory studies uncovered another finding that she found "disturbing": In test groups with female subordinates, they seemed to want the woman who was supervising them to behave in a more dominating way, but gave her low ratings when she did. This seems to suggest, Dr. Watson says, that women want female bosses to behave more aggressively, but they don't like them if they do.

The character of the employees and the nature of their work, more than their gender, may be the deciding factor in how a manager operates. While it's all well and good to debate the merits of authoritarian vs. participative management, your style may be decided by the situation. When Regina Rosenberg worked as the plant manager of a shoe factory in the rough Bedford-Stuyvesant section of Brooklyn, "feminine" leadership was out of the question. Managing was a daily battle to maintain order and keep production going while handling constant clashes with 400 "very chauvinistic" male subordinates. "It got pretty hairy sometimes. Some of the Hispanic men had a

Latin *machismo* thing; they resented being supervised by a women," she says, and would taunt her by muttering insults in Spanish when she passed by.

Seasoned women managers acknowledge the need to learn the games men play—and to sometimes play along.

"You couldn't be sensitive with those men," Rosenberg says. "You had to win their respect and show them who was boss." Although it took her "four or five very frustrating months," she was able to get the men on her side and even "build a rapport with them." They gave a dramatic demonstration of their support when Rosenberg fired a difficult worker and he threatened to kill her, within earshot of the other employees. "The men came running to my defense," she recalls, "carrying baseball bats and lead pipes." Today, managing a staff of men and women in a plush Fifth Avenue showroom, Rosenberg had adapted her approach, "I don't have to use muscle anymore," she says. "I bring the people I supervise into my decision-making. It's important to encourage people, otherwise everyone stagnates."

WHAT'S AHEAD

What's the trend in hiring? Are employers paying attention to the great style debate? "Management style is often the key to getting a job," says Eleanor Raynolds, a partner in the New York-based executive recruiting firm Ward Howell International. "When we put candidates up for a position, they all have the technical skills needed for it, but interpersonal skills will put one person ahead of the rest."

There is no across-the-board preference, however, for executives with a typically male or female approach. "Different openings call for different management styles," she says, "If there are open wounds within the organization—like there might be if they've just let 10,000 employees go—they need a nurturer. They need someone who can wrap her arms around people and say, 'We're here to stay and we need you. Stick with us.'

"But if they have a lot of dead wood and an acquirer is breathing down their neck," Raynolds goes on, "they might need someone with a tougher management style who'll get people to step up to the plate and make a difference."

At this point, it's impossible to say who will have the last word in the argument over how women—and men—should manage. But, for now, the chorus of voices continues from people on both sides of the issue. What's remarkable is that, when it comes to giving bottom-line advice to female managers, they all seem to be in harmony, advocating that women remain flexible and open-mined and learn as much from as many people as they can.

Dr. Dubno says, "The democratic, not authoritarian, approach is best for everybody. Gender has absolutely nothing to do with it. Smarts have everything to do with it, and being able to analyze the managerial situation you find yourself in and adapt to it."

Or, as Grace Lozito puts it, "The way to win is just to try real hard and develop all of your skills—to be on your guard sometimes and let your hair down other times. You have to show all of your sides." And walk like...a manager.

THE FOUR FACES OF SOCIAL RESPONSIBILITY

Dan R. Dalton
and
Richard A. Cosier[1]

Imagine that your company is considering introducing a new plastic container to the market. Your company considers itself to be socially responsible; therefore, an extensive impact assessment program is undertaken. One of your environmentally-minded employees suggests that people might light the containers and then cook their meals over the fire. Although the idea sounds bizarre, you don't want to take any chances, so for over a month you cook hamburgers over a fire made from your plastic bottles. Rats are fed this hamburger, then carefully monitored for negative side effects. Tests indicate that these rats suffer no ill effects.

Of course you also perform an extensive series of tests involving energy usage, disposal, and recycling opportunities. Then you invite the public to carefully scheduled hearings across the country in order to encourage consumer inputs. Finally, you market the new product and land a major soft drink company as a customer.

Sound as if your company has fulfilled its responsibilities and forestalled any possible objections? In the mid-70s Monsanto went through this very process in developing Cycle-Safe bottles and spent more than $47 million to make the product. But in 1977 the FDA banned the bottle because, when stored at 120 degrees for an extended period of time, molecules strayed from the plastic into the contents. Rats, fed with doses that were equivalent to consuming thousands of quarts of soft drink over a human lifetime, developed an above-normal number of tumors.

Monsanto felt that they were providing a product that did something for society—a plastic bottle that could be recycled. But social responsibility is unavoidably a matter of degree and interpretation. Forces outside of the business are liable to interpret a product to be socially unacceptable, even when the company has undertaken an impact analysis.

A precise evaluation of what is socially responsible is difficult to establish and of course, many definitions have been suggested. Joseph McGuire, in *Business and Society*, provided a persuasive focus when he stated that the corporation "must act 'justly' as a proper citizen should." Large corporations have, not only legal obligations, but also certain responsibilities to society which extend beyond the parameters set by law. As the Monsanto case illustrates, the line between legality and responsibility is sometimes very fine.

Peter Drucker offers a useful way to distinguish between behaviors in organizations; the first is what an organization does *to* society, the other what an organization can do *for* society. This suggests that organizations can be evaluated on at least two dimensions with respect to their performance as "citizens": legality and responsibility. The accompanying Table illustrates the

---

[1] *Business Horizons:* Copyright, 1982, by the Foundation for the School of Business at Indiana University. Reprinted by permission.

various combinations of legality and responsibility which may characterize an organization's performance.

These combinations are the *four faces of social responsibility*. Each cell of the table represents a strategy which could be adopted by an organization. It is unfortunate, but we think true, that no matter which strategy is chosen, the corporation is subject to some criticism.

THE FOUR FACES OF SOCIAL RESPONSIBILITY

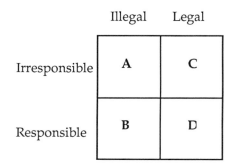

ILLEGAL AND IRRESPONSIBLE

In modern society, this strategy, if not fatal, is certainly extremely high risk. In an age of social consciousness, it is difficult to image an organization that would regularly engage in illegal and irresponsible behavior. What, for example, would be the consequences of an organization's blatantly refusing to employ certain minority groups or deliberately and knowingly using a carcinogenic preservative in foodstuff? Besides the fact that such behavior is patently illegal, it is offensive and irresponsible.

There are, however, instances of illegal and irresponsible corporate conduct which are not so easily condemned.

YOU CAN HARDLY BLAME THEM

Most of us have value systems. They vary, to be sure, from individual to individual and from corporation to corporation. They do, however, have common elements: they are tempered by temptation, consequence, and risk. Sometimes when faced with high temptation, low consequence, and low risk, our value systems are not the constraining force they could be. This may be the human condition and insufficient justification for the excesses which often accompany individual and corporate decision making. Nonetheless, an appreciation of these factors often makes those decisions entirely understandable.

Suppose that the state in which you live invokes a regulation that all motor vehicles operated on a public thoroughfare must be equipped with an "X" type pollution-control device. This law, for the sake of discussion, is retroactive. All automobiles registered in the state must be refitted with such a device, which cost $500. All automobiles are subject to periodic inspection to assure compliance with the law. Assume that the maximum fine (consequence) for violating this statute is $50. Assume, furthermore, that there is one chance in one hundred that you will be inspected and found in violation. The analytical question is simply stated: Would you have the device installed? If you do, it will cost $500. If you do not, the cost will be $500 plus a $50 fine, but only *if* you are caught. Many, if not most, of us surely would not install the device. Strictly speaking, our behavior is both illegal and irresponsible. Our failure to comply exacerbates a societal problem— namely, polluting the air. Our reluctance under the described circumstances, however, is understandable: temptation along with low consequence and low risk.

Compare this situation with that of a large organization faced with the decision to install pollution abatement equipment in one of its plants. Suppose, in this case, the total cost of the installation is $500,000; the maximum fine for noncompliance is $10,000; the chance of being caught is one in one hundred. We ask the same question: Would you comply? We have actually been charitable with the balance of costs and probabilities in this example. The Occupational Safety and Health Administration (OSHA), which was given the charter for establishing and enforcing occupational safety and health standards, has a limited number of inspectors and approximately five million organizations subject to its mandate. It has been estimated that an organization could plan on being inspected about every seventy-seven years, or approximately as often as you could expect to see Halley's comet.[1]   Furthermore, $10,000 is a very large fine by OSHA standards. The fundamental point, of course, is that the temptation to ignore the law ($500,000) is large, the fine ($10,000) low, and the risk (once every seventy-seven years) very small. You cannot be surprised when an organization does not comply any more than you would be surprised that the individual with the polluting car did not comply.

It can be argued that the organization has the greater responsibility. Certainly, a polluting smokestack is more visible, literally and figuratively, than an automobile's exhaust. However, we daresay that the marginal pollution attributable to automobiles far exceeds that of smokestacks in most (if not all) regions. Illegal? Yes. Irresponsible? Yes. Understandable?

Whether or not the behavior is "understandable," the result, at a minimum, is bad publicity. The observation that a corporation is likely to be criticized for operating in that "Illegal/Irresponsible" area is obvious. There has, however, been testimony and documentation that the weight of potential litigations in a classic cost/benefit analysis is far less than the cost of recalling or correcting the alleged deficiencies. While we have suggested that behavior in this area is high risk, there is precious little evidence that it is suicidal.

ILLEGAL/RESPONSIBLE

Being in this cell raises very interesting issues. Monsanto found itself in this cell in the Cycle-Safe incident. The FDA ruled their product "illegal," even though Monsanto felt socially responsible. Many time however, organizations find themselves in ths area because of jurisdictional disputes. Suppose that prior to the Civil Rights Act of 1964 and attendant legislation, an organization chose to embark on a program to employ women in equal capacities as male employees. At the time, this would have been forward-looking and extremely responsible corporate behavior. Unfortunately, much of the behavior involved in implementing that strategy would have been unquestionably illegal. During that period, "protective legislation" was very common. This legislation, designed to "protect" women, restricted working hours, overtime, the amount of weight that could be lifted, and types of jobs (bartending, for example) available to women. These and similar matters were eventually adjudicated largely at the federal court level.

Grover Starling cites an interesting jurisdictional paradox. It seems that the Federal Meat Inspection Service ordered an Armour meat-packing plant to create an aperture in a conveyor line so that inspectors could remove samples for testing. Accordingly, the company did so. The Occupational Safety and Health Administration soon arrived and demanded that the aperture be closed. It seems that an aperture on that line constituted a safety hazard. Predictably, each agency threatened to close down the plant if it refused to comply with its orders.[2] This example demonstrates how an organization could be operating in a fundamentally desirable manner (safely) and yet run afoul of underprivileged children, for example, and find itself in violation of a minimum wage law.

One potential strategy for dealing with problems in this cell is challenging the law. Laws can be, and are regularly, deliberately violated for no other reason that to challenge their application. You cannot get a hearing in a state or federal court on a "what if" basis. In order to get a hearing, someone must be in jeopardy. A classic example is the famous Gideon vs. Wainwright case the Supreme Court ruled that a suspect has the right to counsel and that the state must provide such counsel if the accused could not afford it. This case could not have been decided without an issue—a man convicted without benefit of counsel. Gideon had to be in jeopardy. Courts do not rule on hypothetical cases.

The public is often critical of the corporate use of the courts. It is true that the courts, aside from their jurisprudential charter, are often used as a delay mechanism. There are, for example, legendary antitrust cases which have been in the courts for years. The courts have ruled against the acquisition, but organizations, through a series of legal maneuvers, have managed to stall the actual separations. In the meantime, presumably, the benefits of the acquisition continue to accrue. Interestingly, everyone's "pursuit of justice" is someone else's "delay." Even in Gideon vs. Wainwright, we have little doubt that the prosecuting attorney's office saw the several appeals as both a nuisance and a delay.

Again, organizations can find themselves in a dilemma. An organization in the "Illegal/Responsible" cell faces a paradox. It is likely to be criticized whether it lives within the law or, potentially, challenges it.

IRRESPONSIBLE/LEGAL

Historically, there have been astonishing excesses in this area. Some of them would have been laughable if they had not been so serious. For example, prior to the Pure Food and Drug Act, the advertising for a diet pill promised that a person taking this pill could eat virtually anything at any time and still lose weight. Too good to be true? Actually, the claim was quite true; the product lived up to its billing with frightening efficacy. It seems that the primary active ingredient in this "diet supplement" was tapeworm larvae. These larvae would develop in the intestinal tract and, of course, be well fed; the pill taker would in time, quite literally, starve to death.

In another case, which can only be described as amazing, an "anti-alcoholic elixir" was guaranteed to prevent the person who received the "potion" from drinking to excess. It was *very* effective. The product contained such a large does of codeine that the people taking it became essentially comatose. The good news, of course, is that they certainly did not drink very much. And at the time, this product was not illegal.

There are more current examples with which we are family familiar—black lung disease in miners and asbestos poisoning, among others. Certainly, it was not always illegal to have miners working in mines without sufficient safety equipment to forestall black lung; nor was it illegal to have employees regularly working with asbestos without adequate protection. It can be argued that these consequences were not anticipated and that these situations were not deliberately socially irresponsible. It is, however, less persuasive to make that argument with respect to the ages and extended working hours of children in our industrial past.

But enough of the past. Do major organizations continue to engage in behaviors which, while not illegal, may be completely irresponsible? Among several examples that come to mind, one is, we think, appropriate for discussion but likely to be highly contentious—the manufacture and distribution of cigarettes. Obviously, cigarette manufacturing is not illegal. Is it responsible?

We noted earlier that knowledge of the effects of certain drugs may have been lacking in the past. We mentioned codeine-based elixirs. There are others. Some compounds contained as much as three grams of cocaine per base ounce. One asthma reliever was nearly pure cocaine. Even so, perhaps their effects were little understood and little harm was thought to have been done. Can the same be said of tobacco industry? Is there anyone who is not aware of the harmful effects of smoking? True, there are warning labels which imply that the purchaser knows what he or she is taking. But how many people would endorse the use of codeine or cocaine or any other harmful substance, even with an appropriate warning label. Comparing apples and oranges? Perhaps, but fifty years from now, writers may talk about the manufacture of tobacco products and use terms such as "astonishing," "amazing" and "laughable" as we have to describe other legal, but irresponsible, behaviors.

Certainly, issues other than health are contained in this category. Suppose an organization is faced with more demand for its product than it can meet. Naturally, the organization does not care to encourage competition and would prefer to meet the demand itself if possible. Unfortunately, their plants are already operating twenty-four hours per day, seven days a week. There is simply no further capacity. Management decides to build a new plant, which can be completed in no less than four years.

In the meantime, it is discovered that an existing, abandoned plant can be acquired and refitted in six months. Now, this plant will not be efficient, and will be only marginally profitable at best. It will, however, serve to meet the escalating demand until such time as the new plant is ready for full operation, some four years hence.

Juryrigging this abandoned plant, however, involves several problems. Foremost among them is the fact that the community does not have the infrastructure to serve the plant and the expected influx of employees. School systems will have to be expanded; housing will have to be built; recreational services improved. For the sake of this discussion, suppose that the temporary plant will employ 1,200 persons. It would be reasonable to estimate that this would mean the addition of 3,000 to 3,500 persons in the community. But, remember, this plant will be closed as soon as the new plant in another location is operational.

What is your decision? Do you authorize the refitting of this temporary plant? Certainly, if you notify the community that the plant is temporary, you will pay certain costs. The community would be understandably unlikely to make permanent improvements. Local banks would be somewhat less than enthusiastic about financing building projects, home mortgages, or consumer loans of any description. The simple solution is obvious—don't tell.

The point is that to deliberately use this plant as a stop-gap measure knowing full well that it will be temporary is not illegal. We are aware of no legislation which would prevent this action. There remain, however, some obvious social ramifications of this strategy. The ultimate closing of this plant is likely to reduce this community to a ghost town; there will be widespread unemployment; property values will fall precipitously; the tax base will be destroyed.

Once again, operating in this area is subject to criticism, underscoring our earlier point that being a "law-abiding" corporate citizen is not nearly enough; while organizations may not violate a single law, they may not be socially responsible. What of gambling casinos dealing, not only in games of chance but also offering endless free liquor and decolletage? How about the manufactures of handguns? Automobiles with questionable, if not lethal, fuel systems? Can a society hold organizations to a standard higher than that demanded by law?

LEGAL/RESPONSIBLE

It would seem that we have finally arrived at a strategy for which an organization cannot be criticized. An organization in this sector is a law-abiding corporate citizen and engages in behaviors which exceed those required by law—voluntary socially oriented action. Alas, even this proactive strategy is subject to four severe criticisms.

- Such behavior amounts to a unilateral, involuntary redistribution of assets;
- These actions lead to inequitable, regressive redistribution of assets;
- An organization engaging in these behaviors clearly exceeds its province; and
- Social responsibility is entirely too expensive and rarely subjected to cost/benefit analysis.

INVOLUTARY REDISTRIBUTION

Probably the chief spokesperson of this position is Nobel laureate and economist, Milton Friedman. He points out that today, unlike one hundred years ago, managers do no "own" the business. They are employees, nothing more and nothing less. As such their primary responsibility is to the owner—the stockholder. Their relationship is essentially a fiduciary one. Friedman argues that the primary charter of the manager, therefore is to conduct the business in accordance with the wishes of the employer, given that these wishes are within the limits embodied in the law and ethical custom. Any social actions beyond that amount to an involuntary redistribution of assets. To the extent that these actions reduce dividends, stockholders suffer; to the extent that these actions raise prices, consumers suffer; to the extend that such actions reduce potential wages and benefits, employees suffer. Should any or all of these interested parties care to make philanthropic contributions to fund socially desirable projects, they may do so. Without their consent, however, such redistributions are clearly unilateral and involuntary.

INEQUITABLE, REGRESSIVE REDISTRIBUTIONS

This tendency can be referred to as a reverse Robin Hood effect.[3] Mr. Hood and his band of merry men stole from the rich and gave to the poor, but many programs under the loose rubric of social responsibility have not followed this redistribution pattern. In fact, it can be argued that many programs actually rob the poor to serve the rich. Obviously, the more wealthy persons are, the more regressive this social responsibility "tax."

Many projects which are not commercially feasible are supported by the largest of organizations under the banner of social responsibility. Opera and dance companies, for example, may be subsidized by corporate contributions. Public television is heavily financed by corporate sponsors. The reason that these subsidiaries are essential to the operation of these programs is that public demand for these products is altogether insufficient to defray their costs. Presumably, the money to finance these ventures comes from somewhere in the organizational coffers. Consumers, employees, and other "contribute," as we previously noted, to the availability of these funds.

Who, however, is the primary beneficiary of these subsidized programs? For the most part, it seems fair to suggest that those who regularly attend ballets, operas, dance companies, live theater, symphonies, and watch similar programming on public television are relatively more affluent. It would appear that real income is transferred from the poorer to the richer in this exercise of social responsibility.

EXCEEDING PROVINCE

One, if not the foremost, justification for government involvement in private affairs is market failure. When the market cannot provide, for whatever reasons, that which the public demands, then government is (or should be) enfranchised to supply or finance that product or service. National defense, health and safety, and welfare are a few of the services which the private sector is unable to supply. It may be that libraries, museums, parks and recreation, operas, symphonies, and support for other performing arts are in this category as well. The objection which is central here is that it is not the province of private organizations to decide which of these projects should be funded and to what extent. Such support should not be a function of the predilections of corporate officials; this is the charter of government.

The issue clearly goes beyond fighting over who is going to play with what toys. In theory, public officials are subject to review by the citizenry. If the public does not approve of the manner in which funds are being prioritized for social concerns, they may petition their various legislatures. Failing in this, they may not support the reelection of the appropriate public officials. The public, on the other hand, does not vote or in any other manner approve or endorse highly ranking officers of corporations. By what right should corporations decide what is "good" and what is "right." It may well be that a given corporate image of righteousness is somewhat different from your own.

The potential for corporate influence in this "public" area is enormous. Theodore Levitt, while (we hope) overstating the case somewhat, presents a clear view of the potential of business statesmanship:

> Proliferating employee welfare programs, its serpentine involvement in community, government, charitable, and educational affairs, its prodigious currying of political and public favor through hundreds of peripheral preoccupations, all these well-intended but insidious contrivances are greasing the rails for our collective descent into a social order that would be as repugnant to the corporations themselves as to their critics. The danger is that

all things will turn the corporation into a twentieth-century equivalent of the medieval Church. The corporation would eventually invest itself with all-embracing duties, obligations, and finally powers—ministering to the whole man and molding him and society in the image of the corporation's narrow ambitions and its essentially unsocial needs.[4]

EXPENSE OF SOCIAL RESPONSIBILITY

A final objection to the general issue of social responsibility, whether mandated by regulation or voluntarily pursued by organizations, is that it is oppressively expensive. The necessity to comply with ever-stricter environmental standards, for example, has literally forced the closing of hundreds of industrial locations across the country. Furthermore, it has been argued that these regulations have seriously affected domestic industry's ability to compete in international markets.

No one would argue that expense alone is sufficient to discard programs of environmental protection, employee safety, consumer protection, or a host of other socially responsive concerns. However, it can be argued that these programs should subjected to a cost/benefit analysis. Quite often, this is not done. An automobile, for example, could be manufactured so soundly that driver deaths in accidents could be practically eliminated on our highways. But at what cost? We do not intend to address the question of what a human life is worth. Obviously, its value is incalculable. The fact remains that we live in a finite world; resources are limited. When we choose to make expenditures in one area, we necessarily restrict or eliminate expenditure in another. At what point do safety programs become overly paternalistic? At some time, employees, for example, must bear a certain responsibility for their own safety. The same can be said for those who operate motor vehicles on public byways.

While this principle seems clear, it is often not considered. What expense is justifiable to renovate and refit public buildings to render them essentially fireproof? Or, if not fireproof, at least such that the loss of human life by fire is remote. The hard fact is that very few people die each year in fires in multi-storied buildings. Who is going to pay for such judicious safety? And for the benefit of how many?

The same approach can be pursued with respect to airliner safety. Fortunately very few people lose their lives each year in commercial airplanes. There is no doubt that airplanes could be manufactured so that they would be even safer in accidents. Again, at what cost? We do not wish to appear insensitive; the loss of a human life is a tragedy, especially if it could have been prevented. "Safety at any cost," however, is simply not viable in a society restricted by finite resources.

The objection regarding the expense of social responsibility is easily restated. Aside from its absolute expense, which can be formidable, critics argue that social responsibility is often not accompanied by sufficient benefits to justify its cost.

Once again, even while being both legal and responsible, an organization is likely to receive severe criticism.

We have suggested that every cell (Illegal/Irresponsible; Illegal/Responsible; Legal/Irresponsible; Legal/Responsible) is subject to criticism. Furthermore, the cell that your organization occupies may be determined by individuals outside of your firm—federal agencies or consumer groups, to name a few. It may be a classic expression of the aphorism, "You're damned if you do; you're damned if you don't." Inasmuch as all strategies are subject to criticism, where should the organization operate? Which is the optimum strategy?

We think there are three fundamental principles which should be considered by an organization with respect to choosing a strategy for social responsibility; *primum non nocere*, organizational accountability, and the double standard.

PRIMUM NON NOCERE

This notion was first explicated over 2,500 years ago in the Hippocractic oath. Freely translated, it means "Above all, knowingly do no harm." This would seem to be a sound principle for both legality and responsibility. Organizations should not engage in any behavior if they know that harm will be done as a result. This is not meant to be literally interpreted. Certainly, knowing that some individuals will injure themselves is insufficient to bar the manufacture and distribution of, for example, steak knives. This, like any principle, should be tempered with good sense.

ORGANIZATIONAL ACCOUNTABILITY

An organization should be responsible for its impacts, *to* or *for* society, whether they are intended or not. Ordinarily, in the course of providing a good or a service, costs are incurred. Presumably, the price of the product or service is, at least in part, a function of the costs of its manufacture or delivery. The difference between the cost and the price is profit—the *sine qua non* of private enterprise. This would be acceptable, except for one oversight—very often society underwrites portions of the cost. Historically, given that the production of energy through sulphurous coal leads to higher levels of air pollution, the costs of producing electricity have been artificially low. That pollution is a cost. Sooner or later, someone has to pay to clean it up. But who? The consumer did not have to pay a premium for the electricity to enter a "clean-up" fund. The power company made no such contribution.

Today, we could argue that cigarette manufacturing enterprises enjoy a certain cost reduction. The manufacturer and the smoker can be thought of as enjoying a subsidy. Arguably, the retail price of cigarettes does not approach that necessary to cover its total costs. Where, for instance, is the fund that will eventually be called upon to pay for the medical costs allegedly associated with smoking? The point is that someone should be accountable for these behaviors.

DOUBLE STANDARD

Traditionally, the concept of a "double standard" has had a negative connotation. In the area of social corporate responsibility, we think it is reasonable, even commendable. As we have continuously noted, there are no rules that apply to organizations about what, where, when, how much, and how often they can engage in behaviors *for* society, but a certain power-responsibility equation has been suggested.[5] Essentially, this equation argues that the social responsibility expected of an organization should be commensurate with the size of the social power it exercises. Large companies—AT&T, General Motors, Exxon, IBM, General Electric, DuPont—whose operations can literally dominate entire regions of the country have a greater responsibility than smaller organizations with less influence.

The larger an organization becomes, the more actual and potential influence it commands over society. Society, necessarily, take a greater interest in the affairs of such organizations. Society has correspondingly less expectation of social responsibility from smaller organizations.

This is the nature of the double standard to which we have referred. While any double standard is somewhat unfair, it highlights an observation made by Drucker. He argues that the quest for social responsibility is not a result of hostility towards the business community. Rather the demand for social responsibility is, in large measure, the price of success. Success and influence may well lead to a greater responsibility to society. A double standard, to be sure, but perhaps a reasonable one.

SO WHICH STRATEGY?

We belive that organizations should adopt a strategy reflected in cell D—legal and responsible. Remember, however, that the classification of cell "D" will be determined by the public (or government acting "for" the public). Organizations have to anticipate, and in some cases, influence the public reaction—be proactive. However, a proactive stance involves some risk. As we noted earlier, critics abound regardless of the cell in the table occupied by the organization. A certain risk, nevertheless, is necessary for any business to succeed. Drucker rightly states that to try to eliminate risk in business is futile. Risk is inherent in the commitment of present resources to future expectation. The attempt to eliminate risk may result in the greatest risk of all—rigidity.

We would argue that merely being a law-abiding corporate citizen is something less than social responsibility. It may be that large organizations must "do something." Affirmative action is a compelling analogy. It is not enough not to discriminate. Organizations must "do something" proactively to further the goals of equal employment opportunity. Perhaps this is true for other issues of corporate social responsibility as well. There may be an expectation that organizations must "do something" to further benefit society beyond following its formal laws.

Basically, some action is better than no action. Throughout the course of history, inaction has never advanced mankind. In our view, errors of commission are far better than those of omission. If our ancestors had heeded the critics who were opposed to doing something, we might all still be drawing on cave walls. This issue is not entirely philosophical; there are important pragmatic considerations as well, as evidenced in the remarks of DuPont chairperson, Irving S. Shapiro:

> I think we're a means to an end, and while producing goods and providing jobs is our primary function, we can live successfully in a society if the hearts of its cities are decaying and its people can't make the whole system work...It means that, just as you want libraries, and you want schools, and you want fire departments and police departments, you also want businesses to help do something about unsolved social problems.[6]

Occasionally, it is argued that true social responsibility does not exist. Organizations do not operate out of social responsibility—but good business. Many instances of activities which could be referred to as "responsible" are public relations strategies which are sound business; it pays to advertise. Truly philanthropic efforts occur without fanfare. Some argue that only when organizations anonymously contribute their executives and other resources to socially responsible programs do you have true responsiveness. Perhaps. But we choose not to define social responsibility as philanthropy. We have no objection to enlightened self-interest.

Assuming that society is not totally victimized by actions justified under the banner of social responsibility, then corporations, even pursuing their interests, present a win-win situation. If restoring land to its natural state after mining is *only* done because it is good business, fine. Society benefits. The same can be said for many, if not most, socially responsible behaviors by organizations. We are less concerned with *why* it is done than with the fact that it *is* done. We think it can be best done legally and responsibly.

REFERENCES

[1] "Why Nobody Wants to Listen to OSHA," Business Week, June 14, 1976; 76, from Randall S. Schuler, *Personnel and Human Resource Management* (St. Paul: West Publishing Company, 1981).

[2] Grover Starling, *The Changing Environment of Business* (Boston: Kent Publishing Company, 1980).

[3] Discussion based largely on Dean Carson, "Companies as Heroes?"...New York Times, 1977.

[4] Theodore Levitt, "The Dangers of Social Responsibility," *Harvard Business Review*, 1958:44.

[5] Y.N. Chang and Filemon Campo-Flores, *Business Policy and Strategy* (Santa Monica, California, Goodyear Publishing Company, 1980).

PART TWO
PLANNING AND DECISION MAKING

EXERCISE 2.1 A PLAN TO TRANSPORT

Operational plans are designed to implement strategies. Standing plans, policies, procedures, and rules are to reinforce operational planning in a consistent manner.

As the corporate planner for the newly organized Apex Urban Bus Company you have been charged with the responsibility of developing operational plans before the Municipal Transit Authority can grant you a charter.

In order to give you an idea of what goes into an operational plan—to establish a route—make appropriate responses after each item below:

1. *Family income*: Which income group is most likely to ride buses (low, middle, or high income) and why?

2. *Living density*: Would the better market have people living in single-family homes or apartment dwellers? How does family income impact upon living density?

3. *Where* would these people be transported? What are the people's ages in relation to where they may work, such as: factories, offices, etc.?

4. *How often* should the buses run on this route? What are the important factors here?

5. Any *special considerations*, such as: discounts for senior citizens, charters, Sunday morning church services?

EXERCISE 2.2 CERTAINTY, RISK, AND UNCERTAINTY AND THE REVERSE

Identify three separate events in your academic career or work life involving certainty, risk, and uncertainty.

Describe each situation and single out how each situation could have moved from one position to the other.

Event 1. Certainty:

From Certainty to Risk:

From Certainty to Uncertainty:

Event 2. Risk:

From Risk to Certainty:

From Risk to Uncertainty:

Event 3. Uncertainty:

From Uncertainty to Risk:

From Uncertainty to Certainty:

One of the steps in the formulation and implementation of strategy is resource analysis. Resource analysis involves developing an organizational profile covering the areas of financial, physical, organizational, and human.

Another key step in environmental analysis consists of factors which can impact upon an organization's health such as; economic, technological, sociocultural, and political/legal.

1. Select two companies within the same industry.

2. Through a library research study check *Dun and Bradstreet, Standard and Poor's*, and company annual reports. Designate with a "*Y*" (yes) or "*N*" (no), on each line, if the factors on the accompanying *Goals Table* (on back of this page) are discussed in terms of goals statements, then answer questions 3 and 4.

3. Compare and contrast the two firms.

4. Determine if the firm with more "*Y*'s" is more profitable and if it has more assets than the other company.

(See Goals Table on reverse side)

GOALS TABLE

Company #1	Company #2
Name:	**Name:**

Resource Analysis:	**Resource Analysis:**
Financial:	Financial:
Organizational:	Organizational:
Physical:	Physical:
Human:	Human:

Environmental Analysis:	**Environmental Analysis:**
Economic:	Economic:
Sociocultural:	Sociocultural:
Technological:	Technological:
Political/Legal:	Political/Legal:

EXERCISE 2.4 START UP YOUR OWN MBO

Assume you are the manager of a small hardware store. You have two cashiers, four clerks, and two warehousemen. The cashiers and the clerks do the stocking and the warehousemen handle shipments and do the cleaning.

You wish to implement an MBO program which you feel would be an effective planning and operation strategy.

Below list three objectives for these three jobs and rank their importance on a scale from "1" to "3" with "3" being most important.

Remember objectives must be something requiring the employee to "stretch out" yet be attainable. They must be action oriented and not vague statements such as "to be a good employee."

Cashier	
Objectives	(rank 1 to 3)
1.	
2.	
3.	

Clerk	
Objectives	(rank 1 to 3)
1.	
2.	
3.	

Warehouseman	
Objectives	(rank 1 to 3)
1.	
2.	
3.	

The North Cabinet Company is a family-owned and operated shop. It builds kitchen cabinets for home builders in a metropolitan city in the southwest.

Jeff North is the third generation to join his dad and grandfather's business, but the only one with a degree in Business Administration. As a result of his education and youth, Jeff wants to expand the business and go into residential construction. Jeff grew up in the cabinet business, but feels the business has stagnated. Although his father and grandfather admit Jeff is right, they maintain that the cabinet business is what they know and what they're good, although they admit Jeff is right.

One summer evening, as they were leaving the shop, Jeff's Dad, Harry, said "Let's go to the Pelican Club for a cold one."

As Harry blew off the excess beer foam he said to no one in particular, "It looks like we're going to have the worst summer in our history."

Grandfather Joel set down his glass, "This is 1988 and it's an election year. It's always bad during an election year."

"Bull!" exclaimed Jeff. "Business is bad because we don't know where we're going. We build cabinets when the builders want them. If not, we sit on our duffs."

Joel ordered another round, "Yeah, but we've made a good living for two generations Jeff...and things will get better."

"Bull!"

"You like that word don't you?" remarked Harry.

"Listen," interrupted Joel, "Maybe our college boy has some ideas. Let's listen to him."

"Bull!" laughed Harry.

Obviously there is a goal conflict here and the business is going nowhere. Yet kitchen cabinets are stable items in homes.

The four basic steps in planning are to: establish goals; define the present situation; identify aids and barriers and; develop a course of action.

Assume you are Jeff North. Devise a business plan following the four steps mentioned above.

Joseph Blakely, product manager for the Cereal Division of National Food Corporation, is extremely worried and depressed. Sales for the Wheat-All Brand have fallen 12 percent in the last eight months, profits have declined, and total market share of the wheat cereal is off two percent.

Joseph's depression deepened as he thought of the confidence and optimism his product team exhibited when Wheat-All *hit* the market. All signs during the product development stage were positive; market research had indicated a widening market for a low sugar, no cholesterol, multivitamin cereal with iron and zinc. The Art Department dug deep into their bag of tricks and came up with a unique product design. National's advertising agency, *Smith, Hart, and Nichols* developed an attractive message featuring both female and male athletes. Choice times on TV were bought, aired, and sample Wheat-All packages blitzed a number of test markets. And sales for the first 18 months were higher than expected. But then what happened? Compounding Joseph's worries was a call from Jackson Wertzberg, vice-president of sales for the cereal division. Jackson was viewing the last quarter's sales figures when he called Joseph to ask what was happening. After Joseph responded that he didn't know Jackson retorted with the blunt statement, "Solve the problem!"

The way to proceed on this case is through the rational problem-solving process.

You need to investigate the situation by defining the problem and its causes, develop alternatives, select one, and implement.

As Joseph Blakely you have been given a clear order to solve the problem!

CASE 2.3 BARRIERS AND THE CONVENIENCE STORE

You always enjoyed retailing. The task of selling, stocking, ordering and dealing with people appeals to you. However, you want to be your own boss—you want to be in a position of independence and not having anyone "dictate" to you.

Fortunately, your father has the means to loan you the money for a small business. The only condition is that you graduate from college.

You are now in your last semester. In less than three months you'll have your degree in marketing.

During the summers of your college years you worked at several convenience stores rotating from one store to another as full time employees went on vacation. You enjoyed this thoroughly and you expressed that interest to your father.

"I know I can make it, Dad. I like the work. Being my own boss. Look at 7-11 and other convenience stores," you say over the phone to your dad after completing mid-term exams.

"But what about competition? Specially the one you just mentioned—the 7-11's. Do some thinking on this and let me hear from you."

There are a number of barriers to opening up a convenience store.

1.   Discuss the relevant barriers to your entry in this business.

2.   How would you attempt to overcome these barriers?

Harry Brockton had worked in the grocery business for his entire adult life. First he worked for a large independent, then he moved on to a regional and last a national chain. When the chain merged with another food conglomerate Harry was asked to take early retirement. Although, reasonably young at 49, Harry was willing to take his retirement money in a lump sum and move on.

After an extended vacation to the Bahamas with his wife and two teenaged daughters, Harry began to think of business opportunities. He always had an entrepreneurial spirit but money had always been a barrier. Now, with his retirement money he was ready to "roll" as his wife Betty put it.

After a two-month investigation Harry made a down payment on a small two-person wholesale candy and tobacco operation. His customer base were small independent convenience stores, filling stations, small restaurants and neighborhood bars.

1. How would you describe this stage of development in Harry's business.?

2. The next step is vertical integration evolving into a functional organization. Describe what the structure of Harry's company will be when it reaches this stage. For practical considerations he should integrate forward. How can this be accomplished?

3. The final stage of development is to become a multidivisional firm. What would Harry's firm look like now?

SUCCESSION PLANNING—A BLUEPRINT FOR YOUR COMPANY'S FUTURE

Robert J. Sahl[1]

Organizations can solve succession problems in a number of ways.

Succession planning is a neglected area in much of American industry. Often, the whole topic is ignored until someone either unexpectedly dies, resigns or retires. Obviously, succession planning conducted under these conditions is less than optimal. At worst, in a smaller, privately held organization, the long-term viability of the company can be endangered. This whole topic, however, can be addressed successfully by organizations with varying levels of skill or sophistication. Some organizations do an excellent job in succession planning; unfortunately, however, many others do virtually nothing.

LEVEL I

At the basic level, succession planning is handled quite informally. One executive simply asks another to provide the name of a subordinate that he/she feels is best suited to serve as a backup. This is done throughout an organization and a series of backup individuals is designated for each critical position. The organization draws up a series of back-up charts and considers that it has now done its job and has a full-blown succession plan in place. While this does "get the job done." taking this approach leaves an organization vulnerable to charges of favoritism and subject to having to pay the price of basing a critical decision on insufficient information. When this approach is taken, the Peter Principle can come into play if the plan is ever executed; what started off as a well-intentioned activity instead leads to a whole host of additional problems. An East Coast organization ran into this problem when an excellent marketing manager was shown "on the chart" to be the successor of the vice president of marketing. When this vice presidential position unexpectedly opened up and the marketing manager was moved in, problems quickly developed. The marketing manager was not up to the conceptual demands the larger position required. This had not been apparent in the previous job where analytic demands were much more pragmatic and applied. Within 18 months this organization had two openings—one for a marketing manager and one for a vice president of marketing. Taking the approach outlined at Level 1 can also result in good internal candidates being overlooked since insufficient data about them surfaces. One Midwestern company, after installing a more sophisticated succession planning program, found a wealth of unexpected talent several levels down in their manufacturing organization. It was from this group of people that a vice president of manufacturing and a vice president of engineering ultimately surfaced.

---

[1] Reprinted from the September, 1987 issue of *Personnel Administrator*, copyright, 1987, The American Society for Personnel Administration, Alexandria, VA.

LEVEL II

At the second level of sophistication, not only is the executive requested to identify a backup, but he/she is also asked to provide performance appraisal data in conjunction with the identification process. Any organization, at the very least, should attack the task of succession planning through a combination of Levels I and II. When this is done, assuming a sound performance appraisal system is operating, at least some of the subjectivity and potential favoritism criticism can be eliminated. Backups are known to have a demonstrated track record. This does put some pressure on an organization to have a decent performance appraisal program. This program should yield an appraisal of performance against the "Key End Results" of the job. These should be spelled out before the fact; measurement yardsticks for these Key End Results determined, and performance goals set. Organizations should be doing this as part of their people management process; this is just getting more mileage from a program that should be already in place.

Here, we are talking about a performance appraisal program that is job oriented. Performance is measured against that which the job exists to achieve (i.e., its Key End Results). Every effort is made to hone in on measurable factors. For example, for the position of production superintendent, some of the factors that might be included are:

KEY END RESULTS	MEASURES	GOAL
1. Quality of production	1. No. of units produced	X
2. Quality of production	2. No. of units rejected	Y
3. Human resource management	3. Turnover level	Z%
4. etc.	4. etc.	--

Use of vague traits should be avoided. One executive ran into a real problem along these lines when performance was marked poor relative to "Appearance." The employee was highly insulted and after a thorough hashing and rehashing of the "facts," it all boiled down to taste in clothing—which had nothing to do with the job itself—that of a financial analyst.

While following this path (Level I and II), an organization is in somewhat better shape, but it still is not able to protect itself from promoting somebody to the position just beyond their competence. While Levels I and II are a somewhat sounder approach than just developing a list of backups, much is left to be desired.

LEVEL III

A third level of sophistication is added to the process in some organizations. At this higher level, affected individuals become part of the discussion, and their career goals and potential for growth are incorporated into the plan. This helps an organization avoid the pitfall of promoting individuals into a job in which they may not even have an interest. This process of assessing talent can be substantially enhanced by considering not only the individual's performance and career goals, but also by measuring his/her potential. Potential can be measured by implementing formalized procedures, either through assessment centers or through the use of psychological testing. Either of these procedures enables an organization to look at executive talent in an organized, consistent manner. When properly designed, either approach can shed significant light, not only on overall potential of individuals, but also on the context in which this potential can best be brought to fruition.

A New England bank had one manager who was progressing well within the audit function. This bank then did some developmental testing for identifying high potential people and their growth needs and aspirations. Test results showed that despite top notch performance, this manager was very unhappy in this function, but had been forced into it by family pressures. Additional assessment data indicated that this same individual would be ideal in operations. Some rather careful career path planning resulted in a re-direction for this individual. As a result, the bank changed an unhappy auditor to a most satisfied and effective operations manager in a relatively brief period of time.

An appropriate assessment should consider issues such as:

- aspirations of the individual;
- opportunities within the organization as contrasted to the aspirations;
- intellectual capacity;
- use of intellect, possibly as demonstrated by level of basic skill development (e.g., mathematical skill, vocabulary, reading,etc.);
- interest profile relative to aspirations and organizational opportunities;
- level of management expertise relative to career path position demands;
- job-related traits and/or personality factors (e.g., ambition level, disposition to work with people, things, etc.).

Now the organization is looking at what the individual has done historically through performance appraisal data, and also taking a look at potential in an organized manner and assessing that potential against demands of the next job up the organization ladder. Now, the organization is addressing both succession planning and career path planning.

With this approach, you will have several different personnel systems interfacing and working in support of each other. Performance appraisal is supporting succession planning and this is being amplified to encompass some career path planning.

LEVEL IV

Some companies move to the next level of sophistication in succession planning, Level IV. Having identified the potential of the individual for a variety of jobs and having formulated career paths through assessment, the developmental needs of the individuals can be taken into account and their strengths can be highlighted. Now we have another personnel activity heavily interfacing—management development. At this point, the organization has the option not only of building upon the strengths of the individual, but also formulating developmental plans for him/her so that when the time comes to move into the next position, he/she has undergone the training and development necessary to perform effectively. Having gone this far, the organization can now very easily integrate its efforts in management development with those efforts in career path planning. The contents of these individualized development programs can be based very directly on the career path the executive is following. Necessary development of executives then takes place before they move into the job rather than on the job!

One large Midwest organization carried this to an admirable extreme. This organization developed a listing of courses that the company would underwrite to deal with various developmental needs. These were all courses offered at universities close to their various locations. So, for example, if a manufacturing manager needs to learn more about finance, he could turn to this booklet and under "Finance" would find approved courses such as "Finance for the Non-financial Manager" at the colleges and universities near the company locations. Other headings found in the catalog ranged from "Human Relations Skills" to "Inventory Management." The course listings were reviewed annually and updated so as to maintain an overall quality level.

Undoubtedly, taking the described approach sends a very clear message to all people in an organization. That message says that we are concerned with the long-term viability of our company, but we are also concerned with the long-term growth and careers of our people. Also inherent in this approach is a strong belief in the promotion from within—with actions to back up the message. A side benefit accruing from this method of is that it helps to point out to the individual alternatives that may not even have been considered relative to their career pathing. For example, the individual progressing through an engineering department may well have the opportunity, within a well thought-out career plan, to move into a manufacturing role at a given point. With this planned approach, an organization will have the time for grooming well-rounded managers with broad knowledge in more than one functional area. Many organizations have a need for this level of managerial skill and knowledge within their ranks.

LEVEL V

At the optimal level of succession planning, all jobs within the organization should be measured. Then, after the previously outlined steps are taken, when an opening occurs, the organization can "gauge the size of the promotion." This can be done by looking at the measured job size of the current position of the individual as compared to the size of the job for which the person is being considered. If, for example, a promotion is found to be less than 10 percent larger, it should be recognized as a lateral move. Sometimes a lateral move should be considered within a career path and as a part of a succession plan, but when that is the case, all should be well aware of the fact rather than run into a situation where somebody gets "promoted into a job" that is really no bigger than the previous job and may well not have a higher salary range. With job sizing in place, other guidelines may be formulated such as, if a job if found to be 10 percent–15 percent larger than the job the individual is coming from, this can be viewed as a standard-sized promotion. Beyond that, a 16 percent–25 percent increase in job size can be recognized as a large promotion. Promotions in a succession plan that move individuals into jobs that are 25 percent or more greater than the job they are coming from may well be too large a promotion for an individual to handle; the person might then inadvertently be in a position of being set up to fail. When talking about job size as it relates to succession planning, organizations should focus on their compensation program. This can and should yield job size information rather than just providing a market price for the position. Again, we have an example of one personnel system supporting another. In a sense, we have come full circle. We are seeing that the better the job the organization is doing in succession planning, the better the job the organization is more likely doing in managing their human resources overall. As one executive pointed out, "It doesn't make good business sense to do any less. Our people are one of our greatest cost/assets. We owe it to our shareholders to maximize our return here too!"

To summarize, in an optimal situation where an organization is truly doing a good job of succession planning, an individual possibly becomes a candidate for the program through management nomination. Then, performance appraisal data is reviewed, potential is assessed, developmental needs identified and developmental programs formulated, career paths articulated and promotion into truly "larger jobs" can take place. By following this approach, an organization can avoid panic when somebody unexpectedly dies, resigns or retires. This is truly proactive management rather than management by crisis. To manage a succession planning program at the higher levels of sophistication can take time. However, not to do so can take even more time, and in the long run, be quite costly. The side benefit that grows from all of this is that the stronger your succession planning program is, the stronger all of your human resource systems. The stronger these systems, greater likelihood is for an organization to get the most from its people— and for its people to get the most from the organization.

THE ART OF CRAFTING STRATEGIC PLANS

George S. Odiorne[1]

Strategic planning is no longer a game played strictly by major leaguers. In fact, large numbers of small and mid-sized firms are taking a longer look into the future, trying to prevent it from crashing about them. Too often in the past, organizations found themselves enmeshed in crises that might have been averted by anticipating and preparing for an uncertain future.

One of the newest tools in the strategic planner's repertoire is the "environmental scan." This is the method planners use to try to spy the threats just over the horizon, the risks that must be faced in the next five to 10 years, and the opportunities waiting to be exploited by those with foresight. Strategic planners scan the gamut of environmental factors of environmental factors: governmental changes caused by elections or shifts in administration philosophies, demographic changes brought on by fluctuating population characteristics, social changes in tastes and morals, and many more.

By studying demographics, for example, we can project that in 10 years there will be 7 million fewer workers between the ages of 18 and 24, and almost 20 million more between 34 and 59. The fastest-growing segment of the population will be the elderly, whose middle-aged offspring will face the problem of parental care. Age discrimination laws now enable people to work longer, which guarantees that employers' health-care costs will keep rising.

At the other end of the spectrum, the birthrate is resurging. Phoenix already is planning a dozen new elementary schools and a half-a-dozen new high schools to cope with the current baby boom. As the number of working women continues to rise, demand for employer-supported child care is bound to increase as well.

DATA OVERLOAD

Unless you are a newspaper editor, you probably struggle just to stay abreast of current events, much less sort out issues that might affect your business in the future. One shortcut is to do what professional strategic planners do: Subscribe to information services. Commercial information and data-bank companies such as Lockheed Dialog and ABI Inform can find you everything that has been written on any known subject—at least that's how it will appear to you. You simply send them the key words that interest you, and they return abstracts of every article on that topic from a vast assortment of publications.

Or, if you want to simplify things, you can subscribe to a service that distills information into periodic reports. The Bureau of National Affairs, Commerce Clearinghouse and other companies provide monthly updates on topics ranging from tax laws to personnel practices. Newsbank, another monthly data service, provides an index to every story in every issue of more than 100 U.S. daily newspapers. Subscribers can order the complete text of any story on microfiche.

---

1 Reprinted with permission from the October, 1987 issue of *TRAINING, The Magazine of Human Resources Development*, Copyright 1987, Lakewood Publications Inc., Minneapolis, MN. All rights reserved.

Yes, it's easier than ever to collect mounds of data. But how do you keep from being inundated with the stuff? As consultant Thomas Gilbert, founder of Performance Engineering in Hampton, NJ, puts it: "Data comes in stacks like hay, each straw pointing in a different direction. Information, on the other hand, is like a needle; it points in one direction and has a point."

What you need to plan strategically, then, is more information and less data. With information you can create policies and goals. With information you can turn your analysis into actions that advance your business. The problem remains: How do you turn data into information?

CRITICAL ISSUES

Pop sociologists and journalists like to create monumental trends out of isolated incidents. Managers are ill-advised to listen indiscriminately; we can't interpret each new eruption of media hype as a dire warning of imminent disaster lying square in our path. If we read today's headlines and extrapolate them into the future, for example, we would have a world of cocaine-crazed arbitrageurs using inside information to pull off a leveraged buy out of the entire Milky Way galaxy. Half of our employees would be donating urine samples, while the other half would be jumping at early retirement.

Instead, we must find the few critical issues that must be faced in the future. How do we define the ones we should be prepared to address in our own organizations?

STEP 1: First examine your organization's major problems. What might they be in the future, given recent trends? If your earnings have been flat for four years, you have a problem. If your turnover of key people such as engineers, accountants or other skilled employees is too high, you have a problem. Where are you now and how did you get there? If you didn't do anything differently, where would be in one year? Two years? Five years? Ten years? Do those answers please you? If not, where would you like to be at the end of those periods.

If there is a difference between where you are headed and where you want to be, you have defined the problem: It is the gap between the desired and the projected outcomes. Strategic planners call this exercise "gap analysis." You can use gap analysis to examine your organization's markets, products, customers, employees, finances, technology and community relations.

You're unlikely to find all of your organization's problems in a single department or in a single setting. Problems are bound to surface in several areas of the organization. Similarly, its naive to expect some central staff guru to proclaim the best or even a realistic definition of all of them.

People's Bank in Bridgeport, CT, has an innovative method for identifying such problems, the first step in finding the critical strategic issues. It has established "cabinets" or task forces of managers and staff experts from each area of the business. Their mission: to define the critical long-range problems facing the bank—deregulation, competition and the like.

STEP 2: Next, you're ready to examine outside influences that are important to your organization. When is a change, trend or event important? When it relates to a key problem you have or anticipate having.

While it may be intellectually stimulating to try to keep tabs on the whole world, you have to be selective when it comes to strategic planning. You must focus on those few major issues that could reach inside your business and create problems.

If the cost of energy is crucial for your business, the outcome of the war between Iraq and Iran could be of keen interest, along with the outcome of OPEC's next meeting. Or, if you are being ravaged by Japanese competition, the relative value of the dollar and the yen will be important; a falling dollar against the yen will raise the price of imports, leaving you in a better competitive position.

Fast-food operations, such as Burger King and McDonald's, should be interested in the projected decline in the number of 18- to 24-year-olds by 1990, since this group has supplied most of their store workers in the past. School superintendents, too, should track birthrates and immigration of young families into their region. They must gauge fluctuations in their clientele if they want to do any long-term strategic planning. Facility planning, teacher staffing, budgetary planning, tax requirements and a host of other operating details five years from now will be affected by today's birthrates.

STEP 3: Now you're ready to list the critical issues. As you consider candidates, keep in mind that critical issues used for strategic planning have several distinguishing features:

- They usually affect the entire organization, rather than one department.

- Their impact is usually long-term. Operational issues must be faced next quarter or next year; strategic issues gradually spin out over five or 10 years.

- They are based upon information that is "protracted and robust," to use the jargon of the strategic planner. This simply means that the trend or condition is supported by irrefutable evidence and has been under way for a long time. Strategic planners can't afford to be stampeded by media hype or a single current event, no matter how surprising it may be.

STEP 4: There are several sorting techniques that you can use on your list. First, rank the critical issues according to their importance to your organization. Top priorities are issues that must be turned into programs or operating objectives within the next year. You probably will want to include them in your next budget plan.

Divide your list into categories of urgency such as "must do," "need to do," and "important, but not urgent." The most urgent are the issues that should command management attention now in order to exploit an opportunity that may be five years down the road. For example, if the company doesn't start a research program in a promising area immediately, it won't have a product to meet the competition in five years. This list may also include some areas in which the company has fallen behind and needs to play catch-up.

Divide the items on your list into "success producers" and "failure preventers." Success producers are the top few items that offer chances for big scores in the future. Failure preventers are issues that, allowed to slide, may cause us to stumble.

STEP 5: Describe these critical issues to your organization's management. Make it clear that these are organization-wide goals that should be reflected in the annual operating objectives of every department or division.

At Tenneco, this communication took the form of a letter from the company president. Recently at General Motors, every company manager received a film from the president, who described what he saw as the critical human-resource issues: getting more minorities into dealerships, making factories more human and promoting more women into managerial ranks.

This downward communication is necessary if critical issues are going to be converted into long-term corporate objectives for the operating managers. It's an article of faith in management-by-objectives programs that corporate objectives must be set at the top and passed downward before operating objectives for the coming year are fixed. Similarly, in strategic planning top management must define the critical issues so that line management can figure out how they should be addressed.

STEP 6: Timing is an important element in communicating the critical issues. April or May usually is a good time—issues can be clarified and defined far in advance of budget time. Once critical issues have been "wired into" budgets, they become part of the operating objectives for the following year.

STARTING SMALL

Most people don't define critical issues as part of their daily activities, and learning to do so takes some training. One way to practice the art is to try applying it to your own career.

First, define the major problems in your job and career. If you don't do anything differently, where would you be in five or 10 years? Do you like your answer? Where would you really like to be? The gap between the two answers is your personal career management problem.

Second, look at your environment. Where are some of the threats, risks and opportunities in your world? Examine it from a variety of perspectives: personal, financial, social and cultural.

Next, list the critical issues that must become part of your long-range career development strategy. Rank them according to urgency. Of the things you might do, do differently or refrain from doing, which would be success producers? Which would be failure preventers?

You now have your critical issues list for your career. You are ready to choose actions that will help you close the potential gaps in your future.

You also might practice strategic planning in counseling subordinates. Let's say you have an employee who shows star potential, but is unable to manage her career. Try going through a critical-issues exercise with her. Have her define her problems, environment and critical career issues. Have her rank them, and ask her to define the success producers and failure preventers in her life. The end result just might be a developmental plan that accelerates her achievements and enhances her value to the organization.

These career exercises are good ways to study and practice strategic planning. Having mastered the art of defining critical issues in your career and that or a promising protégé, you are ready to apply the same steps in defining the critical strategic planning issues for your organization.

THEN AND NOW: A LOOK AT STRATEGIC PLANNING SYSTEMS

Harold W. Henry[1]

In the early 1960s, many large U.S. corporations felt a great need to develop a more systematic, longer-term method of planning future business activities. They had increased rapidly in size, product variations, geographical dispersion, and technical complexity during the 1950s. Many investment opportunities existed, new technologies were introduced frequently, competition was intense, and new markets awaited development, both in the United States and abroad.

Planning of a sort existed in many companies, especially product and financial planning, so the scope and time frame were broadened and written long-range corporate plans were introduced. Some alumni of Pentagon planning groups were in management positions. The Stanford Research Institute offered a Long Range Planning service, and the Russian five-year planning experience gave companies some foundation for formal planning. Of course, new positions were needed to perform this important new function, so vice-presidents for corporate planning were created in significant numbers. The pattern of evolution of planning in the IBM Corporation, shown in Exhibit 1, illustrates the type of changes that occurred in many firms. In a study among forty-five companies in 1964 and 1965,[1] I found that a significant number had introduced formal long-range planning procedure, even though simple and number-oriented, while many others were seriously considering such a move.

THE 1960S: ONLY HALTING PROGRESS

More and more companies introduced formal planning in the late 1960s and 1970s, but many experienced problems in their efforts, and some planning systems were abandoned or allowed to stagnate into periodic form-completion exercises of little value. Conflicts developed between staff planners and line managers. Some managers preferred intuition to planning, and some plans were simply projections of historical data with no underlying analysis and strategy. However, pressures of various types increased by the end of the 1960s, so that many firms felt compelled to modify their planning systems radically or to start over in an effort to manage more effectively. The most important factors that led to a rebirth of formal planning are shown in Exhibit 2. By 1973-1974, when I visited twenty-nine companies,many striking evolutionary changes in planning systems had occurred. The major changes were as follows:

- Many new or greatly modified planning systems were introduced in the early 1970s.

- Much more emphasis was given to strategic planning than in the mid-1960s.

- More top executives were involved in strategy formulation, and more seemed committed to formal planning.

---

[1] Reprinted by permission from the *Journal of Business Strategy*, Vol. 2, No. 1, Winter 1981. Copyright 1982, Warren, Gorham & Lamont Inc., 210 South St., Boston, MA. All rights reserved.

EXHIBIT 1

Major Planning Development in IBM Corporation, 1947-1967

- In pre-World War II days, planning was informal and was tied in with operating needs, such as inventory, production, and financing.

- After World War II, as the company's product line, its sales, and its investment needs expanded, and as technological changes became more frequent, financial planning and product planning were set up as separate entities.

- During the 1950s, these same changes accelerated. As a result, planning became a part of each functional area—marketing, manufacturing, service, personnel, and so on—and more concerned with the longer view.

- Toward the end of the 1950s, the need for integrating and enlarging these planning efforts became apparent. A formal strategic (long-range) planning organization was created, and procedures requiring all divisions and subsidiaries to prepare annual strategic and operating plans were instituted in 1959. The strategic plans covered five years, whereas the operating plans were for the current two years.

- Beginning in 1961, each division initiated an effort to systematize its planning procedures for computer operations. By 1965, most divisions had put together various computer programs for planning data recording, including dynamic models of certain business functions, to assist in the evaluation of alternative courses of action.

- In 1966, this divisional planning process was extended to seven years with virtually continuous updating of the summary and back-up data on computer and an official annual review. In addition to this change to continuous divisional seven-year planning, a corporate strategic plan was formalized to provide guidance to divisional planning by establishing a limited number of key objectives for each division and subsidiary.

- Since 1966, increased management attention has been given to planning procedures, and a companywide effort to develop an internally consistent and compatible network of planning data systems has been initiated.

Source: H. W. Long, *Long-Range Planning Practices in 45 Industrial Companies* (Englewood Cliffs, NJ: Prentice-Hall, 1967), p. 144.

EXHIBIT 2

Factors in Formal Planning Rebirth, 1970-1973

- Poor profit performance in the late 1960s and early 1970s.

- Rapid diversification in the 1960s which resulted in poor performing or incompatible operating units.

- Scarce capital funds and high capital costs.

- Scarce natural resources, especially those used for energy and for chemical feedstocks.

- Successful or renewed formal planning by major competitors.

- New top managers with a strong planning orientation and philosophy.

- Unending requests for capital appropriations from unit managers, often for poorly planned and piecemeal projects.

- The influence of a few management consulting firms.

- Some firms developed corporate strategies and plans that went beyond a consolidated set of business unit plans.

- Financial planning had been deemphasized as the dominant thrust in several firms.

- Portfolio analysis was being used in several firms to evaluate the potential of each business and to see a balance in types of business.

THE LATE 1970s: STRATEGIC PLANNING INTENSIFIES

The ten companies selected for analysis in this article were major U.S. firms, with five among the largest ten, and nine in the Fortune 100. Four were petroleum or energy-related firms—Gulf, Mobil, Standard Oil of Indiana, and Union Pacific. The other six produced electronic products, electrical equipment, office equipment, or diversified products. They were General Electric, IBM, Motorola, United Technologies, Westinghouse Electric, and Xerox. Each of the ten had a formal long-range strategic planning system in 1979, and each gave heavy emphasis to strategic planning, even though some still called their results a long-range plan. Four of these firms introduced new or radically different planning systems between 1975 and 1977, thus following the evolutionary pattern of earlier years. Unsatisfactory financial performance, a new top executive, a threatening external environment, or advice from consultants triggered these efforts at more systematic and effective planning.

Most firms planned for a five-year period and utilized all the typical planning activities. Thus, past performance and internal attributes were evaluated to identify strengths and weaknesses. The external environment was appraised to find threats and opportunities. Forecasts and assumptions about future conditions were made, objectives were set, alternative strategies wee identified and evaluated, and a strategy package was selected that included major investment strategies as well as implementation and functional strategies. Then an operation plan for the next year or two that detailed specific programs and financial budgets was prepared.

CHANGES THAT OCCURRED

Reorganizations

Several important reorganizations were found in these firms, including a major change in one petroleum company to shift from a geographical structure to a functional or product basis with seven independent strategy centers. One firm added a new level of managers under the CEO consisting of six sector heads and shifted strategic planning to a three-level activity—strategic business unit planning, sector planning, and corporate planning. Another corporation changed from 137 divisions to thirty-seven business units in 1975 to provide a more rational structure for managerial planning and control. Nine of the ten firms were divided into business units and groups or subsidiaries for assigning profit responsibility. One company had sales and service divisions which did not have control over their products and these operating units. The evolution of corporate structures has clearly been to shift to units that are most logical for strategic planning, profit responsibility, and control.

Length of the Planning Cycle

The planning period varied widely, depending on the nature of the firm or planning unit. One petroleum company shifted from a five-year plan to a ten-year plan, while a competitor went from ten to five. The rationale of the former was that ten years were needed to bring in a new field or to build a new facility, while the latter argued that the environmental uncertainty and turbulence (oil and gas supply and demand) made ten-year forecasts meaningless. A three-year horizon was used for a houseware business, and thirty years for a mining business. One firm shifted from a five-year plan to a seven-year plan to match its equipment replacement cycle.

Nine firms followed an annual planning cycle, but one of these may develop strategic plans on a two- or three-year cycle in the future. One company required business unit plans every other year, and these are staggered over a six-month period to spread the review load of the management committee. These changes probably reflect the fact that companies do not make major changes in their strategy every year. The fact became evident in the 1979 study from comments by planners, such as "If two of 45 (investment) strategies change in one year, that is a lot." In larger corporations with many business units, some strategies may change each year and others may be fine-tuned. Also, the discipline of continuous planning and the knowledge and interaction benefits of annual planning dictate a continuation of this pattern.

Review Procedures

In 1978, a large electronics firm introduced an innovative planning procedure that involved an all-staff review of plans. Business unit staff planners presented their proposed plans to division staff members who later had to integrate and critique them. The division head was not present, and the purpose was to let big issues surface and resolve small ones that the staff could handle.

Staff planners are also being used extensively to train operating managers how to plan in formal classes or workshops. They stress the results expected from the planning process, specific analytical techniques, methods of segmenting business, and ways to size up the competition. Their role in the planning process is viewed by most planners as that of a catalyst—to get managers involved, to get them to focus on issues, and to get them to think in a meaningful way about the best way to run their business.

The task of integrating the planning efforts of business units has not received as much attention as how to differentiate business activities into logical planning units. Two of the firms in my study with a long history of successful planning have focused heavily on the integration problem. One does integrative planning across business units with respect to international concerns, human resources, financial resources, production capacity; and technical resources. Another firm conducts simultaneously "product" and "period" planning activities with special efforts to resolve "issues" that surface.

HOW STRATEGY IS FORMULATED

Strategy formulation is the the most important element and the climax of strategic planning. The process starts each planning cycle when planning guidelines, environmental assumptions,and financial objectives are prepared at the corporate level and sent to each planning unit. In the past, these guidelines have often been very specific regarding the content and format of business unit plans and were considered burdensome and restrictive by business unit personnel. One finding in 1979 was that some guidelines have become simpler and that required plans are less structured. Divisions are told what is expected, but not the precise form. One company has eliminated corporate-level planning guidelines.

A fundamental change in one firm with a well-established planning cycle was to make explicit at the beginning of the planning cycle the corporation mission (strategic thrust) and objectives. Earlier, an analysis of resource allocation at the end of the cycle was needed to identify the corporate strategy. This was done to restrict the amount of additional diversification proposed and to maintain a single-company image rather than one of a conglomerate. Another firm started preparing corporate assumptions on economic and other environmental factors rather than permitting each division to prepare its own, as in the early 1970s. However, if a planning unit feels strongly that different assumptions are more accurate, it may submit two plans, one based on corporate assumptions and one based on its own.

The Importance of Careful Analysis

Careful internal company appraisal is critical for effective strategy formulation, but self-appraisal is not easy for anyone. Several planners stressed that unit managers must be objective and open with top executives in appraising weaknesses as well as strengths. The companies with the most effective planning systems have developed a "planning culture" in which discussion is open and gamesmanship is minimized. One planner reported that "some managers are open with the CEO, while other are not—this is a logjam."

Portfolio analysis continues to be a very important part of internal appraisal, but a new dimension was stressed by some planners in the 1979 study. They pointed out that such a product/market analysis could be applied at any and all levels in the organization, even down to skillets sold in one part of town.

Competitive analysis was also given more attention in the late 1970s and was viewed by some planners as an area seriously neglected in the past. For internal appraisal, a firm must know its current relative competitive strengths and weaknesses. In looking at the environment for future business activities, a firm should anticipate new competition and identify, to the degree possible, new strategies or changes to make old competition stronger.

Human resource analysis seemed to get more emphasis in the past few years, in terms of both existing personnel and those needed to implement new plans. One planner stated that "people are the most critical element of growth," and another said that "manpower needs are stressed heavily in plans." Special techniques to analyze human resources include age distribution graphs, people-in/people-out analysis, and manning charts that show the most likely replacements for key managers.

Some companies gave heavy emphasis to analyzing the external environment as a basis for strategy formulation, while others worried primarily about their competitors. This difference reflects two academic schools of thought on strategic planning. Only a few firms took either extreme position, with most considering both external conditions as well as competition.

Combining the Bottom-Up and Top-Down Approach

Strategic planning was a combination of top-down and bottom-down approaches in the ten firms studied, but most gave the greatest emphasis to bottom-up planning, with broad guidance from the top. One firm had a unique approach in which bottom-up five-year plans were used only as idea generators and the basis for discussing and deciding on strategies and for updating strategic objectives by top management. This was the most centralized approach found, and its major potential limitation seems to be the effect on the morale and level of effort of division managers and planners.

Information on the external environment was obtained from many sources, with heavy dependence on outside economic forecasting services and other specialized service groups. Internal staff groups were also important contributors and one firm had developed a unique census-type method for estimating total market size.

A review team was used in one company to act as consultants to a business unit that was preparing a strategic plan. The chairman of this team was always another business unit manager or staff officer who had been a line manager. The opportunity to interact with "outsiders" during the strategy formulation process was considered very helpful, but the same benefit was obtained in other firms by interaction between line and staff specialists at different levels in the organization. In general, there seemed to be much more involvement of top management in strategy formulation that in the early 1970s.

THE FACTORS AFFECTING STRATEGY IMPLEMENTATION

Matching Manager to the Strategy

One of the most innovative ideas to improve strategy implementation, introduced during the past decade, is to select unit managers according to the type of strategy to be implemented. For example, a "risk taker" would be assigned to implement an invest/grow strategy, a "caretaker" to implement a harvest strategy, and an "undertaker" to gracefully kill off a business. Two firms reported the use of this approach, but one of them which pioneered the idea said it still gave the approach "lip service." Another firm made no effort to select managers to fit strategies since its business differed greatly and little opportunity for transfer existed.

Typing Compensation to Strategy

A few firms are now basing executive bonuses in part on performance relative to strategic factors. One company assigns a weight of 25 percent to strategic considerations and provides qualitative guidelines for this type of performance evaluation. Managers evaluate their own performance, and corporate staff personnel evaluate them also; if they disagree, each presents its arguments and the CEO makes the final decision. In another firm, objectives selected as performance standards for managers are related to the strategies to be implemented. For example, if an invest/grow strategy is chosen, perhaps 60 percent of the bonus will be based on growth and 40 percent on current operations; however, if a harvest strategy is chosen, 70 percent of the bonus may be based on current financial performance and only 30 percent on future benefits. These efforts to relate executive compensation to strategic factors seem very significant and are likely to be followed by other corporations. When rewards are tied to performance, a powerful motivation exists to select and implement strategies in the most effective way possible.

Also the bottom-up approach to strategic planning in which managers are directly involved in formulating a strategy and making commitments to achieve specific objectives provides a strong motivation for effective strategy implementation. When operating managers realize the strategy belongs to them and not to the planning staff, they have no one else to blame for faulty implementation.

The use of the product/market matrix at all levels was viewed as an important implementation feature in one company, for each manager can manage a portfolio of mini-business and is not relegated to a distasteful role.

It is essential to evaluate the effectiveness of a given strategy for achieving present objectives in order to improve on strategy formulation, strategy implementation, and overall business performance. This is an important part of the strategic planning process in all of the companies studied and is done at the beginning of the planning cycle and periodically during a given year. This activity is really part of managerial control, for results are compared to expectations and remedial action is taken by developing new, improved strategic and operational plans. Thus, the trend in the past few years to broaden the concept of "strategic planning" to "strategic management" is valid and logical, for an effective planning system really involves all management functions: planning, execution, and control.

IMPLICATIONS FOR MANAGERS

The findings of my latest field study on strategic planning systems are consistent with the views and results of other management writer and researchers.[2] For example, Rothschild identified the following four factors as ones he considered essential for successful strategic planning:

- Top management commitment to practice of strategic planning precepts,
- The establishment of well-defined SBUs within an organization, based on sound segmentation concepts,
- The training and development of all levels of middle and top management in the use of strategic planning techniques and concepts,
- The development of strategic control systems to determine whether SBU strategies are being implemented as proposed and approved.

These factors were present in the companies I studied, and it seems clear that the rate of evolution of strategic planning systems and the rate of improvement in financial performance are directly related to the degree of top management commitment, the soundness of the organizational design for planning and control, the level of management training, and the amount of care exercised in implementing strategies. Also, the degree to which strategies are evaluated and modified after implementation in light of actual performance is another critical factor for success.

A research survey by Steiner in the early 1970s, with 215 companies reporting, identified many pitfalls in comprehensive corporate planning.[4] Among the ten most important pitfalls reported, five pertained directly to top management attitudes, actions, or inactions, as follows: delegating the planning function; spending little time on long-range planning; viewing planning apart from management; failing to review plans of unit managers; and undercutting formal planning by making intuitive, independent decisions. The other five pitfalls were: failure to develop company goals, failure to involve major line personnel, failure to use plans as performance standards, failure to create a favorable planning climate, and excessive planning formality. All of these problems can be easily corrected by a capable top manager who believes that strategic planning is important. This was clearly the situation I found in 1979, for all ten pitfalls have been overcome or avoided in the companies I studied which had the most advanced strategic planning systems.

Thus, the implications of my results for corporate managers are that management must be inherently "strategic" in nature in any organization if it is to achieve its goals most effectively and utilize its available resources most efficiently. Every manager at all levels in an organization must focus on strategic aspects of management and not merely on administrative, operational, functional, or leadership aspects. However, corporate executives and business unit managers have the greatest responsibility and obligation to all contributors to the firm to manage strategically. This means they must continually think about the resources they can obtain, the goals (short- and long-term) they wish to achieve, and the "best" way to use the resources to achieve the goals in a changing and uncertain environment. Much judgment is required, but planning that is regular and comprehensive will lead to much better results than planning that is piecemeal and expedient.

CONCLUSIONS

The major conclusions from my 1979 study of formal long-range strategic planning system in ten large U.S. corporations are:

- Strategic planning is viewed as a critically important part of business management.

- More companies are introducing or modifying formal planning systems each year, and this trend is expected to continue for many years.

- Wide variations exist in specific planning procedures among companies, so there is no single "best" approach. However, a basic commonality of features exists, and it may be possible to eventually identify the most essential features of formal strategic planning.

- Strategic planning systems evolve in a given firm through a trial-and-error process that is uneven, even within one company. Thus, one planner said, "The state of evolution is dramatically different in each of our businesses for some managers are adept at turning over every rock while others don't have their act together."

- It is essential to involve top executives personally in the strategic planning process in order to make a planning system effective. One planner said he would modify the planning system to keep top management interest high—"to twist, turn, and try new things to get their involvement."

Formal strategic planning is expensive and one executive estimated the cost at $2 million a year, but all of the companies I visited felt the benefits exceeded the cost. Thus, a new management system only two decades old may be the most important development in the management field in the twentieth century.

REFERENCES

1. Harold W. Henry, *Long-Range Planning Practices in 45 Industrial Companies* (Englewood Cliffs, NJ: Prentice-Hall, 1967).

2. Harold W. Henry, "Formal Planning in Major U.S. Corporations," *Long Range Planning,* Oct. 1977, pp.40-45.

3. William E. Rothschild, "How to Ensure the Continued Growth of Strategic Planning." *The Journal of Business Strategy*, Summer 1980, p. 12.

4. George A. Steiner, *Pitfalls in Comprehensive Long Range Planning* (Oxford, OH: Planning Executives Institute, 1972), p. 10.

PART THREE
ORGANIZING FOR
STABILITY AND CHANGE

EXERCISE 3.1 ORGANIZE THE ORGANIZATION

Organizations basically are structured in one of three forms: functional with departments of shipping, manufacturing, sales, etc.; product/market where the organization is organized according to product such as the Cadillac division or the consumer products division of General Electric; and matrix organization which is a combination of functional and product/market.

Before each statement below designate with the appropriate letter the form of the organization: **F** for functional, **P/M** for product/market, and **M** for matrix.

_____ 1. "This will be a special unit. We're going to pull people out of sales, engineering and production to work on this project."

_____ 2. "This organization is out of control, if you ask me."

_____ 3. "Our market isn't what it used to be. It's changing so fast. You never know what people want anymore."

_____ 4. "It takes so doggone long to get a decision."

_____ 5. "Everything is the same. You can't tell a Buick from a Chevy."

_____ 6. "This set-up is great! Everyone has their own skills and we don't have to worry so much about coordinating everything."

_____ 7. "I wish we could experiment on new products, but everyone around here has tunnel vision."

_____ 8. "This way we'll learn each other's jobs. We'll be able to do it all."

_____ 9. "Those easterners are all alike. They want more advertising money and more sales people. They think they should have it all."

_____ 10. "We've got to watch out for duplication. It can happen quite easily when we're organized like this."

EXERCISE 3.2 TO ENLARGE, TO ENRICH AND TO COMPRESS

A motivational approach in job design which seeks ways of making jobs more varied and challenging is through: job enlargement where tasks are combined to make the job more whole; job enrichment where the worker has more autonomy and a greater degree of accountability; and compressed work weeks or flextime where people work 10 hours a day for four days or a varied Monday through Friday schedule centered around a core time.

From your personal job experiences or with jobs you are familiar, select two and identify as follows:

1.   *Occupation*:

      Tasks performed:

2.   *Occupation*:

      Tasks performed:

Describe how you could enlarge the first occupation.

Describe how you could enrich the second occupation.

How would compressed work weeks or flextime impact upon either occupation after job enlargement and job enrichment?

EXERCISE 3.3 HELP WANTED

Recruitment is a critical function of human resources management. It is essential that a pool of candidates be established from which selections can be made. Equally important is that both facets of recruiting; advertising and interviewing be in legal compliance. Additionally, it has been established through court decisions that job requirements must be related to the job.

Examine the ad below. As you can tell there are a number of violations. Reconstruct the ad so it will be in legal compliance.

Janitor Wanted

White, Male, Age 20 to 35

High School Diploma

XYZ Company

P.O. Box 1234

Anywhere, USA

EXERCISE 3.4 RESIST THE RESISTANCE TO CHANGE

A common management problem is workers' resistance to change. People object to changes because they are uncertain how it will affect their work and relationships. But changes are often necessary for company survival.

There are six approaches for dealing with change.

1. Education and commitment: where there is a lack of information or inaccurate information.

2. Participation and involvement: the people do not have all the information they need for the change and others have the power to resist.

3. Facilitation and support: people are resisting because they are having adjustment problems.

4. Negotiation and agreement: those with power to resist will lose out in a change.

5. Manipulation and co-optation: any other tactic will not work or is too expensive.

6. Explicit and implicit coercion: speed is essential and the change people possess considerable power.

Before each statement below indicate, by a number from the above list, which approach would best apply.

_____ 1. "As the new CEO I realize what has to be done. I've been given a 'blank check' by the board. So we're going to move fast."

_____ 2. "This can't be right! And where is the rest of the data we need?"

_____ 3. "Sales are off and we don't know why. But all the regional sales managers have been doing it their own way for a long time."

_____ 4. "We've tried almost everything and nothing works. Anything else might be too expensive."

_____ 5. "The important people in Engineering are fighting this. They know there will be a reduction if this change goes through."

_____ 6. "Those quality control people are all alike. You want to move them around and they get emotional. You would think they need therapy."

EXERCISE 3.5 IDENTIFY THE CONFLICT

Conflict is going to occur in any organization. It can be functional and improve the organization or dysfunctional and hurt the organization. Regardless management must first be able to identify it. There are generally four sources of organizational conflict: shared resources such as a limit on numbers of workers, money, and equipment; differences in goals where accounting wants tighter collection policies to reduce bad debt, and sales wants easier terms to increase revenues; interdependence of work activities when two or more units depend on each other such as sales and shipping; and differences in values or perceptions, like the people in quality control lowering tolerances while the plant supervisor wants to increase production.

After each of the four incidents below identify the conflict.

1. The production superintendent bristled at the suggestion from the sales manger that production be increased. This would result in increased inventories and alleviating shortages. However, quality could suffer and the production people were proud of their work.

2. The Director of Research and Development approached the Budget Director with his request for an increase in funds. Added funds were needed to further modify the new product lines. But the Budget Director shook his head, "New monies are all going to sales promotion. We need more advertising. I'm sorry."

3. The Credit Manager was preparing her report for the upcoming Board of Directors Meeting. She was justifiably proud that receivables and bad debts were each down 12 percent from last year. However, she was concerned that sales had dipped markedly from last year too. "But the bottom line," she said to herself, "is that I've cut our losses by tightening up."

4. The representative from the Occupational Safety and Health Administration shook his head, "Either you put a protective shield here or I'll have to shut down the line," he said to the supervisor as he left the shop. The supervisor wondered if engineering would ever design and install the shield he requested for last month.

Adias' R/D department had developed a personal computer that had more memory and storage than any other on the market, including IBM's, Olivetti's M 20, Xerox 820, or the Apple III.

The president, Joe Adias, has a strong scientific background. Consequently, he spends the majority of his time in the research lab. He enjoyed working with the engineers and technicians and considered them as his "boys."

The sales revenue at Adias had fallen off recently but Joe felt this was due to the general economic conditions of the country as a whole. However, he fully expected this new computer, Adias Supreme, to boost sales tremendously. The retail price is to be $3500 which was higher than competing brands but was justified because of its increased capacity.

Three months after the Adias Supreme had been on the market sales were very slow. Soon economic conditions began to improve but the Adias Supreme sales did not. After some prodding Joe learned from his marketing people that the $3500 was too high in spite of the increased storage and memory.

1. What organizational problem is exhibited here?

2. How could a product/market organization structure have prevented the sales failure of the Adias Supreme?

3. How can a matrix structure better serve Adias?

Maxine Upchurch finally "arrived." After having worked for United Parts for 13 years she made supervisor. But Maxine earned it, she felt. Never missing a day of work, never late and never complaining, she was filled with pride as she moved into her office on this Monday morning. Although a little apprehensive she was confident she could be a good supervisor.

Vern Norris tapped on her open door, "Hi, may I come in?"

"Morning, Vern. Sure, come on in. And how is our personnel director doing this morning?"

"O.K. I guess," answered Vern. "But I know you're busy. I just wanta' tell ya' a couple of things."

"What is it?"

"Don't get too bossy. You're a new super and sometimes that goes to people's heads. Know what I mean?"

Maxine looked curiously at Vern. "I'm not sure I do."

"Well, don't fire anybody or write anyone up. At least not for a while." With a wave of his hand, Vern added, "But remember it's your department." As he turned to leave he bumped into Todd Merkel from Engineering Design. "Hello, Vern. Hi, Maxine. Gettin' squared away?"

Maxine gazed after Vern. "What? Yeah, I guess I am."

"Look, I need to tell you something. I'll be telling your crew about new production schedules since we've made some engineering changes. These changes should bring about increases in productivity."

"But that's my job," interjected Maxine.

"I know. I know. But I have to exercise some authority or we won't get any increases in productivity even with these changes."

Maxine sat down behind her desk.

"Everything will be all right. We'll both run the department." Todd went to the door. "Of course, it's your department."

1. What violation of delegation occurred between Vern and Maxine?

2. What violation of delegation occurred between Todd and Maxine?

3. What is Todd's authority?

4. Do you think Vern's premise of Maxine's bossiness is valid? Why?

CASE 3.3 PLACID PLASTICS, INC.

The absenteeism and turnover rates at Placid have been increasing steadily over the last two years. Although this was disturbing, from a human resource point of view, it was not alarming until the productivity rate began to decrease over the last three months. The line managers were particularly distressed because they were directly responsible for employee performance.

In order to help resolve the productivity problem the reward system was thoroughly examined and compared with other firms in the surrounding area. Placid compared quite favorably. Their wages, incentives, and benefits were as good and in most cases better than others.

Human Resources and Industrial Engineering was called in for their input. I.E. was convinced that job design, productivity rates, and scheduling were well engineered and within tolerable ranges. Human Resources was satisfied that their selection and placement procedure were the state of the art. That is they used the latest testing and interviewing techniques. They utilized job previews and followed through weeks after the employee had been placed. In the selection process Human Resources was careful to employ only trainable people.

1. What is the problem(s)?
2. What solutions should be offered?

CASE 3.4 MORCESS MACHINE CO.

Morcess (a combination of the words more and success) does precision machine operations for a number of large manufacturers. Its technology is state-of-the-art job production. The workers have considerable autonomy and can identify with their tasks. Also, the workers with their supervisors have strong client relationships with their customers. A strong pay incentive program is in place with workers receiving pay which is far above the regional average. Other benefits such as; health care insurance, leave pay, vacation, training, and retirement are comparable with other area industries. Absenteeism and turnover are not a problem because of the excellent reward system and job freedom.

In spite of these positive factors, Morcess doesn't appear to be a company with a destiny - or a purpose. If nothing else it has stagnated and when it moves it moves aimlessly. A typical comment overheard was, "It's sure a great place to work but I wonder how long we'll be doing what we're doing?" This worker did not have in mind profitability because the firm has had slow but steady increase in profits for the last seven years. Obviously, there is some cause for concern, for companies cannot drift for long before serious consequences begin to set in. Such consequences eventually can lead to failure. Obviously some change in the organization is needed.

Assuming this is an organizational development issue, how should you proceed to effectuate a change?

Organizational conflict has always been a problem at Wizard Electronics. Workers arguing and shouting at each other has become a common occurrence, and a source of embarrassment to the company. Supervisors and department heads have been called "on the carpet" by J. E. Carstairs, CEO and one of the two founders of the company. At the conclusion of each session, Mr. Carstairs asks for and receives a commitment from his mangers that they will try to suppress their emotions. Mr. Carstairs feels that is the best solution. He rationalizes the causes of the employees' outbursts to the nature of his business and industry. Computing is a quick growth, high tech, fast moving business. The various departments and subunits often seem to be working against each other, but as Mr. Carstairs figures, they are really trying to out perform each other. That is, the units are highly competitive.

Mr. Carstairs does not want to diminish the spirit of competition for he feels this is the way for the company to maintain its creative edge. The workers, as well as the managers, readily agree that the work is interesting and challenging. There is task significance and considerable job autonomy. However, Wizard is a small firm by industry standards, yet the reward system is better than any other firm in the area.

1. Is Mr. Carstairs correct in his assessment that workers are trying to out perform each other?

2. Is he right in not wanting to diminish the spirit of competition?

3. What do you perceive is the real problem(s) at Wizard Computers?

4. How would you solve the problem(s) and how should you execute their solution?

DELEGATION FOR EMPLOYEE DEVELOPMENT

Donna Vinton[1]

Sometimes thought of as a dirty word in the past, delegation can be just the key managers need to make their employees happy, productive and loyal.

Delegation is generally thought of as a time management tool for managers. But when it is properly applied, delegation can be a tool in developing employees' skills, knowledge, and self-confidence and in increasing their job satisfaction and organizational commitment.

DELEGATION LEVELS

A common theme in writings on the topic of delegation is the idea that delegation is not abdication. The manager does not give up entirely the control of either process or results, if delegation is properly done. However, there are various levels of managerial involvement possible in the implementation of the task. Ross Webber lists the following eight levels:[1]

- Look into this problem. Give me all the facts. I will decide what to do.

- Let me know the alternatives available with the pros and cons of each. I will decide which to select.

- Recommend a course of action for my approval.

- Let me know what you intend to do. Delay action until I approve.

- Let me know what you intend to do. Do it unless I say not to.

- Take action. Let me know what you did. Let me know how it turns out.

- Take action. Communicate with me only if your action is unsuccessful.

- Take action. No further communication with me is necessary.

Whatever the level of delegation, several steps will be included in the process. First, delegation requires selection of employees to do the job. Second, the task must be clearly defined to the employees, including a description of the activities which might be undertaken, the results that are to be achieved, and the context of which the activity is a part. Third, the people receiving assignments need to know how much authority they will have and what resources will be available for the completion of the tasks. Fourth, managers must communicate relevant organizational policy that may affect the carrying out of the task and the factors upon which performance will be evaluated. Finally, managers need to be clear about the type and frequency of reporting and communication they expect.

At its best, the delegation process is one of mutual consultation and agreement. Employees' reactions and ideas can be solicited at any point in the process, and by doing so managers establish the atmosphere of trust, support, and open communication that will be necessary for optimum results to be achieved, both for completion of the tasks and for development of the employees.

ADDING TO SKILLS

Managers sometimes tend to overuse very competent employees, resulting in overloading these individuals' time. At the very least, by not adding to the skills of those less obviously competent, managers deprive themselves of additional resources that could be drawn upon when needed. Delegation to develop employees, then, requires that managers

- be able to determine when subordinates are ready to move ahead and take on more responsibility;
- be willing to let others approach problems in their own way and even to let them make mistakes.

In his article "Delegation—The Essence of Management," in the October 1978 issue of *Personnel Journal*, Francis Tritt makes this observation:

> Every professional can quote in his sleep the results of the famous General Electric study that came out of the 1950s which showed that 90 percent of a person's development is the result of his experiences on the job, *not* the result of formal classroom learning experiences....Knowing then, that development and learning is the result of *doing*, it becomes obvious that what one does on the job is a direct result of what one is *allowed* to do on the job. Hence, the connection between delegation and development is abundantly clear.

Communication in effective delegation is a two-way process, encouraging exchange of ideas and a problem-solving attitude.

A key to using delegation to develop skills lies in identifying employees' task-relevant maturity (TRM). Paul Hershey and Ken Blanchard in their book *Management of Organizational Behavior: Utilizing Human Resources* define maturity in this sense as the "ability and willingness of people to take responsibility for directing their own behavior...in relation to a specific task to be performed." Thus, individuals' TRMs will vary from task to task, and managers must be familiar enough with the employees' current strengths, weaknesses, interests, and needs to identify the task that will stretch those individuals' capabilities without setting them up for failure.

ACHIEVEMENT AND JOB SATISFACTION

Chris Argyris has pointed out what he calls a "basic, continuing problem" in the dilemma of the conflict between the needs of individuals for self-actualization and the needs of organizations for such things as a clear chain of command and task specialization. The results of this conflict for the employee are feelings of frustration and failure and the experience of "competition, rivalry, (and) intersubordinate hostility," along with a "focus toward the parts rather than the whole." The employee may adapt to this situation by such acts as leaving the organization; daydreaming; becoming aggressive, regressive, or ambivalent; and becoming disinterested in the organization. Some managers react to such behavior by establishing tighter managerial controls, a move which perpetuates the original situation. Argyris suggests that the way out of the dilemma is to reduce employees' dependency, subordination, and submissiveness to their work and gives job enlargement as one solution.

But Frederick Herzberg replaces the term *job enlargement* with the term *job enrichment* to distinguish between what he calls "horizontal job loading" and "vertical job loading." The former refers to such strategies as increasing production goals, increasing the number of tasks without increasing their meaningfulness, decreasing the difficulty of the assignment in order to increase productivity: strategies that add to the meaninglessness of the job. Vertical job loading, on the other hand, adds to the meaning. The principles of vertical job loading and their relationship to the act of delegation are examined in Figure 1.

Figure 1—DELEGATION AS A FORM OF VERTICAL JOB LOADING

Job Loading Principle	Guide for Effective Delegation
1. Remove some controls while retaining accountability.	1. Give employees freedom to pursue tasks in their own way, while establishing agreed-upon results and standards of performance.
2. Increase the accountability of individuals for their own work.	2. Encourage an active role on the part of employees in defining, implementing, and communicating progress on tasks.
3. Give people a complete natural unit of work.	3. Entrust employees with completion of whole projects or tasks whenever possible, or at least explain tasks' relevance to larger projects or to departmental or organization goals.
4. Grant additional authority to employees in their activities.	4. Give employees the necessary authority to accomplish tasks and allow them to do jobs in their own ways.
5. Make periodic reports directly available to workers themselves rather than to their supervisors.	5. Allow employees access to the information, people, and departments which may not ordinarily be directly available to them to accomplish their tasks.
6. Introduce new and more difficult tasks not previously handled.	6. Assign tasks that move employees beyond their current TRMs; provide training, instruction, and guidance as necessary to complete tasks.
7. Assign individuals specific or specialized tasks, enabling them to become experts.	7. Assign tasks based on employees' needs and interests.

While job enrichment is not a universally accepted management concept, looking at delegation in this light allows managers to release themselves to do other tasks that need to be done while at the same time enriching employees' jobs without totally restructuring those positions or the department and increasing employee job satisfaction and motivation.

DEVELOPING ORGANIZATIONAL COMMITMENT

How commitment to the organization is developed and maintained is of central importance to organizations and has no easy solutions nor hard and fast answers. But in a 1975 study of 279 managers from eight large U.S. companies—three of which were *Fortune*-500 manufacturing concerns and five of which were federal government agencies—Bruce Buchanan attempted to identify the causes of commitment. The findings identified experiences that fostered commitment among all 279 managers; then multiple regression analysis was used to identify those experiences having the strongest association with the development of commitment.

The five classes of experience having a significant impact on commitment, in order of strength, were:

- a feeling of personal importance from being considered productive and valuable to the organization;
- experience in a cohesive group with positive feelings toward the organization;
- realization of expectations (The question asked was "Has my organization fulfilled its promises to me and otherwise met my expectations in areas I care about?");
- organizational commitment norms (if employees who thought that their organizations expected them to be committed were more committed than those who didn't sense those expectations);
- first-year job challenge.

Buchanan notes that the impact of the last item was both predictable and surprising: predictable in that "a challenging, interesting, and self-confirming work assignment would strengthen commitment," and surprising in that "the job experience of the first year continued to shape the attitude of managers."

The recommendations for managerial motivation that Buchanan draws from his study can be directly related to the process of delegation. Buchanan identifies self-maintenance and self-confirmation as the unifying theme of managerial motivation and makes four recommendations: avoid overstaffing as it dilutes challenge, design jobs with a certain degree of challenge, find ways of bringing to employees' attention the link between their jobs and the whole, and monitor the growth of individuals in their jobs in order to periodically adjust responsibility upward.

Given the findings of Argyris, Herzberg, and Buchanan, several points may be made with respect to delegation as a tool for development of employees.

- Delegate duties that slightly challenge employees but will insure success.
- Relate the delegated task to the overall goals of the department or organization and show its importance in that context.
- Support the notion that employee development must be part of a larger plan, not just an occasional or isolated occurrence that takes place when it is convenient or expedient.
- Use delegation as a tool for development of both the new employee and the experienced one.

MAKING FEEDBACK ONGOING

Feedback allows employees to assess their performance accurately, learn from errors, see how they are perceived by others, replace unproductive work habits, examine alternative modes of behavior, and increase self-awareness. But failure to provide appropriate or sufficiently frequent feedback is a common problem.

Many managers are not trained in coaching or feedback techniques and may rely on the annual performance appraisal to create the vehicle for providing feedback. Yet while performance appraisals are necessary, they have shortcomings if they are the sole form of feedback. They come only once or, perhaps, twice a year; they may be related to salary or other tangible reward systems and thus may create defensiveness on the part of the employee; and they may not be tied to a plan for growth. Managers should have a continuous method of sharing feedback with their subordinates.

Delegation is a way to communicate feedback. The very act of delegating tasks to employees shows that managers trust their subordinates, respect their skills, and have confidence in their abilities and potential for contributing to the organization. Effective delegation processes build-in feedback points as progress on the project is communicated to managers. The feedback is not artificial, as the yearly performance appraisal may seem to be, but is a natural outgrowth of the task. Feedback stemming from this communication process is ongoing, expected, and may even be negotiated as employees' ideas concerning implementation of tasks and reporting possibilities are solicited. Communication in effective delegation is a two-way process, encouraging exchange of ideas and a problem-solving approach.

UNDERUSE OF DELEGATION

There are a number of reasons why delegation is often underused in general and, specifically, as a tool for developing employees. One reason may be that delegation is often seen as a "dumping process" by which managers give to employees those tasks that managers find undesirable and keep for themselves only tasks that afford the most personal enjoyment. When employees see delegation in this light, they view it as merely a transfer of tasks rather than as a tool for development of the individual, department, or organization; will lose respect for their manager because they believe the manager is misusing their time and skills; and will resent what they see as the manager's failure to recognize their potential.

Some researchers take another approach and examine the potential for delegation to trigger feelings of loss in the manager: loss of power, loss of authority, loss of meaning, loss of personal expression, and loss of achievement.[2] The delegation process is seen as subtractive; that is, what is delegated is seen as taken away from the manager rather than as a process that is additive and brings managers and employees consulting together to define tasks, increase productivity, and meet organizational goals. Such a view also ignores the centrality of managers as coaches in effective delegation by providing training, support, and guidance as necessary to see the task through to completion.

Even if managers accept the necessity of developing employees and understand the role that delegation can play in the process, development of employees may not be a recognized or rewarded management behavior in some organizations. Given a low organizational priority, whether or not there is written policy promoting it, employee development may well have to wait for attention until the myriad of daily tasks have been attended to and bottom-line productivity adequately attained.

Effective delegation, whether for the purpose of developing employees or for other reasons, is not easy. It requires the ability to plan, organize, and control many activities with both short- and long-term goals and the ability to manage employees with diverse needs and skills. As such, delegation cannot be expected to come easily or naturally, and unless managers understand the delegation process and work under an organizational policy that both expects and rewards delegation, it is likely that delegation will continue to be underutilized.

NOTES AND REFERENCES

[1]Leboeuf, Michael. *Working Smart: How to Accomplish More in Half the Time.* New York: Warner Books, 1979.

[2]Culligan, Matthew; C. Suzanne Deakins; and Arthur H. Young. *Back to Basics Management: The Lost Craft of Leadership.* New York: Facts on File, 1983.

TOM PETERS INVITES CHAOS FOR SURVIVAL

Perry Pascarella[1]

Excellence guru Tom Peters invites management to bash organizational barriers so that anyone can work with anyone in the company to get things done—thousands of things—and in order to provide the flexibility needed in today's business world. From yesterday's viewpoint, it may look like chaos. From tomorrow's, it may be the only route to survival.

"We need faster failure. It is fair to say that if we can't increase the gross national failure rate, we're in for a very rough ride indeed."

So says Tom Peters, the man who brought you *In Search of Excellence* (with Robert Waterman Jr.) and *A Passion for Excellence* (with Nancy Austin). He's back again with a book entitled *Thriving on Chaos*, published by Alfred A. Knopf this month.

Old industrial economies have two options, writes Mr. Peters. "The first path—toward stable mass production—relies on cutting labor costs and leaping into wholly new product lines as old ones are played out." This has meant layoffs, moving to lower wage areas, farming work out to low-cost suppliers, and diversification.

"The second path involves increasing labor value." This means "continuously retraining employees…, accepting flexible job classifications and work rules, agreeing to wage rates linked to profits and productivity improvements," and more permanent relationships with all of those who have a stake in the firm.

Mr. Peters' book emphatically supports the second path—one that requires a revolution in management practices and structures. The traditional path is causing us to do "dumb things," he says. "we are, for example, letting work drift offshore in pursuit of the lowest-cost production. But to lose control of the plant is to lose control of the future—of quality, responsiveness, and the source of most innovation."

THE IMAGE

Since the publication of his blockbuster book in 1982, Tom Peters has been perceived as an angry young man pacing one stage after another, citing examples of the poor quality of product and service we know all too well. His thousands of speeches and several TV programs have created, in some eyes, the image of a person who is negative on what American business is doing.

But Mr. Peters' early writing was very much grounded in heavy research, and he continues to be the ultimate student of business. His "showmanship" has become a vehicle for further

---

[1] Reprinted by permission, *Industry Week*, October 19, 1987, pp. 48-53. Copyright, Pinton Publishing Inc,. Cleveland, Ohio.

research, drawing to him more and more examples of what to do right. His newest book is thoroughly upbeat, offering enough inspiration and information to feed American management for years to come—plenty for followup action.

If there hadn't been an *In Search of Excellence* to take business-book sales to unprecedented highs, this book might have done it. The content and timing of Mr. Peters' first book helped create this age of concern for excellence and began to raise interest in change that is the route to the ever-moving target of quality. This book could capitalize on that intense interest.

CHAOS NEEDED

Subtitled "Handbook for a Management Revolution," the new book calls for boldness in breaking the corporate mind-set. The man who brought quality to the fore now invites chaos. He demonstrates the advantages of anarchy over the outdated strengths of autocracy.

"To meet the demands of the fast-changing competitive scene, we must simply learn to love change as much as we have hated it in the past," he says. Yet the author's call to action is tempered with the knowledge that a successful revolution comes about through incremental changes—by the thousands. And that includes some wrong actions, some failures. His call to raise the gross national failure rate is a challenge to the nation to increase its hustle. Readers of the Peters-Waterman book will recall that a "bias for action" was one of the eight characteristics of the excellent companies selected.

On the surface, the manager of the future that Mr. Peters has in mind might appear more like a fast-moving video-game player than the chess or poker player of old. But that, by no means, implies being in a reactive mode. Throughout the book Mr. Peters urges developing the skills and flexibility to anticipate and capitalize on market opportunities, rather than letting the market dictate the shape of the company. What could be more proactive?

TOMORROW'S SUCCESSES

Taking what he observes working in Corporate America today, Mr. Peters sketches the characteristics of the successful firm of the future:

- "Flatter [he insists on no more than five layers of management no matter how large the organization].
- "Populated by more autonomous units.
- "Oriented toward differentiation, producing high value-added goods and services, creating niche markets.
- "Quality-conscious.
- "Service-conscious.
- "More responsive.
- "Much faster at innovation.
- "A user of highly trained, flexible people as the principal means of adding value."

This handbook lacks the literary smoothness of *In Search of* but seems better organized than *A Passion for*. But it is a handbook designed to stimulate action. Following its convincing opening chapter on the need for change are five sections that offer 45 major prescriptions, each of which contains still more tips.

In keeping with Mr. Peters' penchant for taking action, each section ends with suggested "first steps." Address all of these prescriptions at once, he advises, since no one technique or area of attention can be successfully dealt with unless the others are being attended to at the same time.

The five sets of prescriptions have to do with:

"1. An obsession with responsiveness to customers.

"2. Constant innovation in all areas of the firm.

"3. Partnership—the wholesale participation of and gain-sharing with all people connected with the organization.

"4. Leadership that loves change and instills and shares a worthwhile vision.

"5. Control by means of simple support systems aimed at measuring the 'right stuff' for today's environment."

TO ACTION

Mr. Peters is at his best in writing about customer responsiveness, innovation, and empowering people. The sections on leadership and corporate systems taper off a bit in originality and care. Yet, overall, this powerful treatment of the issues surrounding industry's need for change and innovation presents a wealth of examples and viewpoints, and at a pace that should stir many management readers to action.

Picking up the "close-to-the-customer" trait cited in his first book, Mr. Peters says: "The customer responsiveness prescriptions add up to a revolution in corporate life—the wholesale external orientation of everyone in the firm, the achievement of extraordinary flexibility in response to what in the past would have been called customer whims."

The company that follows this prescription may have to make a radical change from traditional inward attention to cost reduction. "...Our obsession for the last few decades has been with cost containment rather than revenue enhancement," says Mr. Peters. In an interview with *IW*, he said, "The average senior executive hasn't got his hands around the quality issue yet."

Many managers do not see through the quality/cost paradox "Cost-reduction campaigns do not often lead to improved quality; and, except for those that involve large reductions in personnel, they don't usually result in long-term lower costs either. On the other hand, effective quality programs yield not only improved quality but lasting cost reductions as well. And all this doesn't even touch upon increased revenues from more sales resulting from improved quality." Mr. Peters says.

PEOPLE-DEPENDENT

Each of Mr. Peters' books has stressed the importance of people relationships inside and outside the corporation. This time he points out that "despite the accelerating technology/automation revolution, our organizations must become more dependent on people (line workers)." And a related paradox: "The successful manufacturing firm is turning to a 'service-added/responsiveness-added' strategy that is people-intensive."

As companies become people-intensive, they will have to become less management-intensive. Mr. Peters asserts that self-managing teams should become the basic organizational building block. Management's role is no longer to "give commands and inspect," but to practice Mr. Peters' well-known concept of "managing by wandering around."

When he was interviewed, he referred to *IW*'s companion notion of "managing by stepping aside" (June 1, Page 7). True, you're really in "control" of things only when you can walk away and have them get done, he said. Managing is a balancing act of getting out of the way and letting the regular chain of command perform the followup action, while also being highly visible as a listener and facilitator.

HORIZONTAL MANAGEMENT

We will have to "reconceive the middle-management job as one of facilitator and functional-boundary basher, instead of expert and guardian of functional units," Mr. Peters insists. Self-managing teams make no sense unless we make this change, he tells *IW*.

In this new role, the middle manager "must become 1) expeditor/barrier destroyer/facilitator, 2) on-call expert, and 3) diffuser of good news. In short, the middle manager must practice fast-paced 'horizontal management,' not traditional, delaying 'vertical management.'"

Again and again, in both the interview and the new book, Mr. Peters refers to "horizontal management." The concept is central to his *Chaos* book since the barriers between groups and departments get in the way of responding to the customer and making continual improvements in productivity and quality.

Mr. Peters distinguishes between this "proactive skid greasing" in order to get things done and conventional "coordination," which generally "emphasizes that horrid role of protecting one's function."

LAYING IT ON THE LINE

Self-managing groups need to act horizontally "to seek out fast connections with other functions, without checking up." Unfortunately, Mr. Peters tells *IW*, "the average executive doesn't appreciate the ability of the first-line supervisor to do anything." But successful companies will change the role of this first rung of management. Included in the shift:

- From ten people reporting directly to a manager, to 50 to 75 doing so.
- From scheduler to coach and sounding board.
- From rule enforcer to facilitator.

TOM PETERS DEFINES THE QUALITY REVOLUTION

1. Management is obsessed with quality.
2. There is an ideology.
3. Quality is measured.
4. Quality is rewarded.
5. Everyone is trained in technologies for assessing quality.
6. Teams involving multiple functions/systems are used.
7. Small is very beautiful.
8. There is constant stimulation.
9. There is parallel organization structure devoted to quality improvement.
10. Everyone plays: Suppliers especially, but distributors and customers, too, must be a part of the organization's quality process.
11. When quality goes up, costs go down. Quality improvement is the primary source of cost reduction.
12. Quality improvement is a never-ending journey.

- From planning to wandering.
- From transmitting management's needs down, to selling teams' ideas and needs up.
- From being focused "down" or "up," to horizontally, working with other functions to speed action-taking.

- From providing ideas for workers to helping them develop their own ideas.

Where does this shift from a vertical axis to a horizontal one leave middle managers? Without a job in many cases, Mr. Peters implies. He is concerned about today's huge excess of middle managers. He does not offer himself as an expert on dealing with this national socioeconomic problem.

He does, however, recommend that attention be paid to retraining and repositioning these people as much as possible within a company.

"The manager, in today's world, doesn't get paid to be a 'steward of resources,' a favored term not so many years ago. He gets paid for one and only one thing—to make things better (incrementally and dramatically), to make things different, to change things, to act," Mr. Peters writes.

WHAT'S THE GOAL?

One of the continuing responsibilities of upper-level managers is to set goals. But Mr. Peters stresses the importance of setting goals that create a winning situation. "The prime objective of goal-setting should be to turn 90% of the people in your firm into confident winners who take the new and always greater risks required by the times we live in." Leave room for "stretch," but create achievable targets, he advises. "The right attitude is one I call 'degrees of winning' rather than 'winners and losers.'"

Despite Mr. Peters' invitation to chaos, he warned in his interview with *IW* that a framework of mission, or vision, or purpose has to be put in place before any of his prescriptions will work. In the book he uses the term "vision" and describes it as "the sea anchor—the basis for keeping people from running around as the waves of the change roll in."

Bold change should be called for in top management's vision, but it will materialize only as "the result of a hundred thousand tiny changes...."

The vision provides a form of stability (not the paper-driven kind, he points out). "If there is no vision, or if the edges of the vision are very fuzzy, you don't know what is 'risk in pursuit of the vision' as opposed to 'risk for risk's sake.'"

That's the difference between successful revolution and utter chaos.

A STRATEGY FOR MANAGING CONFLICT IN COMPLEX ORGANIZATIONS

M. Afzalur Rahim[1]

The management of organizational conflict involves the diagnosis of and intervention in conflict at intrapersonal, interpersonal, intragroup, and intergroup levels. A diagnosis should indicate whether there is need for intervention and the type of intervention needed. In general, an intervention is designed to attain and maintain a moderate amount of conflict at various levels and to enable the organizational members to learn the styles of handling interpersonal conflict so that the individual, group, and overall organizational effectiveness are enhanced.

INTRODUCTION

Even though conflict is often said to be functional for organizations, most recommendations for organizational conflict still relate to conflict resolution, reduction, or minimization. Organizational conflict must not necessarily be reduced or eliminated, but managed. This paper attempts to develop a strategy for managing conflict at different organizational levels. An attempt will be made to show how conflict involving tactical and strategic issues should be effectively dealt with.

DEFINING AND CLASSIFYING CONFLICT

Conflict is an "interactive state" manifested in disagreement, differences, or incompatibility, within or between individuals and groups. Calling conflict an interactive state does not preclude the possibilities of intra-individual conflict, for it is known that a person often interacts with himself or herself. Organizational conflict may be classified as intrapersonal, interpersonal, intragroup, and intergroup.

It was indicated in the definition of organizational conflict that it may occur within or between social entities. This distinction between conflict *within* and conflict *between* social entities depends upon a system perspective for a given problem. The classification of conflict into four types, based on the level of their origin, shows that analysis at different levels may be beneficial, depending on the nature of problem(s).

MANAGING CONFLICT

The emphasis of this paper is away from the resolution of conflict to the management of conflict. The differences between resolution and management of conflict is more than semantic (Boulding, 1968, p. 410; Robbins, 1978). Conflict resolution implies reduction or elimination of

---

[1] Reprinted by permission, *Human Relations*, Volume 38, Number 1, 1985, pp. 81-89.

conflict, whereas the management of conflict does not necessarily imply reduction in the amount of conflict.

Several researchers have noted the positive consequences of conflict (Assael, 1969; Evan, 1965; Hall and Williams, 1966; Janis, 1972; Pelz, 1967). Organizations in which there is little or no conflict may stagnate. On the other hand, organizational conflict left uncontrolled may have dysfunctional effects. The concensus among the organization theorists is that a moderate amount of conflict is necessary for attaining an optimum organizational effectiveness. Therefore, it appears that the relation between conflict and organizational effectiveness approximates an inverted-U function (Rahim and Bonoma, 1979). As such, Brown (1983) has suggested that, "conflict management can require intervention to reduce conflict if there is too much, or intervention to promote conflict if there is too little" (p. 9).

Argyris (1976, 1980) and Argyris and Schon (1978) have argued that an intervention for conflict management should promote double-loop rather than single-loop learning. "Learning that results in the detection and correction of error without changing the underlying policies, assumptions, and goals may be called single-loop. Double-loop learning occurs when the detection and correction of error requires changes in the underlying policies, assumptions, and goals" (Argyris, 1980, p. 291). It should be noted that double-loop learning is quite consistent with the approach to conflict management in this paper.

Studies on the management of organizational conflict have taken two directions. Some researchers have attempted to measure the amount of conflict at various organizational levels and to explore the sources of such conflict. Implicit in these studies is that a moderate amount of conflict may be maintained for increasing organizational effectiveness by altering the sources of conflict. Others have attempted to relate the various styles of handling interpersonal conflict of the organizational participants and their effects on quality of problem solution or attainment of social system objectives. It becomes evident from this discussion that the distinction between the "amount of conflict" at various levels and the "styles of handling interpersonal conflict," is essential for a proper understanding of the nature of conflict management.

Amount of Conflict

The previous discussion was mainly based on the notion of the amount of conflict. In recent years, some researchers have used the indices of tension, annoyance, disputes, distrust, disagreement, etc. to measure the amount of conflict at various levels. There are measures of the amount of conflict which are quite distinct from the styles of handling conflict.

Styles of handing conflict

There are various styles of behavior for handling interpersonal conflict. For conflicts to be managed functionally, one style may be more appropriate than another depending upon the situation. Blake and Mouton (1964) first presented a conceptual scheme for classifying the modes (styles) for handling interpersonal conflicts into five types: forcing, withdrawing, smoothing, compromising, and problem solving. Their scheme was reinterpreted by Thomas (1976).

Using a conceptualization similar to Blake and Mouton (1964) and Thomas (1976), the styles of handling conflict were differentiated on two basic dimensions: concern for self and for others. The first dimension explains the degree (high or low) to which a person attempts to satisfy his or her own concern. The second dimension explains the degree (high or low) to which a person wants to satisfy the concerns of others. Combination of the two results in five specific styles of handling conflict, as shown in Fig. 1 (Rahim, 1983d).

A summary of the styles of handling interpersonal conflict and the situations in which these are appropriate have been presented below. The details of these have been presented elsewhere (Rahim, 1983b).

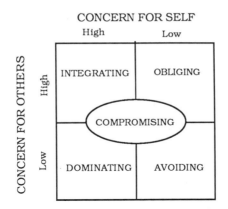

CONCERN FOR SELF

High   Low

CONCERN FOR OTHERS

High

| INTEGRATING | OBLIGING |

COMPROMISING

Low

| DOMINATING | AVOIDING |

Fig. 1 A two-dimensional model of styles handling interpersonal conflicts.

1. *Integrating*: high concern for self and others. This involves openness, exchange of information, and examination of differences to reach an effective solution acceptable to both parties. It is associated with problem solving which may lead to create solutions. Lawrence and Lorsch (1967) found the problem-solving (integrating) mode to be more effective than other modes for attaining integration of the activities of different sub-systems. When the issues are complex, this style is useful in utilizing the skills and information possessed by different parties to formulate solutions and successful implementations. This style may be appropriate for dealing with the strategic issues relating to objectives and policies, long-range planning, etc.

2. *Obliging*: low concern for self and high concern for others. This style is associated with attempting to play down the differences and emphasizing commonalities to satisfy the concern of the other party. An obliging person neglects his or her own concern to satisfy the concern of the other party. This style is useful when a party believes that he or she may be wrong or the issue is much more important to the other party. It can be used as a strategy when a party is willing to give up something with the hope of getting something in exchange from the other party when needed.

3. *Dominating*: high concern for self and low concern for others. This style has been identified with the win-lose orientation or with forcing behavior to win one's position. A dominating or competing person goes all out to win his or her objective and, as a result, often ignores the needs and expectations of the other party. When the issues involved in a conflict are trivial or when speedy decision is required, this style may be appropriate. It is also appropriate when unpopular courses of action must be implemented. This style is appropriate for implementing the strategies and policies formulated by higher level management.

4. *Avoiding*: low concern for self and others. It has been associated with withdrawal, buckpassing, or sidestepping situations. An avoiding person fails to satisfy his or her own needs as well as the concern of the other party. This style is useful when the issue is trivial or where the potential dysfunctional effect of confronting the other party outweighs the benefits of the resolution of conflict. This style may be used to deal with some tactical or minor issues.

5. *Compromising*: intermediate in concern for self and others. It involves give-and-take whereby both parties give up something to make a mutually acceptable decision. It is useful when the goals of the conflicting parties are mutually exclusive or when both parties are equally powerful, e.g., labor and management. This style may be of some use in dealing with strategic issues. But heavy reliance on this style may be dysfunctional.

Although some behavioral scientists suggest that the integrative or problem-solving style is most appropriate for managing conflict (Blake and Mouton, 1964; Likert and Likert, 1976), it has been indicated by others that, for conflicts to be managed functionally, one style may be more appropriate than another depending upon the situation (Rahim and Bonoma, 1979; Thomas, 1977). In general, integrating and, to some extent compromising, styles are appropriate for dealing with the strategic issues. The remaining styles can be used to deal with tactical or day-to-day problems.

The above discussion on the styles of handling conflict and the situations where they are appropriate is a normative approach to managing conflict. Musser (1982) presented a decisional model to show how a subordinate actually chooses a behavioral style to deal with high-stakes conflict with superior(s). A subordinate selects one of the five styles of handling conflict (strategies) depending on his or her response to each of the variables, such as subordinate's desire to remain in the organization, subordinate's perceived congruence between the superior's and his or her own attitudes and beliefs, and the subordinate's perceived protection from arbitrary action.

DIAGNOSIS AND INTERVENTION

The management of organizational conflict involves the diagnosis of and intervention in conflict. The processes of diagnosis and intervention are shown in Fig. 2.

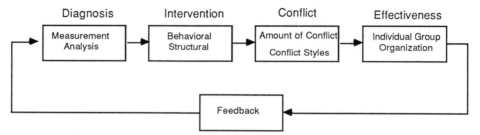

Fig. 2 A model for managing organizational conflicts.

Diagnosis

A diagnosis of conflicts in a system is important because the underlying sources and nature of conflicts may not be what they appear on the surface. If an intervention is made without a proper diagnosis, there is the probability that a change agent may try to solve the wrong problem. This may lead to what Mitroff and Featheringham (1974) call the error of the third kind. This error has been defined by them, "as the probability of having solved the wrong problem when one should have solved the right problem" (p. 383). The management of organizational conflict involves a systematic diagnosis of the problems in order to minimize the error of the third kind. A comprehensive diagnosis involves the *measurement* as follows:

1. The amount of conflict at the individual, group, and intergroup levels.

2. The styles of handling conflict of the organizational members with superior(s), subordinates, and peers.

3. The sources of (1) and (2).

4. Individual, group, and organizational effectiveness.

The *analysis* of diagnostic data should include:

1. The amount of conflict and conflict styles classified by departments, units, divisions, etc., and whether they are different from their corresponding norms.
2. The relationships of conflict, conflict styles, and their sources.
3. The relationships of conflict, conflict styles, and effectiveness.

The results of diagnosis should indicate whether there is any need for and the type of intervention necessary for managing conflict. The results of diagnosis should be discussed preferably by a representative group of managers, who are concerned with the management of conflict, with the help of an outside expert who specializes in conflict research and training. A discussion of the results should enable the managers to identify the problems of conflict, if any, that must be dealt with.

The above discussion presented an approach that may be used to conduct a comprehensive diagnosis of conflict. This should not be taken to mean that every organization requires such a diagnosis. A management practitioner or consultant should decide when and to what extent a diagnosis is needed for a proper understanding of a conflict problem.

Recently, two instruments were designed by Rahim (1983a) for measuring the amount of conflict at individual, group, and intergroup levels, and the five styles of handling interpersonal conflict. The Rahim Organizational Conflict Inventory-I (ROCI-I) was designed to measure the self-report of intrapersonal, and the perception of intragroup and intergroup conflicts. The Rahim Organizational Conflict Inventory-II (ROCI-II) contains three instruments for measuring the self-report of the styles of handling conflict of an organizational member with his or her superior(s) (Form A), subordinates (Form B), and peers (Form C). These instruments use a 5-point Likert scale to measure the amount of conflict at the three levels and the five styles of handling interpersonal conflict. A higher score represents perceptions of greater amount of one type of conflict or more use of a style of handling interpersonal conflict. The test-retest and internal consistency reliabilities and construct and empirical validities of the scales in these inventories were found to be quite adequate (Rahim, 1983 b, c, d). The ROCI-I and ROCI-II were used to collect data from two random national samples of 1188 and 1219 executives, respectively. The percentile and reference group norms of the three types of conflict and five styles of handling interpersonal conflict have been reported elsewhere (Rahim, 1983b).

Data collected through questionnaires should not be the sole basis of a diagnosis. In-depth interviews with the conflicting parties are needed to gain a better understanding of the nature of conflict and the type of intervention needed.

Intervention

An intervention may be needed if there is too little or too much conflict and/or the organizational members are not handling their conflict effectively. The national norms of conflict, discussed before, can provide some rough guidelines to decide whether an organization has too little or too much of a particular type of conflict. In addition to the national norms, data from interviews should be used to determine the effectiveness of the styles of handling interpersonal conflict of the organizational members.

There are two basic approaches to intervention in conflict: behavioral and structural (Rahim, 1977; Rahim and Bonoma, 1979). The behavioral approach attempts to improve the organizational effectiveness by changing members' culture: attitudes, values, norms, beliefs, etc. The behavioral approach is mainly designed to manage conflict by enabling the organizational participants to learn the various styles of handling interpersonal conflict and the situations where they are appropriate. The technique of role analysis may be used to enable organizational members to deal with their intrapersonal conflict functionally. Other behavioral science techniques, such as transactional analysis, team building, and intergroup problem solving may be used to enable the organizational members to deal with interpersonal, intragroup, and intergroup conflicts, respectively.

The structural approach attempts to improve organizational effectiveness by changing the organization's structural design characteristics: differentiation and integration mechanisms, system of communication, reward structure, etc. This approach mainly attempts to manage conflict by altering the amount of conflict experienced by the organizational members at various levels. The structural interventions, such as job design, provision for ombudsman, analysis of group tasks, and analysis of task interdependence of two or more groups may be used to reduce or generate conflict at intrapersonal, interpersonal, intragroup, and intergroup conflicts, respectively.

SUMMARY

Organizational conflict must not necessarily be reduced or eliminated, but managed to enhance individual, group, and organizational effectiveness. The management of conflict at the individual, interpersonal, group, and intergroup levels involves the maintenance of a moderate amount of conflict at each level and helping the organizational participants to learn the five styles of handling interpersonal conflict for dealing with different conflict situations effectively.

An effective management of organizational conflict involves diagnosis and intervention. A comprehensive diagnosis should include the measures of the amount of conflict, and effectiveness. The analysis of diagnostic data should indicate the relationship between conflict, conflict styles, and their sources and effectiveness. Intervention may be needed when there is too little or too much of intrapersonal, intragroup, and intergroup conflicts, and/or the organizational members are not effectively using the five behavioral styles to deal with different situations effectively. The behavioral intervention is mainly designed to manage conflict by enabling organizational participants to learn the various styles of handling conflict to deal with different situations effectively. The structural approach is mainly designed to manage conflict by changing the organization's structural design characteristics. A structural intervention aims mainly at maintaining a moderate amount of conflict by altering the structural sources of conflict.

REFERENCES

Argyris, C. Single-loop and double-loop models in research on decision making. *Administrative Science Quarterly*, 1976, Vol. 21, pp. 363-375.

Argyris, C. Some limitations of the case method: Experiences in a management development program. *Academy of Management Review*, 1980, Vol. 5, pp. 291-298.

Argyris, C., and Schon, D. *Organizational Learning*. Reading, Massachusetts: Addison-Wesley, 1978.

Assael, H. Constructive role of interorganizational conflict. *Administrative Science Quarterly*, 1969, Vol. 14, pp. 573-582.

Blake, R. R., and Mouton, J. S. *The management grid*. Houston, Texas: Gulf Publishing, 1964.

Boulding, K. B. Preface to a special issue. *Journal of Conflict Resolution*, 1968, Vol. 12, pp. 409-411.

Brown, L. D. *Managing conflict at organizational interfaces*. Reading, Massachusetts: Addison-Wesley, 1983.

Evan, W. M. Conflict and performance in R&D organizations: Some preliminary findings. *Industrial Management Review*, 1965, Vol. 7 No. 1, pp. 37-46.

Hall, J., and Williams, M. S. A comparison of decision-making performances in established and ad-hoc groups. *Journal of Personality and Social Psychology*, 1966, Vol. 3, pp. 214-222.

Janis, I. J. *Victims of groupthink.* Boston: Houghton Mifflin, 1972.

Lawrence, P. R., and Lorsch, J. W. Differentiation and integration in complex organizations. *Administrative Science Quarterly,* 1967, Vol. 12, pp. 1-47.

Likert, R., and Likert, J. G. *New ways of managing conflict.* New York: McGraw-Hill, 1976.

Mitroff, I. I., and Featheringham, T. R. On systemic problem solving and the error of the third kind. *Behavioral Science,* 1974, Vol. 19, pp. 383-393.

Musser, S. J. A model for predicting the choice of conflict management strategies by subordinates in high-stake conflicts. *Organizational Behavior and Human Performance,* 1982, Vol. 29, pp. 257-269.

Pelz, D. Creative tensions in the research and development climate. *Science,* 1967, Vol. 157, pp. 160-165.

Rahim, M. A. The management of organizational intergroup conflict: A contingency model. *Proceedings of the 8th Annual Meeting of the Midwest American Institute for Decision Sciences,* Cleveland, Ohio, 1977, pp. 247-249.

Rahim, M. A. *Rahim organizational conflict inventories-I and II.* Palo Alto, California: Consulting Psychologists Press, 1983. (a)

Rahim, M. A. *Rahim organizational conflict inventories: Professional manual.* Palo Alto, California: Consulting Psychologists Press, 1983. (b)

Rahim, M. A. Measurement of organizational conflict. *Journal of General Psychology,* 1983, Vol. 109, pp. 189-919. (c)

Rahim, M. A. A measure of styles of handling interpersonal conflict. *Academy of Management Journal,* 1983, Vol. 26, pp. 368-376. (d)

Rahim, M. A., and Bonoma, T. V. Managing organizational conflict: A model for diagnosis and intervention. *Psychological Reports,* 1979, Vol. 44, pp. 1323-1344.

Robbins, S. P. "Conflict management" and "conflict resolution" are not synonymous terms. *California Management Review,* 1978, Vol. 21, No. 2, pp. 67-75.

Thomas, K. W. Conflict and conflict management. In M. D. Dunnette (Ed.), *Handbook in industrial and organizational psychology.* Chicago: Rand McNally, 1976, pp. 889-935.

Thomas, K. W. Toward multi-dimensional values in teaching: The example of conflict behavior. *Academy of Management Review,* 1977, Vol. 2, pp. 484-490.

COMPARABLE WORTH: AN ISSUE OF EQUALITY

John T. Samaras[1]

What needs to be clearly established in the beginning is what constitutes comparable worth and its difference from equal equal pay.

Equal pay for equal work is now the law of the land expressed by the passage of the Equal Pay Act of 1963. This law clearly mandated that there is to be no discrimination between the sexes for similar work—which is to say that differential wages paid for jobs requiring similar skill, effort, and responsibility and performed under similar working conditions are prohibited.[1]

On the other hand, comparable worth is a concept where pay should be equal between the sexes for performing work which has comparable value but is quite dissimilar. Although equal pay requires male and female secretaries, male and female truck drivers, male and female nurses, welders, and so forth to be given the same pay; comparable worth approaches the issue of the value of the secretary's job vis-a-vis the value of the truck driver's job.

LEGALITIES

Although the Equal Pay Act was a step in eliminating pay discrimination, it did not address the question of pay inequities of other groups. Consequently, Title VII of the 1964 Civil Rights Act was passed to extend protection from pay discrimination to people of different color, race, religion or national origin. Additionally, and equally important, Title VII prohibited discrimination in advertising for open positions, recruiting, hiring, promoting, and terminating of employment.[2]

Neither the Equal Pay Act, nor Title VII clarified the issue of comparable worth. However, in a 1984 Supreme Court case, the County of Washington (Oregon) vs. Gunther, the concept was almost endorsed.[3] In this case, female jail matrons perceived they were being discriminated against because they were receiving only 70 percent of the pay received by male guards. The question was: "Is a jail matron's job similar or dissimilar to a male guard?" Obviously, the work is not quite similar but how much difference is there? On one hand, the Supreme Court ruled that the matron's work was dissimilar but comparable. However, on the other hand the Court did not completely endorse the idea. Consequently, it has not become a precedent setting decision.

In 1981, the American Federation of State, County and Municipal Employees (AFSCME) filed a suit in federal court on behalf of nine female employees against the State of Washington. Their contention was that a job evaluation study conducted years before, by the state, indicated pay discrimination against women. The state was found guilty and was ordered to correct the pay disparities retroactively. However, the state appealed in the 9th Circuit Court of Appeals where the decision was overturned. But before the case reached the Supreme Court, the Washington state legislature had already appropriated $41.6 million to pay for a settlement with the union.[4]

---

[1]Reprinted by permission, *Central State BUSINESS REVIEW*, Summer, 1988, Vol. VII, No. 2, pp. 31-35.

Therefore, in two major decisions, the federal courts have established a basis for comparable worth by putting organizations on notice that the issue of pay disparities has not been settled by the passage of the Equal Pay Act.

HISTORICAL PERSPECTIVES

What is the focus of this issue of comparable worth? The focus is that women earn 64 percent of what men earn, and this is less than what it was more than 40 years ago. In 1946, women were earning 66.1 percent.[5] Is this pay differential justified? Can it be explained? What is the history of pay discrimination? Some perspectives are:

1. Presently the range of occupations for women is half of that for men. Three fourths of all male jobs are distributed among 56 occupations while the same number of female jobs is distributed among 25 occupations.[6] And these are predominantly in lower-paying service industries. They are underutilized in capital-intensive, unionized industries such as manufacturing, which generally offer higher wages and benefits.[7] Why does this exist? Because of historic employment discriminatory practices. Today, women are beginning to move into these industries. And as they do, the earnings gap may begin to narrow, but that in itself does not resolve the issue of comparable worth.

2. Social custom has also led to the difference in earnings. Men, traditionally, are expected to provide for the family. Women are expected to maintain the home and raise children. As providers, it was perceived that men should earn more while women are "temporarily" in the labor force. This social custom applies to all women and men whether they are performing these traditional roles or not. Obviously, these sex roles determine the level of pay for both. The man who is providing for his family is expected to receive more money. There are differing expectations because of this perspective. Men compare themselves to other men, and women tend to compare themselves to other female workers. This difference in comparisons leads to differing expectations, thus many women are less likely to view a low wage as unfair.[8]

3. Carrying this argument of social custom another step—the main concern is when men and women are in the same occupation in the same locale. Companies successfully manage around this concern by segregating women from men. This sex-segregation perpetuates the lower expectations of female workers.[9]

4. There is discrimination in wage classifications. In a New York school district, male bus drivers were classified as maintenance workers earning substantially more than female bus drivers who were classified as clerical workers.

5. A great number of women have short careers because they marry and leave the work force to have children. This cuts down on their careers, which translates into less long-run productivity resulting in lower earnings. June O'Neill of the Urban Institute states that women, on the average, spend 50 to 60 percent of their available years in the job market. The balance of the years off the job are spent primarily raising families.[10]

6. More career minded wives make job sacrifices than of husbands. A woman is more likely to pass up a job move, which could result in increase in pay, than a husband would. Again, the social custom issue surfaces.

7. Fewer women belong to unions than men. This perspective goes back to manufacturing industries which are male dominated and heavily unionized, whereas most female dominated occupations such as; clerical, secretarial, health care, beauty care, and other service occupations are non-union. However, the union has made some headway in organizing school teachers and nurses, thus slightly narrowing the earnings gap.

8. There are less women professionals than men. The highly paying professional occupations are largely held by men. Engineering, medicine, law, university professors, high-tech specialists are male dominated. Although an increasing number of women are entering these occupations, many are being relegated to the lower end of these fields consequently earning less than comparably educated males.[11]

9. Many years ago, statutes were passed to protect women from unsafe conditions and long hours. This resulted in concentrating women in safe, but lower paying occupations. Although legislation has corrected many unsafe conditions and long hours, the Department of Labor statistics show that women are still clustered in traditionally segregated employment areas.[12] As Ruth Blumrosen pointed out, "occupations for women are found to be closely linked to their homemaking role or to their socialization as male helpmates. Such functions include teaching children, nursing the sick or preparing food."[13]

MARKET CONDITIONS

Opponents of comparable worth argue that the market place should be the sole determinant of pay. And if the market decrees through the forces of supply and demand that traditional women's occupations are low paying then it must be right.

First, there is an acknowledged shortage of nurses. Yet in the same hospital in the city of Denver, female nurses earned less than male employees doing outdoor maintenance and gardening.[14] The argument is that the value of a job is determined by supply and demand. And if it pays differently for comparable levels of skill, effort and responsibility, the company is not discriminating rather it is following the market.[15] Evidently there is a greater demand for gardeners than for nurses in Denver consequently the differences in pay.

Another market argument presented by the opponents of comparable worth is the issue of cost. Would not the cost of adjusting female pay upward lead companies to bankruptcy, since it could not be expected that companies would or could bring men's pay downward? Such a specious argument has been presented a number of times in the past on a number of issues: when the Environmental Protection Agency decreed scrubbers in the smoke stack industries, many business leaders screamed that the costs would put them out of business. Virtually every concerned firm survived. Those that failed were facing bankruptcy anyway. When the Equal Pay Act was passed, we heard the same argument from those companies that were discriminating against women and minorities for performing similar work as white men. The successful firms survived and prospered. When the Minimum Wage Act was passed in 1938 setting minimum pay at twenty-five cents an hour, business said they would be driven to the wall. But they survived and that was during the Great Depression. We still hear the same argument whenever the minimum wage is raised.

Successful firms have survived scrubbers, equal pay for similar work, the minimum wage and successful firms will survive comparable worth. A recent survey, funded by the Ford Foundation, found that private employers will support the elimination of pay discrimination between different jobs as "good business" and not inconsistent with remaining in the marketplace.[16]

A GOVERNMENT WAGE BOARD?

A government wage board cannot effectively determine internal pay equity. Companies are unique with each having its own characteristics within a job classification. With several million companies in the United States, it would be impossible to set wages, nor do the advocates of comparable worth recommend such a body. Rather they decry such an agency.

Companies should voluntarily conduct their own comparable-worth job evaluations, and be prepared to defend their compensation practices. Violations should be handled the same as discrimination complaints by the Equal Employment Opportunities Commission. But a federal agency with an army of inspectors would be impractical and too costly. But it could happen—look at the Occupational and Health Administration. The idea is to head off the threat of government intervention. But in order to do this companies must act.

ALTERNATIVES

What are the alternatives to an enforced job evaluation system? The organization of unions in female-dominated occupations could be an answer, but does management want to deal with another union? There is no doubt that with a union, pay for women would increase and possibly increase more than through comparable worth; thus exacerbating labor costs. From the women's point of view, they should understand the union is not going to be all that concerned unless economic conditions are exceptionally good. Presently, and in most circumstances, the focus of union activities is going to be on job security and pay maintenance for their predominant male membership.

Another alternative is to provide for tax incentives to employers who increase the compensation of women relative to men.[17] This would only present another burden upon the business and could result in further increasing the tax burden upon the taxpayer.

A diversionary alternative is to encourage women to enter male-dominated jobs such as; engineering, sales, law; and the industrial trades of welding, machining, plumbing and high tech occupations. This is not the issue. The law and court decisions are quite clear here. There can be no discrimination on entry, pay, or promotion. Comparable worth beaches the subject on increasing pay in present female occupations vis-a-vis male dominated jobs. The issue is not just to open more jobs to women, but to re-evaluate the worth of female jobs to male jobs. This can only be done through a meaningful job evaluation point system that weighs each job or effort, responsibility, skill, and working conditions. Obviously, each of these four items will have a number of sub-factors such as; education, experience, physical and mental effort, hazards, liability and so forth. Job evaluation, to be effective, must be conducted cautiously by Human Resource Managers knowledgeable in the tasks they are to evaluate. There is no question that some subjectivity will enter into the job evaluation process, but the effect would be to weigh each job fairly on the basis of its worth to the organization. At the risk of sounding contradictory, market forces cannot be totally disregarded. Regardless, of the point values attached to each job there needs to be some link to the market. This can never be overlooked in a free enterprise system. The caveat here is not to *depend* upon this system as has been done in the past, which resulted in pay inequities against women.

RESEARCH STUDY

Human Resource Managers from 47 randomly selected organizations within six major industries were surveyed to determine the pay methods their firms were using. Table 1 depicts the industry, firms, number of employees, the method of pay determination and the frequency of each method.

An analysis of this table should be disheartening to the proponents of comparable worth for the pay methods that have been most discriminatory to women, such as "competition" and "market conditions," are the ones mostly in use. This is summarized in Table 2.

Twenty six out of 62 frequencies of the five pay methods were on "market conditions" and 18 were on "what the competition pays." In other words, 44 or 71 percent of the total number of frequencies were of the most sexually biased variety. Compounding this bias is the fact that many firms use both of the discriminatory methods. Referring back to Table 1, it should be noted, a number of organizations use two or more pay methods. For example, 26 manufacturing firms used five methods with a frequency of 36. One large metropolitan health care facility employed three methods, and two manufacturers used four methods (as most students of management know, the Hay Plan is a system for management positions).

It is particularly discouraging to observe that of the health care institutions surveyed, six of the eight frequencies were on "market conditions." This is particularly surprising because there had been a fair amount of job evaluation research done in the hospital setting.

In the same survey, the 47 Human Resource Managers were presented with two scenarios: one dealt with a female file clerk, earning more pay than a male, while the other scenario presented a high school dropout truck driver earning more than a college educated R.N. Specifically, the managers were asked to give their justification. Their answers are portrayed in Table 3.

Table 3 largely reinforces what has been said up to this point, and that is "competition" and "market condition" are primarily the reasons given for the pay differences. A truck driver and a file clerk make more because of supply and demand or the competition for their services. This clearly indicates the mind set of 25 of these managers. Five indicated that unions were the cause. The disturbing point here, for proponents of comparable worth, is that only five Human Resource Managers saw that a job evaluation system could have been the justification for the differences in pay. It is not inconceivable that an objective, purposeful, job evaluation point system could have indicated differences in the earnings between a truck driver and a nurse, and between a file clerk and a skilled craftsman, but only five managers thought so. Twelve managers felt there was no justification for the pay discrepancies.

Although this section of the survey instrument was not designed to indict Human Resource Managers, it clearly establishes the point that a heavy majority are not even "thinking" of job evaluation.

CONCLUSION

What can be drawn from this paper? In spite of the fact that women constitute 50 percent of the labor force they make less than two thirds what men make. Some of this difference can be explained because of fewer women in what have been traditional male occupations. But what of the equally valuable jobs that are female-dominated? Why should their pay be consistently lower than male-dominated work?

Why does a male high school dropout truck driver earn more than a college educated R.N.? Because his working conditions are more difficult? Because of his time away from home? Because he may be hauling hazardous wastes? These are viable considerations, of course, but what of the nurse and the life and death situations she often faces? What of the physical and mental strains in dealing with uncooperative and often hostile patients? Who is the important resource to his or her organization? Comparable worth can work and must work in order to bring about equality in pay for both sexes for comparable work.

Table 1
Firms, Employees, and Methods of Pay Determination

Industry	Firms	Employees			Methods of Pay Determination	
		Female	Male	Total	Type	Frequency
Banking/Finance	6	552	248	800	Competition	2
					Hay Plan	1
					Job Evaluation	1
					Market Conditions	3
Distribution	1	25	179	204	Competition	1
					Market Conditions	1
Health Care	5	5,464	1,530	6,994	Competition	1
					Job Evaluation	1
					Market Conditions	6
Manufacturing (Consumer and Industrial Goods)	26	13,824	55,988	69,812	Competition	12
					Hay Plan	6
					Job Evaluation	5
					Market Conditions	11
					Union	2
Processing (Oil, Gas, Chemicals)	5	307	1,068	1,375	Hay Plan	1
					Job Evaluation	1
					Market Conditions	3
Retailing	4	372	291	663	Competition	2
					Market Conditions	2
Totals	47	20,544	59,304	79,848		62

Table 2
Frequency of Methods of Pay Determination

Methods of Pay Determination	Frequency
Market Conditions	26
Competition	18
Hay Plan	8
Job Evaluation	8
Unions	2
	62

Table 3
Responses to Scenarios

Reason for Pay Difference	Frequency
Market Conditions	15
No Justification	12
Competition	10
Job Evaluation	5
Unions	5
	47

REFERENCES

1. Thomas A. Mahoney and Benson Rosen, "Where Do Compensation Specialists Stand on Comparable Worth?' *Compensation Review*, Vol. 16, No. 4, 1984, p.28.

2. Sandra Hurd, Paula Murray, Bill Shaw, "Comparable Worth: A Legal and Ethical Analysis," *American Business Law Journal*, Vol. 22, Fall, 1984, p. 408

3. 452 U.S. 161 (1981)

4. "Developments in Industrial Relations," *Monthly Labor Review*, Vol. 109, March, 1986, p. 43.

5. Equal Employment Opportunity for Women: U.S. Policies; U.S. Department of Labor, Women's Bureau, 1982.

6. Patricia Yancey Martin, Diane Harrison, Diana Dinitto, "Advancement for Women in Hierarchical Organizations: A Multilevel Analysis of Problems and Prospects," *Journal of Applied Behavioral Science*, January, 1983, p.23.

7. Julianne M. Malveaux, "Moving Forward, Standing Still," in *Women in the Workplace*, ed. Phyllis A Wallace (Boston: Auburn Publishing, 1983) p. 23.

8. Elaine Sorenson, "Equal Pay for Comparable Worth: A Policy for Eliminating the Undervaluation of Women's Work," *Journal of Economic Issues*, Vol. XVIII, No. 2, June, 1984, p. 469.

9. Ibid.

10. June O'Neill cited in San DeForrest, "How Can Comparable Worth Be Achieved?" *Personnel*, Vol. 61, September-October, 1984, p. 6.

11. Hurd et al, p. 417.

12. Ibid, p. 414.

13. Ruth Blumrosen as quoted in Hurd et al, p. 414.

14. Benson Rosen, Sara Rynes, Thomas A Mahoney, "Compensation, Jobs, and Gender," *Harvard Business Review*, Vol. 61, July-August, 1983, p. 170.

15. Robert Livernash as cited in Sorensen, p. 466.

16. National Committee on Pay Equity. "The Cost of Pay Equity in Public and Private Employment." Ford Research Project, January, 1985.

17. Barbara Mackey Carlson and May Pat McEnrue, "Eliminating the Gender-Based Earning Gap: Two Alternatives," *Business Horizons*, Vol. 28, July-August, 1985, p. 79.

BIBLIOGRAPHY

_____ "The Quiet Advance of Comparable Worth," *Fortune*, April 27, 1987, p. 8.

MANAGING STAFF FUNCTIONS IN A LARGE CORPORATION

Jerome Wilkenfield[1]

Senior managements of most large corporations recognize the need for specialized staff experts. Frequently, however, they are uncertain about the best size and location of the staff departments in the overall corporate organization. In large measure, this is due to a lack of clearly defined goals and methods for measuring effectiveness.

Staff functions provide management with specialized expertize in areas not directly related to the primary function of the corporation: the production and distribution of products or services at a profit. These include such functions as research, engineering, quality control, legal services, accounting, employee relations, environment, health, safety, and security.

This paper will define staff functions and explain how they differ from line organizations in structure, authority, and responsibility. Typical methods of operation and reporting, as well as problems in handling specialists and measuring effectiveness, will be discussed. Also, an approach which has been found to be very cost-effective—achieving objectives with minimum-sized staffs by utilizing key experts, sophisticated management by exception, and monitoring techniques—is described.

NECESSARY APPENDAGES

Some staff functions can be integrated into the line organization. No matter where they are, they are considered appendages, albeit necessary ones. This is the result of three elements of staff functions. First and foremost is the fact that, for the short term, business can continue on a day-to-day basis without staff. Second, staffs are made up of specialists who are not in the mainstream of the corporation, and whose functions are not always well understood by line managers and other employees. The third, and very critical, element is that staff effectiveness cannot be measured in the usual business terms of productivity and profitability.

Staffs, by their very nature, are support groups to the line organization. The structure must reflect this reality.

Staffs, by their nature, are support groups to the line organization. To be effective, they must have very few levels within their organization and must report to relatively high levels in the overall corporate structure. Despite this apparent high positioning, however, staff people generally have very little authority to make financial or business decisions in their area of expertise. In most companies, line management is held responsible for profitability, and is, therefore, given full

[1]Reprinted by permission of the publisher, from *Management Review*, June 1986. Copyright 1986, American Management Association, New York. All rights reserved.

authority to make decisions affecting profits. Conversely, staffs usually are held responsible for matters affecting the company in their fields of expertise.

Line organizations are normally clear-cut pyramids of reporting responsibility, ascending in ever-increasing scope up to the chief executive officers. It is rare that line managers are authorized to deal with people several levels higher in the organizational ladder. Measures of effectiveness are based on the quantity of products produced and sold, their quality and cost—items that are normally measured.

However, organizational structures and effectiveness measures usually produce misunderstandings among managers and staff members regarding functions, responsibilities, and value to the corporation. In part, this is due to lack of clearly defined objectives for the staff as well as uncertainty about the full depth and applicability of the disciplines involved in the staff function.

Another problem with staff organizations is the lack of long-term career paths for specialized experts. Methods of recognizing growth and contribution to the organization need to be developed and made clear to staff members. These can include pay commensurate with responsibility—recognizing that staff experts do not manage large numbers of people; titles which confer organizational status; and clearly defined career paths that include opportunities to move outside the discipline.

PROS AND CONS OF SEVERAL STRUCTURES

Currently, major corporations use five primary methods of staffing. These are:

■ *Centralized Staffs*. In these organizations, the corporation has all the required technical experts on the headquarters staff, although not necessarily at the corporate headquarters. When operating units at any level need assistance, they call on the central staff. There may be charge-out on a fee-for-service or allocation basis, either as part of corporate overhead or based on retrospective or prospective usage. Experience has shown that when charges vary by usage, there is a strong tendency by line managers to avoid calling on staff for assistance, and either to make decisions based on the judgment of the line organization or shop for cheaper consultants outside the corporation.

Some benefits of corporate level staff are: easily accessible independent counsel for management; cross-divisional identification of possible improvements or marketing possibilities; and, in technical organizations such as research and engineering groups, the ability to have a critical mass, which can help to identify opportunities for improved performance.

Shortcomings of centralized corporate staffs include increased layers of organization, and a strong tendency to develop bureaucracies. This also sets the stage for possible turf battles between individuals and departments, which take up time that would be better applied to problem solving.

■ *Decentralized Staffs*. In this organizational approach, most staff functions are located at divisional or facility levels; only those required to account for financial matters and provide stockholder and regulatory agency reports are at the corporate level.

This has the advantages of minimizing corporate overhead and maximizing strict profit-and-loss accountability. It also assures that only the staff needed for a specific function is on the payroll, directly reportable and quickly available to the line management of the business group or division involved.

On the other hand, there is a strong possibility of significant problems going unrecognized due to lack of available staff, or provincialism. This can result in uneven attention to problems and compliance with legal requirements in different divisions. This can be interpreted as inadequate management attention at the corporate level by the Securities and Exchange Commission, or by plaintiffs in suits brought against the corporation.

■ *Hybrids.* Depending on the businesses in which the corporation is engaged, some staff groups may be at the corporate level, while others are at the divisional level, while others are at both levels. This is probably the most common corporate staff organizational structure, and it is highly effective. However, it does have all the shortcomings of both of the above structures, with turf protection frequently a major problem. This is tempered somewhat by the fact that, where needed, clearly recognized staff disciplines are employed. Unless there is some central functional direction and management of the decentralized staffs, these specialized experts are rarely known and available to other divisions.

■ *Staffs as training groups.* This approach helps rising line managers obtain a broad perspective and some knowledge of specialized staff technical disciplines as they progress along their career paths.

It also has many disadvantages. These include added cost for training people in the specialized needs of the functions; an increased probability of improper decisions; reduced opportunities for the advancement of professional specialists, leading to higher turnover; and lack of continuity in long-range planning for the function due to turnover in staff. Some of these can be overcome by special incentives, but such measures are costly.

■ *Corporate-level key experts.* This approach is becoming more popular as companies feel an increasing need to reduce costs in the face of domestic and foreign competition. Increasing marketplace, public, and regulatory complexity and sophistication require management to keep advised on the status of highly technical and diverse activities, such as management information systems, the protection of human health, the environment, computer-aided design, and liability lawsuits.

This type of organization calls for very small corporate staffs, made up of very competent experts with broad experience who can keep abreast of developments and programs throughout the corporation in their areas of expertise. They must be able to identify points of weakness in programs and staffs in all areas of the organization, as well as indicate upcoming areas of concern. They must have authority—preferably earned because they are respected—to discuss perceived issues or problems at any level of the corporation. (The ability to water and change water into wine also helps.)

Key expert organizations usually are staffed by one to three experts at the corporate level, with divisional and facility staffs as required to implement plans and conduct the detailed day-to-day activities required for their specific businesses. Lines of communication are usually short, with the staff able to communicate directly with all levels of the organization on a functional basis. The corporate-level staffs need to develop sophisticated "management by exception" monitoring procedures to provide prompt, interpreted information. The system must also provide the staff with sufficient information to allow them to judge what issues are significant to the corporation and whether they are receiving appropriate attention.

Despite the fact that this modification of the hybrid system is most cost-effective, it is not without hazard. The number of specialists able to develop and maintain such a system is limited and, because it depends on management by exception and the judgment of a small staff, it can, on occasion, result in a serious issue being missed. This can be minimized by proper design of the reporting and control system. It can also be minimized if the generated information is reviewed at several levels of the organization and by different employees from varied disciplines. For example, in the environmental protection area, input from both legally and technically oriented experts would assure complete coverage.

LINE AND STAFF INTERACTION

No matter which organizational structure is used, the staff personnel must interact with the line if anything is to be accomplished. After all, line managers are, by definition, the doers. On any specific issue, the initiative can be from either party. The line can request advice or assistance from the staff on an issue; the staff can advise the line of policy or regulatory requirements, or request information needed in developing improved procedures. Almost without exception, a staff-oriented request will be considered with some reluctance by the line managers, who will feel that it is an interference with their authority, might add to their cost, or could affect the efficiency of operation. This is minimized when the line knows that the staff is not only fully supported by senior management, but is required to meet quantifiable objectives.

MEASURING PERFORMANCE

In operating or production departments, performance is readily measured by the establishment of cost, production, and quality goals. Other may be added, but these are the primary indices used. While staff departments usually have budgetary and staff-size goals, they also need goals and indices of performance which are directly related to the functions for which they are responsible. Identifying meaningful indices of performance, and developing data to establish goals by which improvement will be measured take creative effort. Some indices will be directly controllable, while others are only indirectly controllable. Some example of basic indices for measurement of performance of some overall staff functions are detailed in the chart below.

QUANTIFIABLE STAFF OBJECTIVES		
	Directly Controllable	*Indirectly Controllable*
Legal	Actions successfully defended	Actions filed against the company
Environmental	Permit excursions and reportable incidents	Citations and notices of violations
Security	Cases solved or losses prevented	Total losses identified
Safety	Injury incidence rate	Compensation costs
Financial	Operating capital as a fraction of sales	Cost of financing as a fraction of the market average
Stores	Inventory as a fraction of sales or invested capital	Inventory turnover rate
Engineering	Fraction of construction meeting capital estimates	Reliability of facilities (down-time and maintenance costs)
Research	Marketable developments	Implemented process improvements (cost reduction)
Quality Control	Cost of sampling and testing	Frequency of testing

Indices of performance such as these, along with any desired subsidiary terms, permit management and staff to monitor performance on an exception basis. This reduces the necessity for written and oral reports and, by highlighting significant matters, avoids their being lost in the paper storm.

Indices must be carefully designed to assure that they are simple to measure or calculate, yet can objectively measure how well the most important goals of the function are being achieved. It also is best if at least two indices are used, permitting cross-checking for accuracy.

LONG-TERM PLANS

A detailed operating plan for the function should list all issues and programs identified as requiring action, along with a timetable outlining when each item or phase of an item will be completed. This should be developed in conjunction with the operating departments to assure agreement on the short- and long-range needs of the company. By regularly reviewing the status of items in the plan and any needed changes, both line and staff managements can identify the issues that need to be addressed and monitored clearly.

LESS IS MORE

When the kinds of staff structures described above are established, it is usually possible to operate with small staffs at the corporate level. Some functions may need only three or four professionals. Others, such as accounting, legal, engineering, research, and quality control, may need substantially more personnel because of detailed reporting requirements or the performance of semi-operational functions. These need to be reviewed critically after indices, goals, and an operating plan have been established.

Experience has shown that, where corporate level key experts are used, time is not wasted on turf battles. There is also no need to spend time on or hire staff to manage cost chargebacks or distributions. The key experts act as staff consultants who provide guidance to the operating units or divisions, establish corporate policy and programs, oversee regulatory and policy compliance by all units of the corporation, and act as corporate spokesmen. They also provide senior managers with information when they must speak on specialized subjects. Under such a system, line units—with advice from the corporate staffs—establish their own programs to fit their unique needs, with a clear understanding of how their performance will be judged.

I have seen this approach successfully implemented in several of the disparate staff functions mentioned. Staff size and costs have been reduced by installing corporate-level key experts who establish long-range plans, coupled with clearly defined goals and quantitative indices of performance for measuring corporate programs' effectiveness. It has been highly effective in providing the management support and control needed by large corporations at a minimum cost.

PART FOUR
LEADING

EXERCISE 4.1 APPLICATION OF BEHAVIOR MODIFICATION

Imagine you are a machine shop supervisor with a group of twelve machinists. One of your highly skilled machinists is becoming a problem employee by consistently arriving late. Although his work performance is good, his tardiness is creating a disruptive influence on the remaining eleven machinists.

You think, perhaps, that behavior modification might work. First, you review each method of behavior modification: positive reinforcement, reward for desirable behavior such as his good work performance; avoidance learning, which is learning that occurs when an individual wants to avoid unpleasantness such as being "bawled out"; extinction which is ignoring undesired behavior such as not paying attention to the behavior in the hope it will go away; and punishment, an overt action like a suspension or dismissal.

In each box below describe an activity that you think may modify the machinist's behavior.

Positive Reinforcement:

Avoidance Learning:

Extinction:

Punishment:

EXERCISE 4.2 THE WAY TO LEAD

A perspective of leadership behavior is to focus on styles a manager may use in dealing with his/her subordinates. An employee-oriented style is one where leaders try to motivate rather than to control or be authoritative. The leader is supportive and encourages the group to participate in decisions and form trusting relationships. In order to make effective decisions the group must be knowledgeable and skilled in their tasks.

A task-oriented style is one of close supervision where the primary concern is to get the job done. The development and growth of workers is of secondary consideration. This style works best with unskilled workers.

Before each statement designate the appropriate leadership style; "T" for task-oriented or "E" for employee-oriented.

_____ 1. The work is routine with tight production schedules.

_____ 2. To lead a number of farm laborers picking tomatoes.

_____ 3. These are engineers and research chemists working on the space shuttle.

_____ 4. It is urgent to maintain high quality.

_____ 5. The supervisor lets the employees decide on specific work assignments.

_____ 6. The servicing of products is essential for company success.

_____ 7. A decision needs to be made immediately if the object is to continue.

_____ 8. The department chairperson lets the faculty decide on how to cover all the classes.

_____ 9. Migrant laborers working in a meat packing plant.

_____ 10. A new unit is being established to develop and market a new breakfast cereal.

EXERCISE 4.3 COMMIT THE COMMITTEE

There are several types of groups in industry with each having its own characteristics. There is the command group consisting of the work group and its supervision. There are task forces charged with the responsibility of dealing with a particular task. Also, organizations have standing or permanent committees whose function is to review and pass on to a higher authority their formal recommendations.

Lastly, there are informal groups which arise out of the formal organization. This is an irregular group or cliques of workers who tend to be a cohesive unit often led by an informal leader. Informal groups also extend outside of the company such as; bowling teams, or flag football.

Match each statement with the appropriate group type from the box on the top.

Command	**Task Force**	**Standing**	**Informal**

_____ 1. A group assigned the responsibility, by the plant superintendent to solve a production flow problem.

_____ 2. A group of middle managers attending a policy meeting with their CEO.

_____ 3. Twelve employees organizing a weekend fishing trip.

_____ 4. A committee of six workers assigned to hear grievances throughout the year.

EXERCISE 4.4 SEE THE PICTURE

Can communications be enhanced through graphic displays?

The following is an excerpt of a report presented at a recent sales meeting: "Our sales are up 4.5 million dollars over 1986, which was up three million over 1985; and 1985, 1984, and 1983 were two million over the previous year. Sales of 20 million for that year were virtually the same for the two previous years."

You can see how this statement is confusing.

Take the figures and the years mentioned and in the space below, graphically sketch the above statement. If your graph is correct the sales representatives, with a quick glance, should easily understand what was meant to be said.

Gordon Poole is the president and major stockholder of a closely held small microcomputer manufacturing firm. Sales and profits have been dramatically increasing for the past three years. As a result more employees have to be hired in order to keep up with the increasing sales volume. The total number of employees has now reached 165 with more expected to be hired the coming year.

A principal reason for the company's success is the high salaries and wages Mr. Poole pays his employees. The high pay, he believes, attracts the quality people needed to make quality products. Another reason, of course, is that computer manufacturing is a fast growth industry, although a highly competitive one.

It is because of increasing competition that Mr. Poole and his production foreman, Mr. Jake Biggs, have decided to hire two highly skilled electrical engineers, Bob Trackeski and Joan Maras. Their salary was set at $40,000 each plus the standard set of benefits; hospitalization, vacation, sick leave, retirement and membership at a health spa. Each was given a completely refurnished office with an adjoining lab.

Six months later Joan submitted her resignation to a shocked Mr. Biggs. "What's wrong?" he asked after shaking his head in disbelief. " Is it the pay, or what?"

"Oh, its nothing like that, "Joan answered, "I just think I might be happier someplace else."

"I sure would like to know what it is that we can do to keep you here. We like you. We like your work. Hey, if its money-I'll talk to Gordon about a raise-"

"It's not that," interrupted Joan. "It's just that I think I should move on, but thanks for everything." With that last remark, Joan left Mr. Biggs. A few minutes later he called Bob into his office.

"In case you haven't heard," Mr. Biggs started, "Joan has just quit, and for the life of me I don't know why. Do you?"

"No, but I know she wasn't happy. I know we got along well. I enjoyed working with her."

"Is it a home problem? Does her husband want her to quit working?" asked Mr. Biggs.

"I doubt that. They have a big mortgage—she told me. I just think she was not happy with what she was doing."

Mr. Biggs looked closely at Bob. "Well, what about you? Are you happy? Do you like what you're doing. Or are you going to quit too?"

"Well, now that you asked," answered Bob. "Let me say a few things."

1. Taking into consideration Herzberg's Two-Factor Approach to Work Motivation, what response do you think Bob is going to give to Mr. Biggs?

2. Do you feel Joan was justified in resigning?

3. If you were Mr. Biggs what specific measures would you have taken to prevent Joan's resignation?

"He is a born leader," said Frank Wellston, chairperson of the search committee for Empire-Continental Stores. "We need a person to lead us out of the wilderness," he continued. Sue Watson, a committee member added, "What I like about him is he looks presidential. He is tall, distinguished looking and very courteous."

A few minutes later the committee unanimously endorsed the nomination and eventual selection of Clay Enbright as the new company president.

Empire-Continental has been losing money and market share in the department store business for the past three years. Its image as the leading department store chain in the south has slipped as the competition has become more aggressive, both in promotions and in opening suburban stores. Jack Skegstrom, president, was forced into retirement at a stormy board meeting last month.

Two weeks later Frank, whose full time position is vice-president and chief purchasing agent, met Clay in the executive conference room at 9:00 a.m. on the first day of Clay's employment.

"Well, Clay, I hope you like it here," offered Frank.

"I'm sure I will. And I know we'll all get along."

"I'm sure we will too." Frank paused for a moment and then said, "If there is anything I can help you with or anything you need just call me. Remember we have to get moving!"

"O.K. Frank. We'll stay in touch."

With that remark Frank returned to his office and Clay went to the executive suite for a cup of coffee.

The situation over the next six months at Empire-Continental did not improve, and by the end of Clay's first year the business suffered further loses in profitability and market share. Clay enjoyed his role as a department store executive. He liked visiting the department managers and often waited on customers. He asked the clerks and managers for suggestions. He involved the warehouse workers in how best to speed up deliveries. In short, Clay's relations with all employees was good, yet the picture at Empire-Continental was further deteriorating.

1. How do you interpret Clay's leadership style?

2. What are the positive features of his style?

3. Apply Fiedler's Model and identify the pertinent elements to this case.

    a. What is the appropriate match of the leadership style and the pertinent elements you have identified?

Bill Winstrom was the new member in the stamping division of Cross Metals. He seemed like a pleasant, easy going fellow even though he was somewhat different. He wore his hair long, although he tied it in the back, and his beard was a little straggly. He never wore socks and for lunch he always had strawberry yoghurt and a diet soft drink. He preferred to eat alone and although friendly he never had too much to say.

Jack Norton one of the eight other workers in the division was talking to "Pop" Smithson during the lunch break, "I heard that we're going to come under a new incentive system sometime soon."

"What!" replied Pop. "I have a hard enough time keeping up now."

"You don't know what they're going to do yet. They may not be changing too much."

"Bull!" exclaimed Pop. "You know good and doggone well that anytime they change the incentives they increase our rates to make standard."

"Well, don't worry about it. As long as we work at our present output they can't raise the rate very much—if at all."

"You never know what they're going to do. All the big shots think about is more productivity and more productivity."

About two hours later Pop comes running over to Jack. "Winstrom is kicking up a storm."

"Whadda'ya mean?"

"Why he's working fast. I mean real fast."

Jack stopped his machine. "You don't see the 'super' anywhere do you?" he asked referring to the supervisor. "Nah," answered Pop.

"Okay, I'll talk to Winstrom and see what's going on."

Jack ambled the 100 or so feet over to Winstrom. "Bill, do you have a minute?"

"Sure. What's up?" answered Bill as he shut off the stamping machine.

"Well it's like this. We all try to work at an even pace. Not too fast and not too slow. And..uh..of course you're new around here. But anyway, we kinda help each other." Jack paused. "You know Bill, if we work too fast the industrial engineers and the production people might and they just really might raise our standard."

"Yeah and that means more," interjected Bill.

"Not necessarily so," said Jack. "What happens is they may raise the standard rate but not necessarily the money in proportion. If you know what I mean."

"Yeah, I know what you mean all right. But the bottom line is it's more bucks for me the faster I work. Right?"

Jack hesitated for a moment and then answered, "Yeah that's right, but if they raise the standard you'll have to work faster yet just to stay even."

"Maybe so, but I'm new and if I don't work as fast as I can I may not have a job all right."

"No, you're too good of a worker to worry about that," replied Jack.

"What's this beef all about anyway?" asked Bill.

"There ain't no beef. It's just like I said. They'll raise the standard and we'll all have to work harder. Take Pop over there. He has to raise his daughter's kids. His wife is a cripple. If he gets bounced because he can't keep up with the new standards what's going to happen to 'im? Social security and retirement isn't enough."

"Well," said Bill. "I've got a pregnant wife who's always sick and we're living in a trailer. I want to make a down payment on a house and get rid of that clunker I'm driving to work. Besides that Pop has had 40 years to make his nest egg."

"Yeah, maybe so. But I just hope you're not in his shoes some day." With that remark, Jack spun around and went back to his work station.

1.   Would you say that the stamping division of Cross Metals is a cohesive group?
2.   How do you interpret the norms of this group?
3.   How do you perceive the consequences of the non-conformity of Bill Winstrom?

CASE 4.4 THE MEMO

From: The Boss
To: Employees - those that work and those who don't.

There ain't going to be no vacations for nobody if you all don't get to cracking. And I mean it! I come to work at seven when most of you are snoring away. At eight when you're all supposed to be working either you ain't here or you're goofing off or standing around telling jokes. And speaking of jokes I don't want you guys telling the girls dirty jokes either.

Now what I want to tell you besides the above message is about Armistice Day. It's now called Veteran's Day and its on Friday. It may come as a surprise to most of you but Friday is a working day. And Veteran's Day is not one of our regular holidays. And you goof-offs that are going to get sick on Friday you better bring a note from your doctor or else. I have a mind to fire half of you anyway.

I pay you good money and I expect a full day's work from you.

If you don't like it git the hell out!

---

1.   What is your opinion of the memo?
2.   Reconstruct the memo in proper and meaningful but polite terms. Leave out what does not need to be said.

The factors that motivate workers and the things that drive them to strikes and violence cut across cultural differences. This explains why the world economy will be driven less and less by the use of workers who are deprived of motivating work.

Today we have a world economy. But it won't be long before companies will have no place to move in their search for workers who are easy to manipulate.

Strikes are becoming more and more frequent in the developing countries. As workers in these countries develop further, we will see a repetition of the history of industrial relations in the U.S.

Despite sharp cultural differences, there are more commonalities among workers throughout the world than we have assumed. Generally we exaggerate the eccentric attitudes of each culture rather than seek the common characteristics of people at work.

My Motivation-Hygiene theory has shown that managers do not motivate employees by giving them higher wages, more benefits, or new status symbols. Rather, employees are motivated by their own inherent need to succeed at a challenging task. The manager's job, then, is not to motivate people to get them to achieve; instead, the manager should provide opportunities for people to achieve so they will become motivated.

This is not a theory for American workers alone. Recent research by myself and others reveals that these principles hold up in diverse cultures. In other words, there *are* some common characteristics among workers throughout the world.

My early research findings are illustrated in the summary graph of 1,685 employees (primarily American) in 12 job-event studies discussed in my 1968 article for *Harvard Business Review*, "One more time: How do you motivate employees?" The populations surveyed were: Lower-level supervisors, professional women, agricultural administrators, pre-retirees from management positions, hospital-maintenance personnel, manufacturing supervisors, nurses, food handlers, military officers, scientists, housekeepers, teachers, technicians, female assemblers, accountants, foremen, and engineers.

U.S.A.

As the graph shows, about 80% of the factors in satisfying job events come from the motivators (the intrinsic elements of the job): achievement, recognition for achievement, the work itself, responsibility, advancement, and growth.

---

[1] Reprinted by permission, Fredrick Herzberg, *Industry Week*, September 21, 1987, pp. 29-32.

WHAT MAKES WORKERS HAPPY/UNHAPPY?

AMERICAN WORKERS

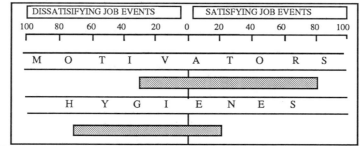

MOTIVATORS are defined as the intrinsic elements of the job—achievement, the work itself. HYGIENES are the job's extrinsic elements—company policy, working conditions.

EUROPE

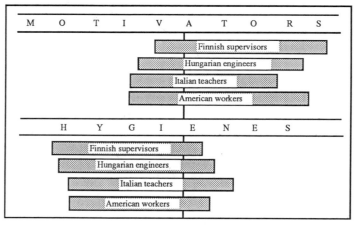

ISRAELI KIBBUTZ

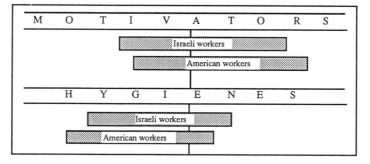

JAPAN

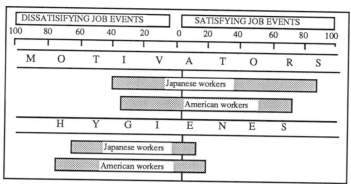

ZAMBIA

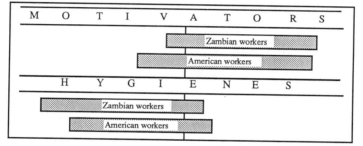

SOUTH AFRICA

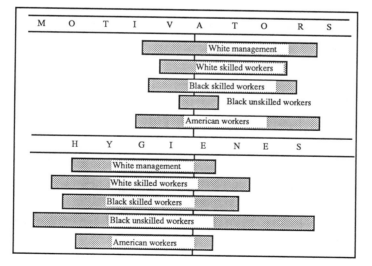

INDIA

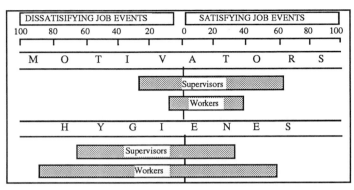

Only about 20% of the satisfying job events involve hygiene factors (the extrinsic elements of the job): company policy and administration, supervision, relationships with co-workers, working conditions, salary, and job security.

In contrast, almost 70% of the *dis*satisfying job events relate to hygiene treatment, and only about 30% to motivator failure—to achieve and grow in the work itself.

EUROPE

Finland in Northern Europe, Communist Hungary in Middle Europe, and Italy in Southern Europe show similar motivation-hygiene patterns.

ISRAEL

In Israel, we studied three motivators—work itself, achievement, and responsibility—and two hygiene factors—working conditions and interpersonal relationships. The last, although a hygiene factor, is so important to the functioning of a kibbutz that it appears as frequently as a cause of satisfaction as it does as a cause of dissatisfaction.

INTERESTING WORK. In other words, my research, and the research of others who have examined real events on the job, show that working people tend to be dissatisfied with the way they are being treated. But, despite the inevitable dissatisfaction with hygiene treatment, healthy human beings can also find motivation and satisfaction in interesting work if their managers will offer them interesting work to do.

As I have often repeated—if you want people motivated to do a good job, give them a good job to do.

DIFFERENT CULTURES. During the '80s there have been some interesting studies of critical job events in Japan, Africa, and India that can offer insights into the motivation of workers in nations that have sharp cultural differences from America. These can be compared with the summary of the first Motivation-Hygiene studies we noted earlier.

Because of the current emphasis on the motivation of Japanese workers, it is perhaps best to begin with a study conducted in Japan.

JAPAN

Here we find 253 workers in public- and private-sector jobs in Japan. To their surprise, the researchers for this study found that Japanese workers are **not** satisfied by hygiene factors such as company policy or interpersonal relations with co-workers.

Contrary to all the conventional wisdom that has grown up about differences between American and Japanese workers, the profile is quite similar. Like their counterparts in the U.S., Japanese workers are made happy by the motivators and unhappy by the hygiene factors.

ZAMBIA

This finding is also very similar to the summaries of American and Japanese studies. It represents 341 public- and private-sector workers from a variety of job levels in 11 organizations in the developing country of Zambia.

SOUTH AFRICA

This study shows part of the 1982 research results of Luther Backer of South Africa. White South African managers show a profile almost identical to that of American workers.

Mr. Backer's studies of 300 skilled black and white workers go on to refute the assumption of the South African Establishment that blacks cannot be motivated by their own achievement and growth in skills. Indeed, with comparable jobs, the black skilled profile is slightly more normal than that of the white skilled workers.

But the motivator and hygiene needs of 789 unskilled blacks sampled from various tribes employed in a variety of companies show satisfaction being dependent on hygiene factors. Mr. Backer believes that the impoverished nature of the unskilled workers' jobs has not afforded these workers with motivators—thus the abnormal profile. Mr. Backer does not speculate on the effect of the lack of motivators on worker unrest, but according to Motivation-Hygiene theory this forcing of human beings to a pattern of seeking satisfaction with hygienes causes great hostility.

INDIA

This study shows that supervisors in textile mills in India have more motivators than do the workers under them. But, like the studies of unskilled black workers in South Africa, this study of 300 textile-mill workers in Bombay, India, by R. Prakasam shows the inversion of motivator satisfaction on the job. The workers are operating on a dependent hygiene continuum that leads to addiction to hygiene, or strikes and revolution.

In this case of the textile workers, they went on strike soon after this study was conducted in 1981. The government finally had to take over the mills in 1983, after they had lain idle for 21 months.

WHAT THEY WANT. When managers deny human beings motivating work, they force them into a pattern of seeking satisfaction with hygienes. This abnormal pattern causes great dependency, rage, and hostility, which must be expressed, in strikes, revolution, or terrorism.

SHOULD YOU CHANGE YOUR LEADERSHIP STYLE?

Lars-Erik Wiberg[1]

Leadership comes in four basic styles and eight combinations of these. Is there a best style for a manager? Yes, it is at once none of them and all of them. In other words, organizational success comes from acceptance of this variety and recognition that each of us operates best from one of these 12 styles of leadership. There is something ungainly about leaders trying to adopt a style that doesn't fit their way of managing.

THE BEGINNINGS

What determines an individual's leadership style? Everybody has one, whatever the extent to which it may be used, but what is its foundation?

Evidence suggests that it is from among several, natural decision-making patterns, at least one of which we all possess. By decision making, I mean personal judgment in action. The underpinning of a person's natural leadership style is the manner by which judgment is expressed through decision making.

PATTERNS OF DECISION MAKING

Let's look at these four patterns, keeping in mind that the designations are arbitrary—the numbers are simply labels.

Decision-making Pattern I proceeds from concepts, theories, or principles. There has to be a fundamental notion of some sort from which conclusions can flow. It is almost like having a formula that can generate the correct answer, but it is not so simple because this decision maker will personally go to great pains to develop the concepts, theories, and principles necessary as the foundation for "good" decisions. Further, just as often as not, Pattern I will not necessarily accept another Pattern I's concepts, so it isn't a question of swapping formulas. It is a matter of high-quality, analytical thinking combined with personal imagination.

Pattern II needs a background of systems, policies, procedures, rules and regulations. A well-crystallized structure is desired so that conclusions can be drawn according to agreed-upon practices. Only then can the conduct of affairs proceed in an orderly way.

The right kind of organization is more important as a proper decision-making framework, and it will usually be considered satisfactory if surprises are few and results can be anticipated with accuracy. Here high-quality analytical thinking combines with common sense.

Pattern III places a premium on precedent, tradition, and experience. It makes a big difference whether this or that approach worked before or whether it is working now somewhere and may be worth emulating. These decision makers refuse to discard any scrap of useful

---

[1] Reprinted by permission of *MANAGEMENT SOLUTIONS*, January, 1988, copyright 1988, American Management Association, New York. All rights reserved.

background that could have a bearing on a present problem; they see no reason to venture into the unknown without solid support based on accumulated, practical knowledge. Since they tend to be persuasive, they are more subject than the other patterns to personal persuasion.

Decision-making Pattern IV depends on impulse, inspiration, and revelation. These are the hardest decision makers to "get a handle on" because they will go their own way, guided as they are from within. There is less centrality of result with Pattern IV. This means that where, in a given situation, others might come to similar conclusion in line with their respective patterns of decision making, Pattern IV will not. This does not mean that individuals with this pattern tend toward erratic decisions; as individuals, they are as consistent as anyone else. However, more than others, they depend on a unique, inner orientation as a personal guide to what they should do.

FOUR LEADERSHIP STYLES

These four basic decision-making patterns lead in turn into some basic leadership styles. It is a natural order since one flows from the other. Where do you fit among these?

Leadership Style I—"Founding." Decision-making Pattern I produces leadership Style 1, which is exercised, as you might expect, through theories, concepts, and principles. Decision making is characterized by rapid identification and integration of applicable data and information. Of special interest is the apparent ease with which such leaders can bring forth decisions and solutions when faced with complicated data and alternatives. Indeed, it is not always apparent that they are leading. But they are synthesizers; they see relationships among facts and phenomena that, on the surface, might appear to be unrelated. They have great skill at decision making in a scientific environment, but they can be burdened by "people problems," which are far more difficult for them to cope with.

Style I leaders are strategic by nature; their capacity to plan effectively well into the future is built in. When called upon to produce written plans, they may find it difficult to generate a good product because they are apt to leave out what is obvious to them; what they perceive as evident, others are likely to find obscure. Because of this, they may often need trusted associates to interpret for them. But they are the givers of models, many of which, once they have stood the test of common sense and experience, become the precedents and traditions for others to follow. They are pioneers and like to experiment, and have high tolerance for ambiguity, including deliberate duplication of effort.

Leadership Style II—"Managing." Whereas Style I has a "blue sky" quality, Style II is grounded in practicality. Here decision making typically involves analysis and testing of available data and information—all of it. This process depends heavily on thoroughness, on "touching all the bases," and judgment is reserved, decisions held back, until all the facts are in. It is noteworthy that this style of leadership has come to be called "management" with its emphasis on controls, rules, regulations, systems, policies, and procedures. Style II leaders have just as much trouble with "people problems" as do those of Style I, but whereas Style I leaders are likely to throw up their hands, Style II leaders will believe in others once they have proved themselves. They are "organization minded" and highly systematic, and their overall plan—they always have one—contains provisions for every pertinent activity. It is within these "slots" that subordinates prove themselves.

Style II leaders are bureaucratic and forensic by nature. They are also naturally tactical and have that strong sense of "what to do next." They are the givers of structures with which to face a given need. When that need changes, they will never hesitate to restructure. Their tolerance for ambiguity is extremely low, and they much prize efficiency and economy of effort.

Leadership Style III—"Developing." Style III leaders are motivated by personal feeling and desire. Issues of character and conviction dominate over those of analysis and testing. Problems are solved and decisions made within a framework of applicable precedent, and which precedent the leader believes to be applicable can be a matter of powerful, personal certitude. Such leaders customarily adopt principles and structure from among traditional models—those that have withstood the test of practical experience and are "tried and true"—and they are likely to stick with the models they adopt "through thick and thin." They are deft in their resolution of "people problems"; they believe that people are good until they prove themselves otherwise and will not only try subordinates in various "slots" in an effort to identify their best niches but even permit subordinates to build their own niches where "slots" can't be found. They are team builders, loyal up and down the line. They place a great deal of faith in teaching and coaching, tend to go the last mile with their people, and become visibly upset if "things don't work out." Style III leaders are neither strategic nor tactical themselves. They try to "do what's right" and get their supporting strategy and tactics from trusted associates.

Leadership Style IV—"Inspiring." Style IV leaders can experience great difficulty in following those who possess the other styles. They have a highly personal, internal guidance system, based on intuition and inspiration, which helps them to make decisions almost instantaneously, and their problem-solving skills appear to be equally rapid and often baffling to others because of their effectiveness in the absence of formal logic. They have the least trouble of all the styles in establishing their leadership credentials; it is almost as if they can't avoid leading. Such leaders have immense confidence in what others can accomplish if only they try, and it is to get them to try that Style IV leaders bend their efforts. They lead chiefly by example in a charismatic way.

Style IV leaders do not plan as such because they feel intimately involved in a large plan that already exists and prefer to seek their place in that plan through intuitive means. Of all the leaders, their accessibility varies the most with prevailing mood; they are the least self-conscious, invariably idiosyncratic, often mysterious, and sometimes scary.

How do the various leadership styles relate to one another? Much depends on the specific nature of the tasks at hand since each style is suited to a particular environment. Nevertheless, there are interpersonal risks generated by certain reporting relationships. In general, Style I should report to another Style I or to Style IV, not to Styles II or III unless the leader is gifted. Styles II and III can report to any style. Style IV can report to Styles II and III for brief intervals, to a Style I leader who is older and wiser than the Style IV, or to another Style IV.

CO-EXISTENCE

How do the various styles co-exist in one individual? The first axiom is that only neighboring styles can co-exist in one person. The second axiom is that they co-exist either by combination or by alternation. In other words, Styles I and III cannot be found in one person, nor can Style II and IV; "neighbors" can occur in the same individual. By "combination," it is meant that the two styles actually blend so that each loses a part of its identity in the creation of a new style that is a sort of "hybrid." By "alternation," it is meant that each style retains its identity for independent, tandem use. Let's see what happens in actual practice.

Leadership Style I & II. In combination, the main emphasis will be on impersonal evaluation—analytical thinking and logical processes. Some practicality and timeliness may be lost, and there won't be much room for hunch playing. The combination favors a lean staff in an austere working environment where both sophisticated strategies and tactics will be thoroughly explored, refined, adopted, and finally implemented.

In alternation, the swing will be between the theoretical and the practical in this highly perceptive pairing. Analysis will be subordinate to synthesis and common sense, but it will play a significant support role. This style of leadership has available a common touch that, along with the vision inherent in Style I, can make for an environment that is fresh and exciting, where new ideas can be freely "kicked around" but for adoption must fill a realistic need that is presently felt.

Leadership Styles II & III. In combination, this pairing of styles produces the utmost in practicality, an exceedingly realistic and down to earth approach to both people and problems. The emphasis is so focused on what to do now that planning, as well as adherence to existing systems and organizational protocol, can be disregarded in the heat of reaction to an immediate problem. Nevertheless, if it is a reliable response in a crisis that you need, this is where you will find it.

In alternation, practicality is ever present, though in a subordinate role. There is a swing between a systematic/analytic emphasis that is strong on tactics and a socially conscious outlook that can actually approximate benevolence. This leader will never lose sight of realistic goals and objectives but will approach them from opposite points of view that, as they alternate, can confuse an observer. On one hand, there is a highly intellectual and impersonal outlook; on the other, a most personal orientation full or warmth and feeling.

Leadership Styles III & IV. In combination this pair of styles produces unquestionably the most activist kind of leadership, not in terms of reaction to problems, though this is possible, but in original action toward a personal goal. There is emphasis on achieving something new and aesthetically satisfying; however, traditional values will not be lost and may be most important. In the eagerness to "get on with it," there may be some neglect of factors that should be taken into account, variables that the exercise of sharper perception would include.

In alternation, we find a reemphasis of perception with the activist influence subordinate though present. Thus is produced a more calm and considered leadership environment in which there is a swing between outgoing and effective communication of realistic and pertinent traditional values, and a sort of uncanny, even evangelical expression of what the future might bring.

Leadership Styles IV & I. In combination, vision and intuition are most prominent. This is a highly future-oriented brand of leadership, in which the present will be subordinated to the leader's perception of the future and what must be done to prepare for it. This leadership is not only prophetic but also theoretical, and of all the styles it is the most difficult to understand yet not hard to get along with because what others are doing and thinking is usually not the leader's main concern. It may take such leaders more time than most to "get moving" but when they do, it is with unique assurance. Their outlook is uncluttered by precedent.

In alternation, the influence of future-oriented perception is diminished as two startlingly different behavioral modes alternate. One is that of the aesthetically sensitive leader who actively pursues goals in which artistic beauty predominates. The other is the analytical experimenter who methodically pursues objectives that have an applied scientific scientific or strategic business purpose. In either pursuit, invention is a likely outcome, one rich in feeling and character, the other in intellect and rationality.

Do you see yourself among these 12? With all the styles and variations available, there is no reason for anyone to attempt a style at odds with "what comes natural." Should you believe it a good idea to adopt an expedient pattern and consequently style, remember that it is always best to "stick to one's last," not to waste time and effort that could be put toward cultivation of a natural strength on self-improvement in an area of natural weakness.

If your forte is "developing," don't try to make yourself into a pioneer. The real pioneers will skin you alive as long as they aren't trying to give themselves a developmental veneer. If your great strength is "inspiring," make peace with your inefficiency. Try to make yourself systematic, and you will be about as effective as the "managing" production wizard who attempts to succeed as an epic poet. If it is at all possible, refrain from a style that is less than your best.

You have seen how, for example, "managing" is long on tactics, short on strategy, deficient in inspiration, strong in organization, and weak in development. "Founding" is adept in strategy, inept in development, weak in tactics, indifferent to precedent, unparalleled in pioneering.

Tradition-rich "developing" is unexcelled in team building and conservation of useful experience, strong on communication, yet indifferent to theories and weak in planning. With "inspiring" you get charismatic personal example at the expense of efficiency and organization.

It is possible to have many leaders and not enough leadership; just gather an overabundance of the same style in support of the same effort. Think of the weaknesses that could show through. There has to be a leadership mix. One comes to the inescapable knowledge that a balance of leadership styles is essential for any enterprise that wishes to excel.

ESTABLISHING AND SUSTAINING MANAGEMENT SUPPORT FOR QUALITY CIRCLES

R. Douglas Allen[1]

SIGNIFICANCE OF THE ISSUE

Quality circles (QCs), since their importation by U.S. industry from the Japanese in the mid-1970's, have expanded in use at an enormous rate. The International Association of Quality Circles reported some 200 member organizations in 1979 while today that number has expanded to include approximately 6,000 members; nearly a thirty-fold increase in eight years.[1] While this may be considered a somewhat remarkable statistic and may be interpreted as strong evidence in support of the efficacy of the QC concept, it should be pointed out that many organizations that joined the QC "movement" over this time period have since abandoned the use of QCs due to their operational failures.[2] QCs, by way of definition, are small homogeneous work groups composed of from three to twelve volunteer members from a given organizational work area. These employees meet regularly (usually once or twice a week) in the work environment to identify, analyze, and resolve work-related problems through the process of group decision-making.[3] The QC effort is designed to be a highly participative endeavor on the part of all group members.

The results of research on the factors or conditions impacting on the success or failure of QC programs suggest strongly that management support and involvement, at all organizational levels, may be the single most critical factor with regard to determining the success and longevity of any given QC program.[4] Antecedent to this factor is the need for the existence of the proper organizational culture. That is, one in which a participative philosophy of work, as required by QCs, can flourish.[5]

CULTURAL AND MANAGEMENT STYLE

Any organization attempting to intelligently undertake a mission to introduce and effectively utilize QCs would be well advised to examine its existing culture to determine if the culture supports, or is capable of supporting, a participative style of management. The participative approach to management, as previously suggested captures the essence of the QC's operational design.

The culture of an organization, with specific focus on its dominant management style, has been discovered to be a major variable affecting the success of QCs and thus should be carefully evaluated to determine the readiness of any given organization to implement a QC program.[6] Research suggests that a Theory X philosophy of management, which involves a directive, controlling,unyielding autocratic style, is simply not compatible with the participative philosophy of QCs.[7] Successful QCs programs have been reported where management has a sincere commitment to employee participation throughout the organization, honestly perceives its

---

[1] Reprinted by permission, *Central State BUSINESS REVIEW*, Summer, 1988, Vol. VII, No. 2, pp. 13-15.

employees as valuable resources, and has a strong "people building" attitude toward QCs.[8] Without the existence of this philosophy or orientation on the part of all levels of management, the odds are stacked against the successful implementation and sustainment of a QC program by any given organization. Far too frequently it seems, organizations fail to recognize or underestimate the degree of change that must necessarily take place in attitudes as well as organizational structure and operations when participative programs, such as QCs, are introduced.[9] One theory based approach to addressing the necessary organizational change is presented next.

DEVELOPING MANAGEMENT SUPPORT THROUGH PLANNED CHANGE

As one conceptual approach to the problem of building and sustaining management support for QCs, the follow change model is suggested.[10] The model was designed and developed to address planned organizational change (e.g., the introduction of QCs as a major organizational intervention) with a view toward the long-run effectiveness of the change.

The model contains four stages as indicated in Figure 1. The first stage, **Unfreezing**, suggests that before any significant and meaningful change can take place within a given organization there must be a willingness on the part of those employees to be involved in, and affected by, the change to want to make the change. That is, they must first be significantly dissatisfied with the status quo. When this condition prevails, it suggests that their attitudes toward the current organizational environment and/or operations are "unfrozen" and thus ready to welcome change. For those situations where change is needed but existing attitudes are such that the unfreezing stage cannot be properly entered into, the following techniques for attitude change are suggested. Two of several available techniques or mechanisms for attitude change appear to be appropriate with respect to generating managerial support and enthusiasm for change involving the introduction of QCs.

The first technique involves providing "new" information to managers (as well as all affected employees) at all organizational levels in the form of actual cases of production and quality improvements that have been associated with successful QC implementation in other organizations.[11] This information should be a part of in-depth discussions focusing on how QC programs were typically structured and operationalized in these organizations. Formal instruction and training as to the integrative and participative orientation of QCs should be a very important part of this communication effort.[12]

The second technique available for attitude change involves fear arousal or reduction of fear depending on the particular situation.[13] Attempts to reduce change induced fear might take place with respect to communicating to middle and lower level managers the fact that they have very little to be apprehensive or anxious about concerning QCs as a threat to their power, authority, or job security. On the other hand, fear arousal may be appropriate with respect to creating in managers a healthy respect for the consequences of losing market share to the competition due to quality and other production related problems that may, to an appreciable extent, be alleviated through the introduction and sustainment of QCs as a major organizational intervention.

The importance of attitude change with respect to building strong and viable support for QCs at all levels of management cannot be overemphasized.[14] It is crucial to the success of any such change effort as suggested by the Theory of Cognitive Dissonance.[15] This theory argues, in essence, that when people find themselves acting or behaving in a manner that is inconsistent with their attitudes they will experience undesirable tension as a result. In order to reduce or eliminate this tension, a person has two basic options available. First, they may change their attitudes so that they are compatible with their behavior, or second, change their behavior, if possible. If middle and lower level management, for example, have had QCs more or less "crammed down their throats" by a rather autocratic top management, then it may be very difficult, if not impossible for some, to behave in a very positive and supportive fashion toward QCs because their attitudes

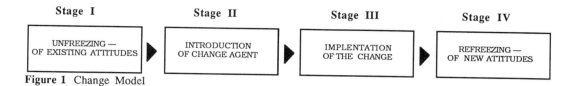

Stage I	Stage II	Stage III	Stage IV

UNFREEZING — OF EXISTING ATTITUDES ▶ INTRODUCTION OF CHANGE AGENT ▶ IMPLENTATION OF THE CHANGE ▶ REFREEZING — OF NEW ATTITUDES

Figure 1 Change Model

are entranced, so to speak, in support of the status quo and thus in conflict with expected behavior. To increase the likelihood of successful QC implementation, it is necessary that no significant discrepancy exists between attitudes and behavior on the part of those managers and other employees to be involved in the change.

Stage two of the model, **Introduction of Change Agent**, usually involves bringing in someone from outside the organization that management at all affected levels would view as an expert with regard to QC program design and implementation. That is, they would occupy a position of high prestige in the eyes of management; their opinions and expertise would be highly valued.

The primary role or function of the change agent is to act as a consultant or resource person with respect to the required changes surrounding a decision to develop a strong and viable QC program.[16] They would play an active and significant role in helping a steering committee establish the general objectives to be accomplished by the QC program. Additionally, the change agent may also have been involved in the unfreezing stage of the change process by helping top management and/or the dominant organizational coalition, understand the need for change.

It should be heavily emphasized that the change agent's role is to serve primarily as a catalyst or facilitator for change. Their job is not to dictate what specific activities and events are to take place when a QC program is introduced; rather their role requires that they actively seek and encourage significant involvement and participation by all levels of management with respect to all pertinent phases of the QC program design and development. The fundamental rationale for doing this is to develop in management a sense of identification with, and commitment to, the QC concept and resultant program as the change process proceeds through its final two stages.

Stage three, **Implementation of the Change**, requires that management and labor together operationalize the design for the QC program that was developed by them in stage two. The roles that both management and labor are to play in this stage should have been previously clearly delineated. Because "Murphy's Law" to some degree always seems to prevail, it should be expected that in this stage the plans for change will not always mesh with the realities and demands of the transition in the workplace. In other words, both management and labor should expect some problems associated with implementation of the QC program regardless of how extensive the training and communication efforts have been. When these problems occur it is extremely important that management and labor not engage in "fingerpointing" with respect to blaming one another, but instead approach the problem and its solution in a sincerely cooperative and collaborative fashion. This near collegial approach is a necessary prerequisite to effectively resolving implementation problems and creating the type of organizational climate where essential mutual trust and confidence between management and labor can take place.[17]

The change agent's role in this stage of the change process involves once against acting as an advisor or consultant to both management and labor in their efforts to effect the change and satisfactorily resolve any implementation problems that may arise. If the change agent has preformed his or her role satisfactorily, then the change itself will be attributable in the greatest sense to the creative efforts, involvement, and commitment of both management and labor. This condition is a necessary prerequisite to the final stage in the change process, refreezing. It insures that the refreezing stage can be effectively initiated and carried to a successful conclusion.

Stage four, **Refreezing**, is concerned with the notion that new attitudes and behaviors within the workplace have been created in both management and labor as a result of the change that has taken place. This stage is effectively achieved when management and labor truly feel that they have: (a) played a major role in developing and implementing the change, and (b) that their efforts have resulted in a QC program that will be a valuable part of the overall organizational structure and operations. A characteristic comment associated with success in this stage is for those involved in the change to state that they were in large part responsible for the change themselves and that they feel the change will be for the better. From perceptually based comments similar to this, it can be concluded that pride and an accompanying elevated sense of self-worth exists in the end results of the change as well as establishment of desired positive attitudes. In essence, those involved in the change have internalized it to such a significant extent that it has become a viable and very meaningful part of their world at work.

SUSTAINING MANAGEMENT SUPPORT FOR QCs

As just discussed, if the final stage of the formal change process has been successfully completed then management (as well as all other affected members of the organization) will have internalized the change to a significant extent. Stated another way, management will have developed a sense of ownership in what has been created and accomplished. At this point, it may be reasonably concluded that a strong commitment of the part of management to the QC program exists. This commitment will, in all likelihood, translate into the support necessary to insure the operational success of the program.

Beyond this point in time, no guarantees exist in terms of sustained management or labor support. Future support by management must be keyed to the degree of success of the QC program in terms of formal goals and objectives accomplished. To determine the degree of QC program success objectively, formal review and evaluation on a regularly scheduled basis has been found to be a necessary and invaluable process.[18] The information and feedback from such a process should be used as an important and integral part of the effort to sustain the long-run vitality and strength of an effective QC program.

REFERENCES

1. IAQC—International Association of Quality Circles, Vol. 2, 1987, p. 3.

2. Ferris, Gerald R. and Wagner III, John A. "Quality Circles in the United States: A Conceptual Reevaluation" *Journal of Applied Behavioral Science*, reprinted in *Current Issues in Personnel Management*, Rowland, Kendrith M. and Gerald R. Ferris, Allyn and Bacon, Inc., Newton, Massachusetts, 1986, p. 350.

3. Mento, Anthony J. "Demystifying the Mystique of Quality Circles," *Proceedings of the Southern Management Association,* 1982, p. 179.

4. Steel, Robert P., Mento, Anthony J., Dilla, Benjamin L., Ovalle, Nestor K. and Lloyd, Russell F. "Factors Influencing the Success and Failure of Two Quality Circle Programs," *Journal of Management*, Vol. 11, No. 1, 1985, p. 117.

5. Napier, Rodney W. and Gershenfeld, Matti K. *Groups-Theory and Experience,* Houghton Mifflin: Boston, 1985, pp. 530-531.

6. Whitehead, Carlton J. and Blair, John D. "An Analytical Perspective on Quality Circles," *Proceedings of the Southern Management Association*, 1982, pp. 183-184.

7. Flippo, Edwin B. *Personnel Management*, McGraw-Hill: New York, 1984, pp. 420-421.

8. Ingle, Sud "How to Avoid Quality Circle Failure in Your Company," *Training and Development Journal*, Vol. 36, No. 6, 1982, pp. 54-59.

9. Op. Cit., Napier and Gershenfeld, p. 530.

10. Szilagyi, Jr., Andrew D. and Wallace, Jr., Marc J. *Organizational Behavior and Performance,* Scott, Foresman: Glenview, Illinois, 1987, pp. 627-631.

11. Steers, Richard M. *Introduction to Organizational Behavior*, Scott, Foresman: Glenview, Illinois, 1984, pp. 425-426.

12. Saporito, Bill "The Revolt Against 'Working Smarter'," *Fortune*, July 21, 1986, p. 64.

13. Op Cit., Steers, pp. 425-426.

14. Dale, Barrie and Barlow E. "Facilitator Viewpoints on Specific Aspects of Quality Circle Programmes," *Personnel Review* (UK), Vol. 13, No. 4, 1984, pp. 23-24.

15. Festinger, Leon *A Theory of Cognitive Dissonance,* Stanford University Press: Palo Alto, California, 1957.

16. Dale, B.G. and Hayward, S.G. "Some of the Reasons for Quality Circle Failure: Part III," *Leadership & Organization Development Journal* (UK), Vol. 5, No. 4, 1984, pp. 28-29.

17. Imberman, Woodruff, "How to Make Quality Circle Programs Work," *Chief Executive*, Vol. 22, Winter 1982-83, pp. 21-22.

18. Conklin, Diana "Evaluating the Quality Circle Activity: An Effective Leaders' Circle Project," *Transactions of the International Association of Quality Circles 9th Annual Conference*, April, 1987, pp. 270-273.

TWO-WAY COMMUNICATION PRACTICES FOR MANAGERS

John T. Samaras[1]

It is up to you, the manager, to make the message understood.

The success of any organization depends on how effectively its communication network functions. There is no possibility of a coordinated effort toward common goals without organization-wide exchange of information and understanding. This effort must not only obtain its intended results—the exchange of information—but must also help to build positive human relations in the bargain. Such communication takes the form of a four-step model:

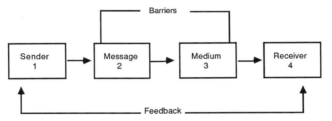

WHO'S RESPONSIBLE?

Step 1 is the sender—in this case, you, the manager—who is responsible for making the message (Step 2) understood, and for this to happen, he or she must fully understand the substance of what is to be communicated. However, one of the most common organizational communication problems is that managers are frequently so vague about the exact information to be transmitted. And if the message is vague in the sender's mind, then it is going to seem vague to the receiver, too.

Once the sender has formulated the message, then the appropriate words or gestures which symbolize its meaning must be found. Remember, though, that words take on a meaning relative to the sender's background. Regardless of how skilled a sender you are, the message will seldom coincide with the meaning the receiver will attach to it. Therefore, you should take into consideration such factors as the receiver's education, experience, training, and cultural background.

Step 3, the medium, is that through which the message is transmitted. The following two rules about media can generally be applied to communication:[1]

---

[1] Reprinted by permission, *PERSONNEL JOURNAL*, August, 1980, Costa Mesa, California, All rights reserved.

1) **If the content of the message** is complex, then the use of more than one medium is suggested.

2) **Where persuasion is needed,** face-to-face contact is more effective than other media, since it provides a better opportunity for the manager to observe reactions and to adapt the presentation to obtain the desired results.

It is at this step that the sender begins to relinquish control of the message. Not only must the sender cope with the receiver's background, but other things begin to interfere with the message's transmission: interruptions, distractions, noise, etc.

(Timing is as important as choice of medium. It should be such that you have the information in hand before people hear about it. Then you must schedule the communication so that everyone in the department receives it at the same time, if at all possible. This keeps rumors and distortion to a minimum.)

The receiver is the fourth step of the model. If the message isn't "read," then all the work

---

The communication process isn't complete until the desired action has begun. This is where feedback is so important.

---

that went into it is lost. In other words, if there is no interest, there is no communication. (A proven solution has been to say more with less talk and to write shorter messages.)

THE IMPORTANCE OF FEEDBACK

Despite all this preparation, the communication process is not completed until the desired action, as sought by the sender, has begun. This is where feedback is so important. Feedback determines the degree to which the message has been understood and accepted by the receiver. In oral communications, you can often get a quick feedback from the look on the receiver's face.

Every manager must accept the fact that at least some workers are going to misunderstand communication efforts at least some of the time. The most effective defense against it it to take nothing for granted. Some managers are content to rely on a simple question after giving involved instructions or directives, asking "Have you got that?" or "Do you understand?" Such questions invariably obtain an affirmative response, but what the employee frequently means is, "No, I don't understand, but I'm too afraid (or shy or proud) to admit it." Rather than ask for clarification, the employee will muddle along trying to work things out alone, sometimes with disastrous results.[2]

One way to obtain feedback from oral communications is to ask the receiver to repeat the message; however, this may appear too condescending, particularly when dealing with professionals who have attained a certain degree of sophistication and status. A more effective and mature method is to create a climate in which all employees feel comfortable asking questions.

THE COMFORTABLE CLIMATE

How is this climate created? In five different ways:

1) **You have to gain employees respect** regarding "technical knowledge": you must be knowledgeable in the field and aware of future development.

2) **You must be able to explain** in precise detail all organizational policies and procedures—from the top down and as they affect that particular unit.

3) **You should possess a flexible style of leadership** that can adapt to different situations while always getting the maximum effort from each individual.

4)   **You must be empathetic** with each employee's feelings, needs and expectations and know how to channel them toward accomplishment of the unit's objectives.

5)   **In order to do this,** you must know and understand everyone's job description.

A good organizational climate is not as difficult to achieve as it may sound. All that is required is a determined effort. The reward: that unit will be the most efficient and productive in the entire organization.

Barriers to Communication

Everyone brings personal experience, values, attitudes, motives, assumptions and expectations into the working world. It is these background factors which affect people's perception of communication's intent. To reiterate, you should be aware of the receiver's background, and, of course, how you perceive this background will affect the message also.

There is no such thing as an "open mind"—every person already has a set number of ideas. For example, if an employee feels he or she has gotten a bad deal from a former employer, then that person is going to be distrustful of future employers. Therefore, most communications will be met with resistance, which can be overcome in time with persuasion and persistence.

---

*There is no such thing as an "open mind"—every person
already has a set number of ideas.*

However, the greatest barrier to surmount is attitude, which can be interpreted as your approach or position to a topic, question or event. Attitude is particularly important in a face-to-face, two-way communication.

Your attitude and behavior will play a vital role in either encouraging or discouraging effective two-way communication. If you appear anxious to get a conversation over with, or annoyed or distressed by the subject being discussed, then you may well be building an insurmountable communications barrier.

Managers often resent and resist communication which indicates that their actions have been less than perfect. Where this attitude is evident, loyal workers will often withhold valuable information. In other words, unless you are willing to hear criticism freely, much that you learn about the operation will come from those who are least loyal to it.

Moreover, managers often resist becoming involved with their subordinates' personal problems. This resistance may also affect employees' willingness to communicate on other matters more directly to the job. Since job problems and personal problems are often closely linked, it can be difficult to discuss one without the other.

One of the strongest deterrents to two-way communications is the attitude of managers who ignore undesirable conditions previously brought to their attention. The result is that workers lose

---

*Your philosophy of management determines the value
you place on communication.*

---

faith both in the sincerity of management in general and in the value of communication in particular. These are the managers who think that they have too many daily problems and responsibilities to provide adequate time for listening fully to their subordinates' ideas, reports and criticisms. Nevertheless, many time-consuming problems could be minimized or eliminated if superiors were free to listen to their employees, for in listening, they can discover solutions to present problems or anticipate causes of future ones.

A manager's philosophy of management determines the value placed on communication and the time given to it. The manager who has built a people-minded philosophy and who is engaged in developing both individual employees and group teamwork will rank communication high in priority and will allow time for it, since communication is the nerve center of such a leader's

---

Since we were given only one mouth but two ears, perhaps we were meant to listen twice as much as we talk.

---

management process. In contrast, the manager who acts alone, attempts to solve the department's problems alone, and ignores the growth of subordinates may well be headed for problems down the line.

Employees can also be emotional and prejudiced. Their feelings, too, mix freely with their facts, creating further attitude barriers to two-way communication. But developing a people-minded attitude will help you understand and interpret what employees are trying to say. Of course, you must recognize and minimize your own prejudices and idiosyncrasies before you can do this.

THE ROLE OF LISTENING

Did you ever stop to wonder why we were given one mouth and two ears? Perhaps we were meant to listen twice as much as we talk. This is a point worth keeping in mind and which could lead to improved two-way communication.

If you stopped to observe, you would find that most people spend about half their time in the "act" of listening. The point is, however, do we really listen? Dr. Ralph Nichols of the University of Minnesota has found that most people retain only about half of what they hear immediately after listening to a short talk. And after a short period of time, the same people can recall only about 25% of what was said.[3] Putting it more dramatically, most people are operating at 25% efficiency when listening. Imagine the consequences if a health care supervisor conducted all of his or her responsibilities at 25% efficiency!

The importance of effective listening is that it stimulates interpersonal relationships by showing willingness to understand the other person. There is no better way to improve a dialogue

---

Hearing is a physical act, but listening is an active mental effort in the form of concentration.

---

than to be a good listener, and failure to be one invites many problems that could otherwise be avoided.

Hearing is a physical act and requires no effort. However, listening is an active mental effort in the form of concentration. Whereas hearing is done with the ears, listening is done with the mind.

Good listening, like good speaking, must be learned, which may involve changing some habits. Here is a short test devised by Ralph W. Reber, supervisor, training and development, at Champion Papers in Pasadena, Texas, and Gloria E. Terry, training and education coordinator at Memorial Hospital System in Houston.[3] These nine questions may give you an idea of whether you have any bad listening habits.

1) You think about four times faster than a person usually talks. Do you use this excess time to think about other things while you're keeping track of the conversation?......... Yes   No

2) Do you listen primarily for facts, rather than ideas, when someone is speaking?......... Yes   No

3) Do you avoid listening to things you feel will be too difficult to understand?............. Yes   No

4) Can you tell from a person's appearance and delivery that he won't have anything worthwhile to say?.. Yes   No

5) When somebody is talking to you, do you try to make him think you're paying attention when you're not?... Yes   No

6) Do certain words or phrases prejudice you so that you cannot listen objectively? .... Yes   No

7) Do you turn your thoughts to other subjects when you believe a speaker will have nothing particularly interesting to say? .... Yes   No

8) When you're listening to someone, are you distracted by outside sights and sounds?... Yes   No

9) When you are puzzled or annoyed by what someone says, do you try to get the questions straightened out immediately, either in your mind or by interrupting the speaker?... Yes   No

If you answered no to each question, you can classify yourself as a perfect listener, provided you were truthful.

Let's discuss each of the above items.

You think at a rate of 400 to 500 words per minute, which means you talk about 125 words per minute. This difference cause you to have an unused capacity which then wanders off thinking

---

Don't try to memorize any facts as the speaker makes them;
facts are meaningless unless connected to the ideas of the message.

---

about next Saturday's football game, or what's for dinner, or the report you should have gotten out yesterday. So what you need to do is to get more involved in listening than hearing. You can do this by summarizing the points the speaker has made, stopping him or her and asking, "Let's see if I understand what you're saying," and then reviewing what has been said.

Don't attempt to memorize any facts as the speaker makes them. Facts are meaningless unless they are connected to the message's principles or concepts.

If the subject is unusual or unfamiliar, many people tend to tune out the message. Everyone has come across a difficult passage in a textbook, but after repeated readings and thinking, it finally made sense. It isn't much different if you listen and continue to listen. You may discover the subject wasn't so hard after all.

Do not allow prejudices to reduce listening effectiveness. If you become emotional about an issue because of prejudices, you may find yourself in an awkward position. The thing to do is to let the speaker finish before judging what he or she had to say. If there is still disagreement, then perhaps a third party's opinion should be consulted.

Don't be a phony listener. Your reaction will reveal whether you're listening or not. And if you're not, you will have cut off any effective upward communication. But more important, you're cutting yourself off from a potentially good source of information.

Anther bad listening habit is allowing certain words or terms to block rational listening—words such as welfare, computers, income taxes, unions and inflation. The point here is to keep in mind that words are symbols and don't always express the same meaning you attach to them.

All the information you listen to isn't necessarily going to be interesting—to you, that is. But since you have to sit and hear out what the speaker is saying, you should concentrate on sifting out whatever information may be meaningful. Seldom is there a speech or talk that doesn't contain a bit of important information which can be used somewhere in your work.

Discourtesy and poor listening go together. Discourtesy is letting outside interruptions interfere with your employees' conversations with you. What you are telling your speaker is, "Go ahead and talk, but I'm not really interested in what you have to say!"

Impatience is another bad listening habit, because silence is often so difficult for many of us. We spend so much time thinking about what we are going to say next that we miss much of what the speaker is telling us. Let the speaker know he or she has your full attention by making a brief comment, such as, "O.K." or "I see" or simply nodding.

COMMUNICATIONS IN SUM

1) **Effective communication is a vital element in the managerial process,** since it is through some form of communication that supervisory and planning activities are carried out.

2) **Communication can be judged effective** if it produces its intended results—in this case, positive employee behavior.

3) **As a process,** communication consists of four elements: sender, message, medium and receiver.

4) **For communications to be effective** in management, not only are those four elements important, but the receiver's response to the message as well. This two-way feedback process between sender and receiver is called two-way communication.

5) **For two-way communications to be effective,** there must be channels open to all members of the organization.

6) **While there are many barriers** to effective communications, the prevailing one is the attitudes of the sender and receiver.

It is worth repeating that communication is the most significant ingredient in any sort of management, for it is mastery of this function that will lead to managerial excellence.

REFERENCES

1. James E Morgan, Jr., *Principles of Administrative and Supervisory Management* (Englewood Cliffs, New Jersey: Prentice-Hall, Inc., 1978) pp. 63-66.

2. Ralph W. Reber and Gloria E. Terry, *Behavioral Insights for Supervision* (Englewood Cliffs, New Jersey: Prentice-Hall, Inc., 1975) pp. 170-172.

3. Ralph Nichols, "Listening Is Good Business," *Management of Personnel Quarterly*, Winter, 1963, pp. 2-10.

4. Reber and Terry, *Behavioral Insights for Supervision*, pp. 170-172.

PART FIVE
CONTROLLING

EXERCISE 5.1 APPROPRIATE CONTROLS

There are four basic types of control:

1. Pre-action controls require that the necessary resources, such as: people, money, and equipment, have been budgeted. This type of control makes sure that all the resources are available in the manner required.

2. Steering controls are designed to allow corrections to be made before a particular series of actions is completed. This control is effective if the manager can obtain the necessary information ahead of time.

3. Screening controls provide for taking corrective action while a project is underway. It is a "go or no-go" device requiring that a specific procedure must be approved before continuing.

4. Past-action controls evaluate the completed action. Any discrepancies from the predetermined plan are applied to future plans.

The left column lists a number of actions to be undertaken. The right column lists the aforementioned controls. Match the columns by placing a number in the space provided at the left.

ACTIONS	CONTROLS
____ 1. Distributing bonus checks.	1. Pre-Action
____ 2. Weekly reports to the division office indicating sales and sales quotas.	2. Steering
____ 3. Quotas assigned to sales representatives at the beginning of the year.	3. Screening
____ 4. Copies of weekly reports sent to the national sales office for future decision-making.	4. Post-Action

EXERCISE 5.2 BUDGETS OR MISBUDGETS

There are two broad categories of budgets: operating and financial. A manager needs to be familiar with each one.

In the category of operating budgets there are four types; engineered cost budgets which describe specific costs involved in each production item for efficiency; discretionary cost budgets are used for certain administrative functions which cannot be measured accurately; revenue budgets measure marketing and sales efforts; and profit budgets measure costs and revenues and are sometimes called master budgets because they are used by managers who have responsibility for revenue and expenses of their departments.

There are also four types of financial budgets: capital expenditure budgets are for future investment expenditures into physical assets, cash budgets show the cash flow and the pattern of revenues and costs, financing budgets are to make certain about the availability of money to meet shortfalls of revenue, balance sheet budgets are developed in conjunction with cash sheet budgets which bring together all of the budgets for projection purposes and give managers an indication of problems or opportunities.

The column on the left lists a number of business activities. The right column lists all eight budgets. Match the columns by placing a number in the space provided at the left.

BUSINESS ACTIVITIES	BUDGETS
_____ 1. Consideration of purchasing new trucks.	1. Engineered Cost
_____ 2. Measures liquidity and costs.	2. Discretionary Cost
_____ 3. Costs associated with each production model.	3. Revenue
_____ 4. A measure of costs in the human resources department.	4. Profit
_____ 5. To make sure funds are available when needed.	5. Capital Expenditure
_____ 6. How well sales and their related costs are doing.	6. Cash
_____ 7. A necessary budget for managers who have responsibility for revenues and expenses of their departments.	7. Financing
_____ 8. An accounting of all other budgets.	8. Balance Sheet

EXERCISE 5.3 TO PRODUCE OR NOT TO PRODUCE

The question of productivity has been on the minds of management professors, industrialists and government leaders for a number of years. There are a number of factors that have contributed to America's decline in productivity and in some instances those very same factors are beginning to cause an increase in productivity. Such a factor is the shift in workers' attitudes and motivation.

Based upon your personal knowledge and job experiences answer each question below.

1. The contention is that workers today no longer have the work ethic. What could have caused the loss of the work ethic?

2. What management practices may have demotivated workers?

3. What internal values and beliefs do workers want to possess about their jobs?

4. What can management do to help instill such values and beliefs?

EXERCISE 5.4 INTRO TO MIS

Managers of the future must be able to understand the basics of management information systems and its potential.

As a library project, research the history and development of MIS and answer briefly the three questions below.

1.   How did MIS develop?

2.   What is the need for MIS?

3.   How has MIS affected decision-making?

Makins is a rural department store in a small but affluent southeastern city close to the Florida panhandle.

Max Rumfelt has been the store manager for four months having transferred from Ft. Worth.

The store employs six women and seven men plus Max's secretary. The women and six men are sales clerks. The seventh man, Stanley Steele, is the stocker and delivery man.

Max welcomed the opportunity to become a store manager. After graduating from the state university he accepted a job at Makins as a management trainee. He had been in appliance sales for three years before he was made assistant store manager. The transfer was a promotion and a chance to relocate in a small community which Max preferred.

However, now after four months, Max was confronted with a serious pilferage problem. Merchandise from costume jewelry to small appliances; toasters, blenders, coffee makers, were disappearing.

Max had always assumed that rural people were always honest, but now he was having doubts. He began to wonder about Stanley who opened and closed the store each day and supposedly kept track of the stock in the storeroom.

1. What controls should you implement in trying to eliminate the pilferage problem?

2. How should you handle Stanley Steele?

3. Should you give lie detector tests to all your employees?

"We never know what is going on!" shouted Marshall Stroud, Brocton's Healthcare Division sales manager. "Those sales guys are nothing but order takers," he continued, "and not good ones at that."

Craig Summerwaite was wondering why he was asked to attend this meeting of bigwigs. After all, he was only the comptroller and he certainly had no understanding of selling pharmaceuticals.

"Our competition always gets an edge on us. They come out with deep discounts and get all the business before we can do anything. They take on new lines and hit the streets with it before we know it," said Estes Murdoch, Brocton's newly appointed manager.

"Yeah, and somethin's got to be done," offered Marshall.

For a few moments nothing was said and Craig continued to wonder about his presence.

Estes shuffled some papers and then looked around the room. "Our sales for this quarter are down 7% and that's continuing a trend that began two years ago," he said.

Marshall nodded in agreement, "And, you know, Estes, our products are the top of the line. Both in quality and price. That is, we have value."

Estes held up his hand, "But our competition always has a little edge on us. We never know what's up 'til it's too late to act."

One of the other executives, Wilbur Comstock from advertising looked over the rim of his glasses, "Well we can't tap their phones and we certainly shouldn't try to bribe anyone. I think their sales reps are just better hustlers than ours."

"I think it's more than that," remarked Estes. "And that's why I asked Craig to come to this meeting. Sometimes we can't see the forest because of all the bushes."

"Trees," interrupted Wilbur.

"Trees, bushes, whatever," replied Estes as his face reddened.

Craig squirmed uncomfortably in his seat.

Estes cleared his throat, "Craig, you're comptroller. You look at figures all day long. You know what's going on. Do you see anywhere where we can tighten up?"

Craig shook his head. "The business just isn't coming in. Are the guys making their calls?"

"Well, of course they are!" he retorted.

Craig uncrossed and crossed his legs. "We don't know that for sure. We pay 'em their salary and commissions and whatever expenses they send in."

Marshall looked sternly at him, "Well, what do you propose?"

Suddenly Craig realized why he was summoned to the meeting. The other were reluctant to make a hard decision on the issue of expense reports.

1.　As Craig Summerwaite, what type of information would you require on an expense report?

2.　What other general information should be asked?

3.　To whom should these reports be sent?

"What the devil can I do? What is it goin' to take to git more business?" muttered Tim as he started to make out the checks for the rent, utilities and insurance premium for his Tim's Automotive Repair and Service. "I don't know if I'm going to have any bucks to pay my men. All two of 'em!"

Tim Woodson started his garage two years ago from his brother's military insurance. Martin was killed in Vietnam. The two brothers talked about opening a garage when as teenagers they were constantly "souping up" their own buddies' cars.

Tim and Martin had both worked at the local General Motors assembly plant but had always planned on their own business but Tim had never thought it would be so difficult to "git more business."

He looked at the sign behind his desk posting service charges for various basic auto repair work. "We charge 'bout the same as anyone else and less'n most. I cain't lay one of the guys off 'cause that'll throw too much work on the other one and me and besides they're both good mechanics and they're hard to find." Tim closed his check book and began to address the envelopes. "I can always advertise but I don't have any dough and all the banks around here are in so much trouble I'm 'fraid to ask."

Harry, one of the mechanics, poked his head through the doorway. "Wanna call 'ole lady Simpson and tell 'er her car's ready?" Tim nodded as he licked a stamp. "Hell, our service and quality are good. Nobody complains."

1. In analyzing this case an obvious strategy would be promotion, however, as mentioned, this is a limiting factor. This factor also inhibits any possibility of updating equipment. Therefore, identify other productivity improvement factors.

2. Select the one you feel is most appropriate.

3. Justify your selection.

Evelyn Yauncy was recently appointed to the position of Assistant Vice-President for training and development of the Hargrove Manufacturing Corporation, a unit-type production firm making custom machine parts for small appliance motors for a number of national companies.

Before Evelyn was promoted she had spent twelve years in the personnel office serving primarily as a recruiter and interviewer. Occasionally she performed job analysis in the various machine shops scattered throughout the main plant. It was through her experiences of these tasks that led Evelyn in formulating a plan of placing all personnel and training data into a computer data base. The objective is to develop a profile for each employee; job title and job description, wage record, evaluations, discipline, and training needs.

An information system (IS) would make personal data very accessible, save a considerable amount of time, and make for greater efficiencies.

In order to make an effective presentation to the vice-president to implement this system Evelyn began to think of all possible ramifications, positive and negative, of a personnel information system such as:

1. What should be the back-up in case the system failed?

2. How often should there be an update?

3. How should controls be established?

COORS: BREWING A BETTER CONTROLLERSHIP

Kenton B. Walker[1]

In 1982, Adolph Coors Company, the nation's fifth largest brewer, began an ambitious program to sell its products nationwide. Coors had been a highly profitable regional firm, but increased competition forced the company's management to extend its market more quickly in order to maintain its position in the brewing industry.

Al C. Pipkin joined Coors in early 1981 as controller. Profits were declining and the need for new direction in business was apparent. Previously, Mr. Pipkin had worked at Iowa Beef Processors and at Monsanto Company. His background included extensive experience in the application of computer systems for business. He also was instrumental in the start-up of new businesses, both domestic and international.

PIPKIN'S PLAN

Mr. Pipkin reviewed the organizational structure of the department he inherited. While it recognized the typical functional responsibilities of the controller, it did not support the specialized needs of operating management (Figure 1). The director of internal accounting was responsible for the day-to-day accounting activities, producing the company's monthly financial report for management, and coordinating the annual audit. The company's internal financial statement was the typical 20-to-25-page accounting report that was issued to the board of directors and the company's officers.

The director of financial planning was responsible for managing the company's annual profit-planning efforts, producing departmental operating income and expense budgets, preparing updated quarterly profit projections throughout the year, and explaining variances between plan and actual results to the board of directors. The remaining two directors were concerned with the SEC, shareholders, and IRS compliance reporting.

Realizing the need to dramatically reshape the controller and management accounting functions, Mr. Pipkin developed a plan based on these proposals:

- Use a top-down approach to sell management on the need to restructure the controller's department.

- Assure personnel that no jobs would be eliminated and opportunities for advancement would continue to exist.

- Create "functional" responsibility centers within the controller organization to accommodate the key areas of responsibility represented on the board of directors and/or other significant operating units requiring attention.

- Transform "accounting" reports to "management" reports, and

- Place more emphasis on a forward financial perspective rather than on historical reporting of the company's financial results.

---

[1] Reprinted by permission, *Management Accounting*, January, 1988, pp. 23-27, copyright 1988 by National Association of Accountants, Motvale, NJ. All rights reserved.

COORS FINANCE ORGANIZATION CHART BEFORE

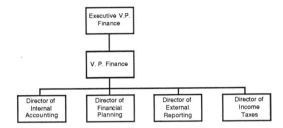

COORS FINANCE ORGANIZATION CHART AFTER

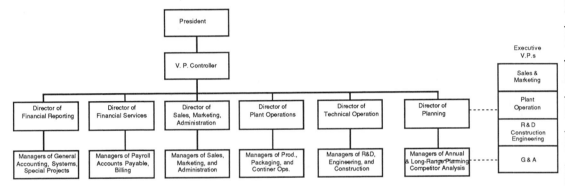

Knowing that his plan would not be successful without the support of top management, Mr. Pipkin familiarized himself with the attitudes of the senior management team toward the controller's function. Some did not have a high regard for accounting reports and their usefulness for decision-making purposes. The information they received was too late, too accounting oriented, and did not focus on data relevant to their specific operations.

When Mr. Pipkin took charge, accountants were considered "bean counters" rather than active participants in managing the company. He encountered skepticism when he described how accounting reports could be produced to create a new perspective for managing operating departments that might result in improved operating performance. Today, Coors' accounting system produces management reports that present a combination of financial and nonfinancial data important for performance evaluation, forecasting, and strategic planning.

Mr. Pipkin then outlined the major categories of services the controller should provide:

- Financial control and reporting for routine accounting functions including error corrections, account code verification for accounts payable, payroll, etc., and variance analysis and investigation.

- Financial planning and control, including in-depth knowledge of a functional group's personnel, language and terminology, cost behavior, nature of operations, and organizational considerations potentially affecting budget allocations.

- Financial reporting for each specific function on a timely basis.

CONTROLLERS' QUIZ

These questions are based on Coors' philosophy of what characterizes an effective controllership. Your answers may reveal how important you are in directing your company's activities.

What is your relationship with your staff? Staff members should have clearly defined roles within your department and specific responsibilities and working relationships should be identified. You should meet with your staff members on a regularly scheduled basis to discuss their performance and potential areas for improvement. A working environment for fosters new ideas and encourages interdepartmental communication will be more effective in meeting the information demands of senior management.

Are you consulted before any short- or long-term corporate decision are implemented? You should not be surprised by what other executives are doing or thinking of doing. An effective controller occupies a unique position within a firm to integrate financial and nonfinancial information in formulating informed business decisions. The controller should hire individuals whose thinking extends beyond mere management by the numbers to considerations of strategic, political, social, and moral issues confronting contemporary business. Other corporate officers should actively seek your advice and that of your staff on almost all decisions.

What is your grasp of the business? You should understand what occurs on the shop floor as well as in the boardroom. You should be able to converse equally well with a marketing executive who is introducing a new product and a production manager who has material quality problems. Ask yourself if you can identify the major problems facing the business and its industry and where your firm will be in the next five to ten years.

What is your level of participation at management meetings? First, you should be a member of key committees such as capital expenditures, new products, and strategic planning. Are your recommendations requested at these meetings? The ability of you and your staff to provide informed advice on the contemplated activities of the firm is an additional indication of your involvement. The controller should be able to identify duplication of effort, spot potential conflicts in planned activities, and resolve demands for scarce resources.

How expert are you in cost and financial systems? You should understand the company's costs and how they are related to products. Knowing the information needs of operating management is crucial to the usefulness of management accounting systems. You should be prepared to provide reports that are valuable for current operating decisions and future plans—they should be timely, easy to read, and relevant. Today's rapidly changing technology and global business environment require constant attention to the financial systems used in managing the business of the future.

- Forecasts and analysis of functional financial performance against the plan. These reports are prepared at the end of each period and forecasted results are presented for the coming period, next quarter, and remainder of the fiscal year. The projections incorporate knowledge of forthcoming events and planned management actions obtained from close association with the organization.

- A full-time finance staff to support each major function of senior management to provide financial control and accounting services. One individual is designated to serve on each senior executive's staff, and one accounting staff member is assigned to each vice president.

Because managers do not make decisions on the basis of dollars alone, it is beneficial to combine accounting and operations data to produce useful management reports. Realizing this fact, Mr. Pipkin also requested that some existing information-gathering functions in other areas of the company be transferred to the controller's department. This data could then be more easily integrated into the management reporting system.

Compromises in this area were necessary. The requests to absorb information-gathering departments were sometimes regarded as a potential loss of power and resistance was encountered. Some requests were compromised, but the broader objectives of providing a greater understanding of and control over company costs were achieved. Also considered key to success of the reorganization was the transfer of short- and long-term planning to Mr. Pipkin.

COMMITTED TO STAFF DEVELOPMENT

Coors' financial organization is decentralized with strong central control. All staff members report to Mr. Pipkin who reports to Peter H. Coors, president of the Brewing Division. With this type of structure, personnel have a comprehensive overview of what's going on in the company. In fact, they are expected to interface with members of other departments so that they have a total grasp of the business and industry they work in.

Proud of its long record of employee job satisfaction and retention, Coors has maintained a philosophy of no layoffs throughout most of its history and has discouraged employee terminations in management reorganizations in favor of transfers to other departments. Mr. Pipkin also realized any changes in upper-level management would create apprehension and uncertainty among employees, and that his plan would more likely succeed if the threat of job loss was minimized. Employees in the controller's departments were assured that their jobs were secure and there would be additional opportunities for advancement.

The reorganization also called for the creation of three "functional" director positions to conform to the major divisions of authority within the company. The board of directors includes executive vice presidents of sales and marketing, finance and administration, plant operations, and corporate development and technology. The new controller's organization includes an accounting director to support each of these areas as well as two directors of internal accounting (one for general ledger accounting and top level corporate financial reporting and another to oversee financial services such as accounts payable, payroll, billing, and property accounting functions) and another director for corporate financial planning. Each "functional" director serves as an active member of his assigned executive vice president's staff while the directors' respective managers serve the needs of the vice presidents who report to the executive level. The accounting personnel have a dotted line relationship to the functional VPs and direct reporting responsibility to the controller. (See Figure 2).

Preliminary skepticism occurred, however, in the attempt to convince vice presidents to accept the accounting personnel as members of their staff. Initially, some were regarded as outsiders. Previously, the accountants had little or no contact with operating management. Some vice presidents considered it an attempt by the accounting department to "check up" on how well other organizations were being managed. There was a suspicion that the information obtained by controller employees attending other officers' staff meetings could be used to question management in some areas to the benefit of the controller. Instead, this was quickly dispelled as the philosophy was readily accepted. The suggestion was made that the functional financial directors report directly to the operating executive vice presidents. However, this would destroy Mr. Pipkin's centralized control over the management accounting and report system. The ultimate loyalty of each finance director would have rested with several senior executives and lacked a set of well-coordinated, corporate financial system objectives.

The enhanced ability to integrate information across the company's operations was the primary selling point for the arrangement, in addition to the capability to satisfy the needs for more specialized information. This was made possible by combining the technical knowledge of trained financial personnel with dedication to a specific area of the company's business. Company vice presidents were no longer required to devote manpower resources to quasi-financial functions. The officers of the company were provided full-time financial staff support they could direct but would not have to include in their operating budgets. The vice presidents further retained the right to approve the personnel assigned to their area.

BETTER FINANCIAL REPORTS

The first planning season revealed benefits of the new organizational structure. Accounting personnel now had in-depth knowledge of the company's accounting system and the cost behavior useful for planning the amount and timing of expenditures. Because of their awareness of the company's overall financial objectives, the accountants were able to provide valuable advice concerning planning strategies. In addition to annual planning, they also began handling various types of management analyses, monthly cost variance reviews, financial systems development, and contract and purchase order review and approval.

The new structure also calls for accounting managers to attend the monthly staff meetings of their respective vice presidents while the directors attend meetings of the executive vice presidents. The controller conducts his own monthly staff meetings and reviews information for each functional area. He looks at what has occurred and plans for the future. This type of overview permits a comprehensive financial assessment of contemplated management actions for the entire company, identification of potential problems and conflicts in planned programs, and the ability to bring this information before the board of directors along with recommendations for future action. The information network created by Mr. Pipkin has impressed the board of directors. They are now presented with a comprehensive view of corporate activities support by detailed analysis.

The expansion and redirection of the company's approach to internal financial reporting was another major change in the operating environment. Internal departmental expense reports were redesigned to assign costs to the appropriate level of responsibility. As a result, many expense items were transferred to higher levels in the organization. These reports are now considered by management to be accurate and reliable measures of performance.

A financial book for each functional area is developed by the managers of the areas and their accounting staffs. These reports, which are prepared each accounting period, are adding value to the management of the respective operations.

The operations report emphasizes product costing, manpower utilization, inventories, productivity, and material usage. The sales and marketing report centers on sales volume data, pricing, and advertising expenses. The technical operations report is concerned with project costs, engineering and construction overheads, and the status of projects in progress. The statements emphasize controllable factors by presenting only selected profit and loss information and using standard costs for items beyond the control of the functional executive.

For example, standard product costs are reported in the sales and marketing executive's financial statement and standard revenue in the report to the operations executive. The focal point of variance presentation is to direct attention to the factors under the control of the respective managements rather than to recapitulate total company operating results. Only members of the board of directors continue to receive actual historical financial results in their entirety. This report has been changed to emphasize financial highlights rather than accounting detail. Many schedules have been replaced or supplemented with graphic analysis for ease in absorbing important information.

Reports now emphasize the financial future of the company rather than historical reporting. In addition to the annual plan, the financial planning department is responsible for long-range planning, competitor analysis and a systems/modeling area that supports planning efforts throughout the company. The department also prepares special reports for the monthly board of directors' meeting to give members estimated financial results for the remainder of the current accounting period and forecast data for the remainder of the current quarter, current year, and subsequent year. Most of the forecast data are obtained from the corporate officers' staff meetings and by asking key personnel in the functional areas about any significant changes in spending plans. The objective of the forecasts is to focus the board of directors' attention on decisions that will improve company operating performance.

ELECTRONIC BOARDROOM

As part of Mr. Pipkin's objective to have the right information at the right time, the company is modernizing its planning and financial systems with the implementation of leading-edge, user-driven, fully integrated mainframe software technology.

According to Darwin C. Niekerk, Coors' manager of modeling, technology, and analysis, the focus is on having both a high volume transactions-oriented traditional system and a new user-driven decision-support and reporting system. It includes Thorn/EMI decision support software and an IBM SQL/DS relational database. The traditional systems will provide data to the new modeling database system. A Thorn/EMI 4th-generation language provides modeling and data manipulation. IBM's database is the system's reservoir of information.

It's expected that improvements in traditional systems will improve staff performance and substantially reduce information processing costs. These savings, according to Mr. Niekerk, will be used to fund the development of the new user-driven systems. In turn, once the new user-driven systems are developed and implemented, overall system costs are expected to be reduced by 20% or more.

Why did Coors select a relational database? Because as Mr. Niekerk explained, data structure are defined in a conceptual rather than physical manner. Productivity is improved because very high-level and easy-to-use languages can be used to access the database.

The new technology will change the way employees work at every level. Jeff Coors, president of Adolph Coors Company, plans to have a terminal on his desk to be able to access information and perform "what if" scenarios about the company's various operations from the sophisticated financial database. At weekly production variance meetings, management will analyze on an on-line basis shop floor productivity yield variances. For example, when discussing why variances occurred, the managers can query the database directly and electronically to develop solutions.

The system also will be used for the company's designated marketing area (DMA) project—making it possible for the executive vice president of sales and marketing and his his staff to access and analyze the profit and loss results of 250 geographic market areas.

Coors understands the psychological impact this new technology will have on the corporate culture and therefore has invested time and effort in education and training to gain employee acceptance. Mr Pipkin scheduled several off-site breakfast meetings with outside experts to explain the impact of new systems in a "user-friendly" atmosphere.

Coors recognizes the necessity of adequate investment in training. It is perhaps considered as important as the investment in hardware and software. An innovative arrangement was made with Regis College in Denver to give three hours of college credit for in-house training. Coors financial staff members are certified as adjunct Regis faculty members.

ACCOUNTANTS PARTICIPATE

Whether you are the controller of a *Fortune* 500 company or a small firm, you should be concerned about what impact your department has on the day-to-day running of the business. According to Al Pipkin, his department is an integral part of the decision-making process and is supportive of the company's efforts to achieve national distribution. Accounting staff members function at every level in the company from the shop floor to the board of directors. His department's information network and system of financial reporting and forecasting enables top management to make fast decisions about Coors' various operations.

Although the methods used by the controller at Coors may not be entirely appropriate in other organizations, the philosophy behind it is solid and worthy of careful consideration if you want to broaden your management role.

WHATEVER HAPPENED TO ZERO-BASE BUDGETING?

Stanton C. Lindquist and R. Bryant Mills[1]

In this paper the authors review the Zero Base Budgeting concept, and address the problem of why it has not achieved more widespread adoption in both public and private organizations. They state that they found from their consulting experience that managers in both types of organization often had difficulty in understanding ZBB and how it could be used as a management tool. As to its potential, they suggest that ZBB should be viewed as an evolutionary step rather than a final solution in the planning/budgeting process.

INTRODUCTION

During the mid and late 1970's the concept of "zero base budgeting" (ZBB) was set forth as a new approach to controlling operational activities and their related financial expenditures. Since ZBB was first publicized several years ago by the then Governor Jimmy Carter of Georgia (who claimed that it had been implemented in his state with startling results), numerous books and articles, both pro and con, have appeared dealing with the theory and application of ZBB in both private and public organizations.

Peter A. Pyhrr has defined ZBB as:

An operating, planning and budgeting process which requires each manager to justify his entire budget request in detail from scratch (hence zero base) and shifts the burden of proof to each manager to justify why he should spend any money at all. This approach requires that all activities be defined in 'decision packages' which will be evaluated by systematic analysis and ranked in order of importance.[1]

ZBB is characterized as a general management tool to be used in providing both a systematic evaluation of operations and programs, and a mechanism for shifting resources into what are considered high priority programs or services. Theoretically, the ZBB process offers managers opportunities to: (1) recommend how much money should be spent; (2) evaluate and possibly change operations to improve efficiency and/or effectiveness; and (3) participate in a more meaningful way in program planning and budgeting, thereby encouraging management development, better communication, and discussion of key issues and problems. In summary, the fundamental objectives of ZBB are to improve managerial performance and facilitate efficiency and effectiveness in achievement of organizational goals.

The transition of ZBB theoretical concepts into practice requires two steps. First, each manager must develop "decision packages" which state expenditures and personnel required at different levels of departmental and/or program activity. Second, these decision packages must be evaluated and ranked to determine the best decision package according to predetermined

---

[1] Reprinted by permission *Managerial Planning*, January/February, 1981, pp. 31-35.

operational objectives. The best decision package for each managerial level must then be integrated with the best decision packages from other managerial levels to form an overall operating budget in accordance with the broad company or agency operational objectives.

If ZBB (as a total concept) is such a vast improvement over traditional planning and budgeting, why has it not achieved more widespread adoption in both public and private organizations? This question is addressed in the following paragraphs based on the authors' experience in applying ZBB in public as well as private organizations.

IMPLEMENTATION PROBLEMS IN PUBLIC AND PRIVATE ORGANIZATIONS

Although many of the problems encountered in implementing ZBB are similar for public and private organizations, our experience with county governmental units, school districts, and with private firms of varying size lead us to conclude that there are special problems in the public sector not present to the same degree in a private organization. For analysis purposes we have enumerated three important and meaningful problem areas: (1) people or personnel problems; (2) system or process problems; and (3) legal and political problems.

PEOPLE RELATED PROBLEMS

Invariably, when attempting to implement a ZBB system in both public and private organizations, the first problem area that must be dealt with are people, specifically the managers who must make the system work. The "people problem" has several dimensions. First, a lack of understanding as to the purposes, objectives, strengths and weaknesses of ZBB often exists within a particular organization. ZBB has been viewed as having universal applicability to all organizations and over-sold as a cure-all for planning, budgeting and operating problems.

The point to be made here is that in most of the public and private organizations we have been involved with, managers, particularly those at the top, have failed to clearly define and understand the total concept of ZBB within the context of organizational structures and objectives. They have assumed that ZBB would fit nicely in with whatever planning and budgeting system they were presently using.

This problem is particularly pronounced in private profit-oriented organizations where not all departments and functions can utilize ZBB. For example, planning and budgeting for line operations (such as various production departments) are driven by a combination of unit volumes and standard costs. While ZBB will significantly influence the planning and budgeting process in line operations, it is intended primarily for those departments and functions such as manufacturing staff, plant and sales administration, R&D, personnel, and accounting. ZBB is ideally suited to these staff functions because cost/benefit analyses can be made which are not a direct result of units being produced or predetermined standard costs. Failure by private enterprise managers to clearly understand the type of operational areas suitable for ZBB as well as how ZBB integrates with other on-line planning/budgeting systems can only end in a failure of the entire ZBB process.

A closely related problem is the inability to define the "zero base" from an operational manager's viewpoint. Each manager is running an ongoing department or program with existing budgets and personnel. Is the zero base 50 percent, 30 percent, 110 percent, or 125 percent of existing expenditures and personnel? Managers often take their existing level of operations as the zero base and view any reductions from this base with extreme alarm and any increases from the base with extreme delight. Thus, the whole concept of ZBB becomes confused in the operational manager's eyes.

The second dimension of the people problem has to do with attitudes. Our experience has shown that when attempting to implement a ZBB system in a public or private organization, common human reactions of suspicion, cynicism, and direct opposition are encountered from those with managerial and budgetary responsibilities. Opposition from agency heads or department managers may be caused by a variety of factors, internal and external, but more often reflects a fear of change and insecurity in learning a new "system." Although irrational from the managerial point of view, opposition to change should be viewed as a normal response. After all, by introducing a new method of operation, one is in fact implying that the old method, and those responsible for it, were in some way ineffective.

Fear and suspicion are heightened when attempts are made to radically change the planning and budgeting system. Managers view the budget as crucial to their survival and to the future of their operations. In those organizations with internal morale problems, managers at the bottom of the organization often view the ZBB process as a tool of top management and as a reflection of top management's dissatisfaction with lower level managerial performance. In essence, suspicion of change may be a reflection of internal organizational conflicts. If implementation is to succeed, ways must be found to bring into the ZBB planning process all those persons with budgetary responsibilities. Each participating manager of a department or functional area selected for ZBB implementation must be convinced that the ZBB concept is good for the organization, good for the manager, and operationally feasible. In addition, each manager must understand how ZBB will be used to evaluate his or her managerial performance. If the above cannot be accomplished successfully, ZBB as a management tool will not work.

The high degree of cynicism often found among managers in both private and public organizations can be viewed as a response to past attempts to "implement a new system." This is particularly true in the large public agency. It is the rare public manager who has not been subject to frequent attempts to "change things" or to try something new be it MIS, MBO, PPBS, or ZBB. Thus, ZBB must contend with past attempts (some successful and some not) to improve operations. Cynicism then, is probably a healthy bureaucratic response and must be recognized as such.

Since opposition to change and cynicism regarding new systems are common among operating managers, it is particularly important that top management give its unequivocal support to ZBB prior to undertaking a project. Top management support must be communicated to those down the hierarchy clearly and precisely so that no one is in doubt as to what is expected. However, our experience has indicated that even with the strongest backing from top management and with the clearest statement of what is to be done, it is not unusual to find managers unwilling to support the change. In the public agencies, because of civil service status or other reasons peculiar to the public service, managers may oppose introduction of a new system for a considerable length of time and not be sanctioned.

Although the factors listed above may account for most cynicism and opposition to ZBB, an often neglected consideration is a deep fear of failure resulting from a lack of skills normally expected of a person occupying a managerial position. The fearful, incompetent, or marginal manager projects his or her fears on the new system and often invents elaborate justifications for why the system cannot work.

The final human dimension that should be mentioned, and one that closely correlates with the above is an inability to collect, interpret, and utilize performance data required for implementing a ZBB system. Although this problem was found in private firms, it seems more pronounced in public agencies. It is often amazing to those trained in the rigorous world of business management to view the absence of common analytical skills and the paucity of analytical performance data characteristic of many public managers and agencies. As mentioned earlier, ZBB requires that performance criteria be established, that tasks and functions be clearly understood, and that methods be developed to provide meaningful feedback information for control purposes. This is particularly important to those persons formulating decision packages, attaching costs to them, and ranking them. Unfortunately, the manager responsible for collecting data may be unskilled in doing so. If this is the case, then implementation of ZBB must be preceded by a basic training of the unskilled administrator or the whole process will be put in jeopardy.

SYSTEM AND PROCESS PROBLEMS

ZBB in public and private agencies has to do with operational processes and management systems. Basically, these difficulties are: (1) failure to properly supervise implementation; (2) lack of well-defined feedback procedures; (3) lack of an adequate revision process if found necessary at a later date; and (4) lack of performance and work load measurements.

Assuming the ZBB can be defined and conceptually understood by all levels of management, the next major problem area requiring analysis and attention is the actual implementation of a ZBB system. All too often top management assumes that lower level managers can and will follow through without further help and supervision. Unfortunately, this may not be the case. Our experience indicates the need at this point to reiterate to unit and functional managers that implementation is largely *their* responsibility. Managers must be convinced that quality preparation and defense of their decision packages, and modifications (if necessary) are up to them and that they will be held accountable. If the managers believe that what they propose will be superceded or materially altered by other individuals and/or committees they will not only fail to prepare quality materials and support the system, but may actually attempt to sabotage its implementation.

Secondly, participating managers often do not receive the detailed on-going technical assistance and supervision in designing and collecting work performance data and in preparing decision packages. Participating managers have difficulties in defining their departmental and functional objectives, determining effective levels of performance within a particular department or function, preparing decision packages in a consistent manner, and keeping the entire ZBB process on a master time table. In short, our experience indicates that organizations attempting to implement a ZBB process have failed to develop a "ZBB strike force" composed of knowledgeable specialists whose primary function is to assist participating managers with their problems.

If ZBB is to work as planned, it is necessary that a comprehensive management information system exist. All too often, public and private agencies have not developed a method of providing managers with data indicating performance of on-going operations. In ZBB this is particularly important as feedback data is needed for future decision package formulation. What feedback exists often is of a financial nature required by the accounting system and of limited value to a program or departmental manager.

Part of any management information system involves the development of procedures which can be used to adjust current operations from predetermined operational and budgetary activities. Our experience indicates that organizations attempting to implement a ZBB process did not give adequate consideration to the development of a mechanism for review and adjustment throughout the operational year. Consequently, once a level of program, departmental or agency activity (decision package) is set, very little managerial attention is given to changing decision packages if adjustment in current operations take places. Too often managers spend most of their time making expenditures fit into predetermined levels of activity rather than revising decision packages according to actual levels of activity. Managers view ZBB as a once-a-year phenomenon rather than as an ongoing system of management.

As stated earlier under people related problems, ZBB requires the collection and analysis of large amounts of work performance and work load data. In larger public and private organizations with staffs of productivity experts, this usually does not pose an insurmountable problem. But in smaller public and private organizations, procedures to collect this data on a needs basis have not been developed. The charge of "too much paperwork" is an understandable one from the point of view of the lower level manager, but what is neglected here is that the collection of work performance information and assessing it for control and budget-making purposes is an important function of a manager. Yet, from our experience this managerial function is often neglected and even resisted.

The last major process problem we have identified in implementing a ZBB system in public and private organizations involves the need to design a *logical, workable,* and *acceptable* process for evaluating and ranking hundreds of ZBB proposals. To be logical the ranking system must reflect the goals of the organization and the objectives of individual units within it. A workable and acceptable ranking system should be understandable to all concerned, and hopefully, acceptable as well. In practice, however, the ranking of decision packages often becomes illogical due to the fact that individual unit objectives are not coordinated with the goals of the organization. Also, the ranking system may become unworkable due to inadequate design and preparation thereby necessitating an inordinate amount of work in processing hundreds of ZBB decision packages. Finally, the ranking system often becomes unacceptable to the participating managers if they are left our of the final ranking process. Participating mangers will be very reluctant to prepare future decision packages if they see their work "go down the drain" through a faulty ranking system.

LEGAL/POLITICAL PROBLEMS

Students of public administration often emphasize the legal and political environment of the public agency as a major factor explaining differences between public and private management. Our experience with ZBB in public agencies would seem to support this contention. Although politics, rules, and regulations are found in the private organization, these factors take on a unique and often overriding role in public agencies. The budgeting cycle and support operations are determined by state laws, county or local ordinances, and must be compensated for if they cannot be changed. A ZBB system must take into account legal requirements of reporting, required periodic review of financial data, and other legal requirements. When implementing a ZBB system, care must be taken to design the system to "fit" the legal requirements governing the agency.

An important legal problem encountered in our work in Michigan, a highly unionized state, were rules regarding personnel placement, functions, job tasks, transfers, and other personnel related matters contained in union contracts. Many times, these collective bargaining agreements made it difficult for managers to consider reallocation of personnel necessary for formulation of decision packages. Also, union contract agreements often specified wages, location of jobs, and assigned duties, and thus were major considerations when lower level managers attempted to attach costs to variable levels of service in their decision packages. Attempts to force arbitrary decision package funding levels on a manager when 80 percent of his or her budget was personnel costs and over which the manager had no control, were highly unrealistic. Managers were often concerned about reaction from union representatives if they proposed levels of funding and changes in services below established current allocations. When decision packages suggested reassignment of personnel or reduction in staff, union contracts become prime considerations. These problems were particularly important in a sheriff's department where the sheriff and his chief budget officer were unable to attach cost to personnel for the coming year until completion of a new contract with the Teamsters Union. Attempts to estimate probable salary ranges were resisted by the sheriff for several reasons including his unwillingness to "give away" the bargaining position of the county in advance. The union contract also specified duty stations and numbers of officers assigned to them. Consequently, the sheriff was restricted in shifting personnel to maximize efficiency.

Many researchers have commented on the politics of budgeting in public agencies and the literature is rich in case studies of how politics rather than "rational" management decision determine final budget amounts. Political concerns account for an unwillingness even to think about a reduced level of service or of a reduction in expenditures for special programs. Either it was recognized that the controlling political officials would not support a reduction in favorite programs, or increases in others, or that clientele groups in the community would intervene to continue and hopefully increase current programs benefiting them. Under such conditions, public managers responsible for making up decision packages at different funding and service levels were reluctant to commit themselves below previously allocated amounts. Although the final ranking of decision packages and the attachment of funding to each must by necessity be a political decision of top management and the elected officials, and is proper, political pressures at the lower levels cause difficulties in considering a ZBB process.

SUMMARY AND CONCLUSIONS

When comparing the problems of implementing ZBB in public and private organizations, more similarities appear than differences. The people problems encountered were essentially the same in both public and private organizations. Managers in both types of organization often have difficulty understanding ZBB and how it can be used as a management tool. We also found that in several cases ZBB was used primarily as an attempt to accomplish budget reductions which led to opposition from lower level managers. In essence, people problems encountered in implementing ZBB in both public and private organizations were of degree rather than of substance.

The process problems involved in implementing ZBB in public and private organizations were also very similar. Both types of organizations generally did not spend sufficient time and effort in designing the ZBB system for their particular organizations nor in providing everyday supervision and technical assistance required for successful implementation. Also, both types of organizations evidenced a reluctance to replace traditional planning/budgeting systems with a new untried system.

Legal and political problems in involved in implementing ZBB constituted the most significant area of difference between public and private organizations. Public organizations are political entities created to serve political purposes. Even the most rational management and budgeting system must give way to this fact. Thus, a ZBB system may improve the allocation or reallocation of material resources with public organizations or programs, but those supporting the system must be prepared to adjust to political decisions when the final budget is prepared. On the other hand, private organization did not encounter outside legal and political restrictions in terms of implementing ZBB. The lack of outside legal and political restrictions appears to make ZBB easier to implement in private organizations. However, in the final analysis, implementing ZBB depends much more heavily on internal commitment than on any outside legal and political restrictions.

Several conclusions can be drawn about ZBB as it currently exists and about its future potential. First ZBB is not a panacea for curing planning/budgeting problems nor should it be judged in terms of a "total" success or a "total" failure. While very few public and private organizations currently employ ZBB as a total concept, they do utilize elements of ZBB in their planning/budgeting process. For example, new programs and capital expenditure proposals are ranked according to organizational priorities. Also, operational audits are being performed to evaluate managerial performance on the basis of end results compared to predetermined objectives. Currently the sum of ZBB elements being applied to organizational planning/budgeting do not equal the total ZBB concept.

In terms of its future potential, perhaps ZBB should be viewed as an evolutionary step rather than a final solution in the planning/ budgeting process. As resources dwindle and costs spiral upwards, managers in both public and private organizations will utilize a planning/budgeting system which can provide more accountability to tying expenditure, expenditure results, and personnel to organizational objectives and goals. Ultimately, the future work of ZBB (as a total concept or piece-meal) will be determined by how it is used within a particular organization.

REFERENCES

[1] Peter A. Phyrr, "Zero Base Budgeting," unpublished speech delivered at the International Conference of the Planning Executives Institute, New York, May, 1972.

A CRITIQUE OF PERFORMANCE APPRAISAL SYSTEMS

Ed Yager[1]

Many systems are poorly designed because of a lack of clear objectives.

Emphasis on pay for performance, federal employment guidelines, government employee reform acts, promotional policy, motivational research and MBO all culminate in the performance appraisal process. It is hard to imagine any personnel relations topic currently receiving more attention than performance appraisal.

Over the years the literature has been loaded with expert counsel on how to conduct performance reviews. Nearly every professional and management journal has published articles dealing with this topic. Dozens of training programs, models, films and tapes are available which show how to conduct performance reviews. Yet, problems persist. I still find an incredible number of major shortcoming in the performance appraisal process. I have worked in hundreds of management workshops with thousands of managers, and I seldom find managers satisfied with the systems adopted within their organizations. As I review various formats of personnel appraisal, many traditions seem to hang on—even in the most sophisticated of systems. I do not intend to cover the entire subject in detail. Instead, I have raised issues for the reader to consider when evaluating current and proposed performance appraisal programs.

Most performance appraisal methods are based on inferences, assumptions of cause and effect, and theories that a particular review system will impact some other more distant relationship for which other research has been accomplished. Because feedback is good, one assumes a performance review program that provides feedback is inherently good.

Too many performance appraisal systems are designed and installed ineptly because of a lack of clear objectives. Organizations and managers have not yet determined what they want the performance appraisal or performance review system to do, and they try to accomplish too much with one singular system. There seems to be a nagging orientation to numbers plaguing many organization as they try to come up with scores, ratings, or singularly unrealistic-simplistic global statements of performance.

In my view, performance appraisal, performance planning, and salary planning are distinctly different phases of the supervisor/worker relationship. All require different skills, have different goals, and should be practiced individually. Below, I have defined performance appraisal, performance review and performance planning, and their applications:

■ *Performance Appraisal* is an interpersonal process that occurs regularly and frequently between supervisor and worker. An appraisal of some sort, causal or formal, general or specific, should follow each task or project as it is accomplished. Some

---

[1] Reprinted by permission, *Personnel Journal*, February, 1981, pp. 129-133. All rights reserved.

acknowledgement, praise, correction or comment should always occur. This is an essential role of a manager—indeed, it may be the primary role of the manager.

Continuous appraisal is a simple pattern of behavior that distinguishes the most effective managers. This practice alone does more to motivate, encourage, build, train, reinforce and modify behavior than any other single action or series of actions that a manager might take.

■ *Performance Review* should be a periodic summarization and review of preceding performance appraisals. There should be no surprises, and, in fact, the employee should be able to do as accurate a job of reviewing performance as the supervisor. If this is not the case, then the supervisor has not done an adequate job of providing appraisal along the way. The employee and the supervisor should have developed a common bond so that either could write the annual review and gain total agreement with the other. Any focus on the past is not to generate a score card, but rather to formalize a statement of "where am I" so I can plan in more detail "where am I going," and "how am I going to get there."

■ *Performance Planning* is a third and higher level of communication that grows out of the performance review. It is during performance planning that the employee and supervisor agree on "where am I going," "how will I get there," and "how will I be measured." A well-designed performance planning process should allow managers to outline the consequences of various agreed-upon performance levels.

Too many employees find themselves playing the game with no clear understanding of the payoffs. A generalized "if you work harder, you will get ahead," substitutes for specific planning which says, "this level of work is required for this much increase, or for consideration for this type of promotion, etc."

The actual systems used will be quite different depending on the outcomes required:

	Performance Appraisal	Performance Review	Performance Planning
To provide feedback on performance	X		
To establish plans for development		X	X
To share ideas and concerns: working relationships		X	
For salary planning		X	
For job placement		X	
For improved work performance	X		X
For behavior change	X		
To determine work goals	X		X
To establish measurements of work output			X
To provide information for promotion decisions		X	
To guide and control work	X		
To coordinate department and interdepartmental planning			X

Notice that none of these systems include ratings of promotability. Neither do they include salary planning decisions even though some of the information is subsequently used for that purpose. I feel strongly that these are totally separate systems. I have yet to see a system that effectively gains the full commitment of managers and employees by combining the review, salary planning and potential ratings at the same time.

Systems that combine all appraisal functions into one package rarely win both employee and management support.

TRAPS AND PITFALLS

Some of the most common traps in the performance appraisal or performance review process are outlined below. Evaluate your own program to see if it includes any of these pitfalls.

■ *Separate rating and evaluation processes*

Attempts to combine all systems into one master rating, combining performance appraisal, development planning, ratings and salary decisions all on the same form to be done at the same time will cause severe problems. The performance review and the planning should be separate from ratings of potential and promotability, and pay decisions. Of course, they are going to be affected by the performance review or the performance plan. But if the performance review or plan is allowed to lead these decisions, then the degree of honesty, help and feedback will be inaccurate as the information is manipulated in order to meet pay plans or to serve other agendas and needs.

Every additional purpose added to performance review information decreases the accuracy and value of the total process.

■ *Maintain the lines of authority*

Too often performance reviews are written for the wrong audience, such as the boss or the organization. I believe an organization should keep the performance review within the lines and limits of authority. Each manager should be held responsible for evaluating the employees who report directly to him or her. This rating should not be influenced by the thinking of other managers at higher levels or in other areas.

A senior manager should be concerned about his or her subordinate supervisor's ability to appraise others, and should rate them on the kind of appraisal job they do. If not satisfied, then that manager has the responsibility for improving the quality of performance reviews given in his/her area, but he or she should not interfere with the review that has already been done. The subordinate supervisor should be challenged to improve his or her performance reviews in the future.

Despite what some legal authorities may say about the requirement for a second-level concurring review, the manager should not intervene between a subordinate's rating of his or her employees. Concurrence could easily mean understanding; it does not have to mean agreement. Intervention in the rating process undermines the authority of the supervisor. It may disrupt the relationship between the supervisor and worker and it forces written reviews that reflect what will be accepted "upstairs" more than what is good for the employee. An employee knows if the performance review is the review of their immediate supervisor or is a reflection of a manager two or three levels above. If this is the case, employees lose confidence in their supervisor's authority and credibility.

■ *Report Card Type Ratings*

Many performance reviews are based on vague generalities and are not specific. A reviewer should avoid report card ratings of traits or generalized ability factors. These are seldom helpful and are subject to an extreme number of rating errors. If ratings are needed, they should be based on behavioral descriptions of the activities. Some systems try to overcome these problems by asking the manager to comment on the rating, or to comment on all high or low ratings. The comments are seldom more than vague references to performance, and few managers will write reviews where they have to comment on anything.

Many appraisal systems provide a checklist of factors like initiative, interest, ability, etc. These are all rated from high to low on some particular scale. This is often a hopeless endeavor—not that the rating are unimportant—but because most of these factors are unrateable. The anchors are of little help because of extreme subjectivity and variability of definitions and interpretation between readers.

One common attempt to solve this problem is to use behaviorally anchored rating scales. In this type scale, a descriptor is placed at key points along the scale to try to provide a common interpretation of the factor. For example the most common strategy is like this one:

Initiative

Does only what is told.   Will occasionally initiate some project and generate some ideas.   Consistently finds work to do, adds extra elements to assigned tasks.

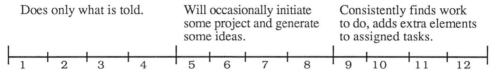

Although a major improvement, this type scale frequently falls short. Scales of this sort are seldom behavioral. They add some definition to the rating, but they still require much subjective interpretation. A better example of a behavioral scale could be directly related to a job analysis and could list a series of critical behaviors with ratings on each. For example:

Initiative

When a customer asks for merchandise which is not on the selling floor, employee:

Tells the customer, "We are out: and does nothing—or says, If it's not out, we don't have any."   Volunteers to help locate the item and to check the back room to see if any have come in.   Does this and also asks customer to place a special order so a call can be made when it comes in. Brings outage to manager's attention.

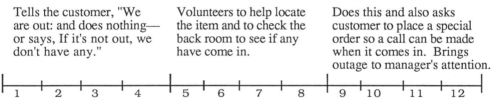

This type of rating takes time to develop, but is much more meaningful and helpful. It also provides models of behavior for training and allows for more specific ratings and descriptions of factors.

■ *The Use of Single Ratings*

Many systems, even though utilizing an otherwise acceptable system, force the manager to arrive at a single overall rating. I have a strong bias against overall ratings, in the performance review. I suppose, realistically, they are inevitable, but they affect the accuracy and balance of the appraisal or review. I have yet to see an organization that is able to obtain anything approaching a normal distribution of ratings without forcing the curve, and few managers support forced curves. A single rating is a barrier to meaningful performance discussions because it puts all of the focus on the single rating and its defense. This single rating does not permit indepth reasoning, and yet will singularly influence most of the decisions regarding the person's future. It will probably be the only other factor that goes into the computer or into an employee's personnel record.

Whenever a single rating is used, it is more a rating of the relationship between the rater and the employee than anything else. If a single rating is required, then it might be done separately from the performance review—perhaps based on statements comparing this person's overall performance to others, or this person's overall performance compared to the expectations of the job. This type of overall rating could then be used for pay plans, but it should not be used as part of the actual performance review itself.

Comparison rating allows employees to gauge their performance against that of their colleagues.

Many organizations have had great success using comparative ratings by comparing employees to one another. This seems risky, and yet this is exactly what is being done every day. It is a more honest and easier way for a manager to rate. By rating on a comparative basis, there will be more value to employees, allowing them to know how they compare to others in the same job. One scale that might be used is:

Compared to others I know doing the same job:

- This person's performance is not as strong as most others.

- This person's performance is comparable to most others.

- This person's performance is better than most.

- This person's performance is far better than most.

- This person's performance far exceeds most.

This rating does not require the manager to defend a definition called outstanding, average or poor, but it simply a comparison. Managers frequently find this a better rating system because they can call all employees outstanding if they want to. The ranking just makes some employees more outstanding than others.

A next step is to compare all of the people of like positions from all managers, thus providing an overall percentile ranking for each employee. The employee can then be told, "You are in the top 20% of all who are holding this position." An additional advantage is that the organization is able to observe each manager's rating tendencies.

■ Managing by Objectives

Misunderstandings about the misuse of MBO concepts causes problems. MBO can easily be used in Theory X or Theory Y managing, with totally different outcomes. Many managers base this rating on the number of objectives met. This simply increases the manipulation of the measurement or of the objectives. This manipulation can be solved by focusing on the level of difficulty of the objectives to the overall department goal—not on how many objectives are achieved. An outstanding performer could have a limited number of extremely high, stretching objectives, yet they may not achieve 100% and could still greatly outmatch their peers. Weak performers or new performers, on the other hand, may have many more basic objectives and may exceed this simple measurement and meet all their objectives. This does not mean that they are doing an outstanding job when compared to other employees. To some employees, meeting all the objectives (assuming the objectives are set within their level of ability) may simply mean continued employment. Other employees with much more difficult objectives may not reach any of them and still be qualified for promotion.

Some systems emphasize the number of objectives met. These systems unrealistically assume that a manager has the ability to set accurate objectives a year in advance. It also encourages the MBO game. Once objectives are written, they become next year's performance review, so employees are forced to write sure-thing objectives.

Another frequently witnessed problem of MBO utilization is the manager's inability to select good measurements. When managing by objectives, the objectives and their measurements must be within the employee's control. Too many objectives are measured by ambiguous or difficult to obtain criteria. Many are evaluated by measurements which are not within the control of the employee.

For example, a safety director who accepts an objective to reduce loss time accidents has little control over obtaining his or her objectives. He or she cannot control the measure because there are so many other factors like employee concern, supervisory activity, weather, employee relations, capital, budgets and other factors beyond his or her control. Because he cannot control these factors, even though the goal is very desirable, the exercise become a game of chance more than a real measure of the safety director's work effort. Measures should be established which the safety director can control, such as elimination of a certain number of hazards, changes in equipment to make them safer, administration of policies, or other similar goals upon which it is assumed a reduction in loss time accidents relies. These are measures over which the employee has direct control, which should result in the ultimate objective of reduced loss time accidents. This also allows the employee and his/her supervisor to discuss specific expectations in terms of work output and responsibilities.

■ *Measure Results Not Activity*

Too many managers measure activity and become overconcerned with what employees are doing with their time instead of what they are accomplishing. It is important that one avoids measures of activity and instead focuses on results.

Measures like "number of students in class" or "numbers of classes taught" show up in training directors' objectives. All this serves to do is increase nonproductive activity or activity for its own sake. Indeed this may be one cause of the national decline in productivity in past years.

Most often, MBO forces employees to be more concerned with how time is spent, rather than with real accomplishments.

An expert's review of MBO reports would probably help most organizations solve this problem. From the reports I have seen, it might be concluded that accountants are paid to account; trainers are paid to train; lawyers are paid to defend. Seldom do measures appear to be focused on results. When a trainer is paid to train, and when his or her promotions and increases are based on an MBO system that emphasizes the amount of training done, training will proliferate. The same is true with accountants who are paid to account. If no measurements are established on the contribution of the accounting or the usefulness of the accounting, then accountants will continue to account, establishing pyramid relationships to increase responsibility and accounting.

CONCLUSION

Because of the tendency to respond to manager's complaints that the traditional performance review is too time consuming and too burdensome—which in itself is an indictment of the value of the typical system—we have taken too many liberties in combining, shortcutting or eliminating critically important aspects of managerial work. Performance planning, MBO, performance review and performance appraisal are distinctly separate and valuable management processes. They all have separate purposes and separate payoffs. The organization should decide what information is needed, what decisions will be made based on that information, and then devise separate systems which:

- *Provide the precise information* that is needed by the organization, or by the employee, as efficiently and accurately as possible.

- *Emphasize feedback and build relationships* between managers and subordinates.

- *Avoid a once-a-year, form-filling-out chore* which could not possibly meet all of the essential objectives.

- *Separate ratings of performance, potential, promotability and pay* as separate decisions which are arrived at using different comparisons and inputs.

The organization must be sensitive to these various differences and provide better information, feedback and performance at numerous levels throughout the organization. This is the essence of managing.

PLANNING AND CREATING AN INFORMATION SYSTEM

Joseph E. Izzo[1]

Harold Laski, one of England's leading twentieth-century economists, once said, "We must plan our civilization or we must perish." In like fashion, companies that lack an overall plan for their computer system architecture seriously jeopardize their chances for growth and success in the future.

An architecture helps a company determine how, and in what form, computer technology will be implemented to achieve the firm's goals. When I go into a company, one of my first questions is, "Do you have a system architecture?" The answer is invariably, "Yes, we do"; however, in viewing that architecture, I find it relates primarily to a hardware or a communications network. Such an architecture addresses only how the technology is connected, but not necessarily the needs of the users or the business itself. I ask further, "How will the technology be used?" I am told that the users will be better able to share information and to communicate with one another. If I ask why they need to do this, or how this will benefit the company, the answers become considerably more vague.

What's the problem here? Quite simply, there is no strategy for the computer systems architecture. When I say strategy, I mean the art of planning and directing activities to achieve a goal. It is difficult to use the technology properly when there is no business purpose in mind. I have no problem with the idea of a hardware or communications network architecture nor with users communicating with each other. In fact, both are essential. But these are the means, not the end. My point is that without a strategy that produces a desired business goal the technology is going to waste.

Historically, the firm's goals and the business technology department's goals have not been the same. A primary reason is that the business people have never taken the time to develop a true system architecture strategy that responds to the overall needs of the business. This essential first step must be taken before we can begin using technology as an enabling device.

We are at a major crossroads in deciding how computer technology is going to be used in the future. The problems are detailed in frequent cover stories in every business magazine. You must make a decision about your company's computer resources. Don't say you can't afford to make the time or the monetary commitment; you can't afford not to. The problem is already costing you hundreds of thousands, perhaps millions of dollars a year in lost opportunity and overhead.

It's not that we have been without a planning strategy or methodology in the past; it's simply that the methodologies of yesterday and today are woefully inadequate. Their purpose, for the most part, was simply to help perform tasks more quickly, which at one time was probably considered a "productivity gain." But they cannot help us implement a future architecture that

---

[1] Reprinted by permission, *Information Center*, September, 1987, pp 28-35.

addresses the changing needs of the users or that helps us produce products or services better, faster, or cheaper.

OLD PLANNING TECHNIQUES

Many of the old methodologies were, in the parlance of business technology, "information-driven," such as IBM's Business Systems Planning (BSP). Others incorporated such things as "functional activity models" with "information flow models" that created "business models." The process began when the programmers-analysts diagrammed the business operation, noting where every scrap of information came from and went to. This took months, and was often frustrating and exhausting. In many cases, this data collection became so complex that it would require a miracle to design a system that accounted for every need.

Perhaps the greatest drawback to diagramming business functions and activities is that it only accounts for where a business is right now. It doesn't consider where the company is going, and so is doomed to be out of date before it is even implemented.

In most cases, the concentration is on "information." This supports the prevailing myth that information is the computer's end product. Though the various ways in which computers are able to manipulate and deliver "information" fascinate business technology personnel, there are no inherent productivity gains that benefit the business.

To underscore my point, consider this description of a seminar for executives:

This program will give executives a solid basis for directing the implementation of technology for the information age in which we live. Meetings will focus on devising strategies for controlling the costs of handling information.

There are probably some useful and worthwhile techniques presented in a seminar like this, but it's still yesterday's thinking. It promotes what I call ephemeral planning, because it make everyone feel good for a few fleeting moments, but can rarely be implemented in the day-to-day business world. If we are going to see the benefits of computer technology as an enabling device that truly benefits the company, we must begin what I call sensible planing: not what we'd ideally like to have in a perfect world, but what is realistic and achievable.

One more point: conventional planning strategies are concerned with managing the data we have collected and plan to collect. These strategies assume we will continue to amass more and more data on more and more functions, and never address what I consider of greater importance. If computer technology can be properly deployed, isn't it conceivable that we could reduce the amount of data we collect and retain, and perhaps eliminate some redundant functions as well?

There are certain points in a company's business cycle when extraordinary effort is required to make a major shift or change in the way things are done. At these points, standard methods for creating change are not adequate. New approaches must be sought. How to begin? By bringing the firm's movers and shakers together to plan the strategy.

THE SKUNK WORKS

Many years ago, Lockheed came up with the idea of gathering a team of people together in some off-site location for brainstorming new products. They called the idea "the skunk works." The term "skunk" comes from the notion that these people are isolated and that no one wants to be around them. It was an immediate success at Lockheed, and now many other companies have adopted the concept. Great ideas almost always emerge. One of the most famous skunk works projects was creating the MV-8000 super minicomputer at Data General, which was chronicled in Tracy Kidder's Pulitzer Prize-winning book, *The Soul of a New Machine.*

I believe the skunk works is the best environment for tackling something as important as a new computer system architecture. First of all, it allows the team to break away physically and mentally from the everyday corporate culture. It also gives them freedom to identify new ways in which computer technology can be used to support the business and help it thrive. The skunk works allows people to get rid of their inhibitions and innovate without restrictions. The goal is an environment where they can think and talk without the conventional business constraints.

Senior management should demonstrate their support, and must remain visible and involved throughout the skunk works. This is important because it shows their confidence and trust in them. The team needs that because they are changing the way computer technology is going to be used, and thus changing some fundamental ways you do business. Involvement says you are willing to accept the risks in giving them this assignment. Without the outward signs of confidence, it will be more difficult for the team to innovate or to take the risks the project needs. They must feel confident, inspired, and secure.

As their leader, senior management must initiate the skunk works project and give the team its mission and focus. Skunk works participants must be clear and precise about their task; no one should think this is just another bull-shooting session or a low-level, busy-work project. It must be clear that change will emerge. The team must have access to the firm's goals for the next five to ten years. The team must understand senior management's thinking and strategy in planning those goals. If they can grasp how that thinking came about, they have a much better chance of turning those goals into reality.

Depending on the size and complexity of the company, it may take three to six months for the skunk works to create its plan for the new system architecture. The team must understand that the project requires their full attention for the duration, no matter how long that is.

THE COMPOSITION OF THE TEAM

The members of the skunk works should be people respected by their departments and the rest of the company. These people should be in a responsible line capacity, people who are committed "doers." The ideal mix is two-thirds line people from the user organizations and one-third technology people.

The line people should be from different departments and should be people who represent their organizations and can speak for them. You want departmental line people who understand the business. You want operational people—those who meet the customers and are involved with the firm's product.

You do not want staff people who are steeped in procedures. Nor do you want backroom people who are interested in data for data's sake. You want the people who make the difference in the company.

From the technology side, you want people who are perceptive and can think in conceptual terms. These should be people who are clear thinkers and problem solvers, not those mired in yesterday's technology. They should have a broad understanding of the technology and its uses and applications, but not necessarily detailed knowledge.

The skunk works leader should be someone who embraces the concept of technology as an enabling device, who is able to create an open and frank discussion environment, and who is not encumbered by company politics. The leader should be a senior manager who understands the business in its broadest perspective, and who is highly respected by both peers and management.

THE SKUNK WORKS DEN

To be truly effective, the skunk works team should meet in an off-site environment. "Off-site" means far enough away from the daily operating environment to avoid constant interruptions about everyday matters. The actual place the team meets may be a conference room in the far corner of one of your buildings, a rented trailer, the company apartment, or in a hotel meeting room.

The team members should have only the task at hand before them: planning and designing a new system architecture. The corporate culture drives us to certain preordained conclusions, and the team must break free of them if it is going to innovate. There are the interruptions in our daily routines for phone calls and supposedly important messages, even at the most tightly-closed-door meeting. All these influences and interruptions must be eliminated for the skunk works to be successful.

The team members work every day at the off-site location, just as if they were going to the office. Three weeks is a long time for people to be away from their normal jobs, let alone three months. Participants often grow anxious about what is going on in their absence. Some may feel they will lose their positions to competitors if they're away too long. They must feel assured that their positions are not in jeopardy. In some cases, it may be necessary to let the team go to their offices one day a week. Be aware, however, that this creates a mind shift and may slow down the creative process.

There is no question that the company pays a price by sacrificing these people for the duration of the skunk works. But there is a payback as well. First, the new system architecture will be significantly more appropriate in supporting and advancing the business. Second, skunk works members, ostensibly the rising stars in the firm, receive a broad education in the combined aspects of business and technology. This unquestionably valuable experience puts them in a strong position to offer additional benefits to the company for a long time.

Once the team is formed, the work begins in earnest. Almost. To be realistic, not all skunk works team members will be available immediately. Most will need a little time to transfer their responsibilities to others while they are gone. This need not deter the start-up phase, however. There are many preparatory steps that need to be taken so the team can work effectively and efficiently once things are in full swing.

For example, let's say the project length has been set for six months. The first two months can be designated as preparation time, and the remaining four months as the actual skunk works project. Under such a plan, the two most important tasks during this period are establishing goals and building the business model.

ESTABLISH GOALS

Of all the skunk works activities, setting goals is the most important. If the goals are inadequate in the beginning, they will produce inadequate results at the end. They should be broad, general goals, but not easy ones; each should require a lot of thinking and hard work for the team. The goal setters shouldn't be immediately concerned about whether or not the team can actually achieve the goals they set; rather, they should be good, desirable goals that are potentially achievable. One company, a diversified manufacturing concern we helped to develop a system architecture, set these goals for their skunk works team:

- Reduce the total cost of the divisions' direct and indirect nontouch labor by 30%.

- Reduce the full-scale product development schedule spans by 33% and initial production spans prior to full production by 50%.

- Reduce internally generated changes to product definition by 75%.

- Improve the time span for incorporating changes by 50%.

- Improve shop floor direct-touch labor and equipment costs by 25%.

- Reduce the factory work-in-progress inventory by 50%.

DESIGNING A SYSTEM ARCHITECTURE

What is meant by the term system architecture? It's the same process as designing a building. It is a set of design principles that define a relationship of, and interaction between various parts of a system or network of systems, including the organization of functions. System architecture starts with a look at the business as a whole to determine the best way computer technology can be used to support the business and its mission to produce its products better, faster, and cheaper. It's not just looking at the individual functions, but the relationships between all the functions in the business.

The best computer system is a simple computer system. The way to achieve this is to disperse the computer power throughout the organization, moving applications away from the centralized computer and as close to the user as possible. The application strategy I present here is conceptual in nature. The method of implementing it into a system architecture can vary significantly, depending on the nature of the organization and its size.

Most companies don't have an overall system architecture. If they do, it usually is a patchwork of current technologies serving the existing, time-worn approach to applications. The inherent problem with this approach is that it assumes those 10- to 15-year-old applications are satisfactory. Thus, whatever exists becomes, by default, the foundation for further architectural developments.

Any future systems architecture must address three different missions: company needs for system integration of functions and data, organizational or departmental needs for applications that are responsive to their unique requirements, and an application environment that provides individual users with the tools they need to accomplish their work. I call these three levels of systems architecture enterprise level systems, departmental level systems, and ad hoc level systems.

Enterprise Level Systems. These systems maintain the primary management and operational data that cut across the company as a whole. Enterprise level systems should be limited to only processes that integrate key business functions. These systems are both a transporter of data between entities and a maintainer of data that are shared between multiple entities. I view an enterprise level system as the primary means of achieving control between various organizational entities within a business unit. This assures that a common operating philosophy is achieved.

Notice the enterprise level systems normally are not involved in creating data or in determining the manner in which data are used. These activities are best performed at the other two levels of the system hierarchy. By taking this approach, you will greatly reduce the complexity that could result from the mixing of departmental requirements with overall company requirements.

Departmental Level Systems. These are systems that are placed within a departmental or even an organizational unit within a department. Their purpose is to achieve the unique objectives of that entity. For example, consider how different the needs are for processing, managing, and controlling a purchase organization versus a marketing department of a manufacturing organization. Although these various departments may share some data, most of their data processing can be self-contained and should be treated that way. These organizations should have the authority and responsibility to select and implement their own solutions to satisfy individual objectives.

Departmental level computer application processes deal with a variety of situations and special cases, which makes the application software design relatively complex. This complexity should be addressed by those people who are familiar with the functions their departments perform. Further, the definition and implementation of data that is created in the department should be their responsibility as well. The software design and maintenance demands of department application functions are thus isolated from the enterprise level applications.

The system hierarchy concept suggests that large central programming staffs may no longer be required. Some of these people can be moved out to the departments to directly support them. This will give departmental managers not only the responsibility, but also the capability to use their computers as they deem necessary.

Decisions about the number and capacity of the company's computers are more manageable when the system hierarchy is applied. Growth in central capacity is more easily controlled when it is no longer driven by departmental processing demands. Computer resource needs at the departmental level, on the other hand, are influenced mainly by the number of terminals and workstations those computers must support. With a dispersed computing approach, functional managers find that they can decide for themselves whether to increase computer capacity or to buy more terminals because they alone make the terminal response time versus computer cost trade-offs. Their computer cost decisions are not compromised by priority or peak processing demands of other users. Departmental managers are out in a position to better control their work.

Ad Hoc Level Systems. These are not systems in the usual sense of the word, but rather a variety of tools and techniques that let individual users set up their own systems. We have found the most innovation at this level of the architecture, so these systems have the fewest controls and permit the greatest freedom.

Here we find a high proliferation of personal computers, personal productivity software, English-like languages, and 4GLs that tie into relational DBMSs. Often we find software and other capabilities provided by the company's information center, that allow PCs to act as on-line terminals.

Even though I say control is slight at this level, it is important that users adhere to conventions established for the architecture. If the corporate standard is set for IBM PCs and compatibles, or the approved data base software is, say, *dBase III*, then all users must adhere to those products. This facilitates a degree of compatibility for future systems planning, which would be essential if, for example, a local area network were installed. It also means data can easily be distributed and shared. And last but not least, it facilitates learning efforts, because an experienced user can help the novices.

The enterprise, departmental, and ad hoc systems together make up the integrated application environment of the future. The main goal always is to move the technology out. A well-planned, well-executed, dispersed architecture is essential for using computer technology as an enabling device and moving the business aggressively into the future.

- Facilitate improved information exchange standards and practices between the company and vendors, other contractors, and the customers.

Any skunk works team members examining these goals would have no doubt about what the team's objectives were. Equally important, goals like these demand that people look at the computer in an entirely different way: as an enabling technology for achieving the goals set forth.

And with such specific goals the business technology department will grow, not in a purposeless manner, but as an organization with a strong, directed mission.

I learned this lesson the hard way. Back in the mid-1960s, I was asked to head a project to develop an automated production control and material management information system. And that's exactly what I did. Furthermore, when we completed the design we offered it to the president with great pride. We explained how the system was going to reduce inventory by 10%. We showed how the time to build a product would be shortened by five days. Best of all, we said, the new system would produce tons of "information" that would help to manage and control various processes.

After spending more than an hour listening to our presentation, this patient and polite man quietly complimented us on the exquisite design we had created. Then, less quietly, he told us we were not to continue with the project. "If this company is going to be in business five years from now," he said, "we must reduce inventory by 30% and the time it takes to build the product must be reduced by 45 days. That's what we need, and as for the information, if some is available, well it might be nice."

We went away, properly admonished, to reconsider what we had done. Two months later, we went back into the president's office and made quite a different presentation. Our new system was far less complex that the previous one, produced quite a lot less "information," and met every goal he asked for.

Bold, clearly stated business goals are essential prerequisites if the skunk works team is to develop a new computer system architecture. And these goals are not simply to automate a manual function or, worse yet, to create another information system. These goals are to be developed by the skunk works team, working with senior management. During the first two months, the team might meet once a week to agree upon the goals. Once the goals are set, it is the skunk works team's responsibility to develop a strategy for achieving and implementing them.

IT'S A FULL-TIME JOB

While the skunk works team's goals are being outlined, one or two of the team members are permanently assigned the task of building a high-level model of today's business practices. This is referred to as the "as is" architecture model. Several of the business technology department staff may be assigned to this group on a temporary basis to assist in the definition. The "as is" model is necessary as a tool to help the entire team when they meet later, on a full-time basis, to discuss the overall aspects of, and the interactions between, various business functions.

The first month of full-time involvement is hard on the team. It is also a chaotic time. People are getting used to one another and trying to become comfortable away from their normal work. They have to adjust to spending day after day together, often in one room. They want structure and duties, which are not forthcoming unless they themselves create them.

There is also a lot of negativism at first. As the discussions begin and people start making suggestions, you hear of lot of we-can't-do-that or they-won't-let-us or that-can't-be-done comments. These are simply excuses people sometime make up to justify flaws in the system.

This is when the leader begins to make his or her presence felt. The leader has to give the team permission to break rules, knock down defenses, and be innovative and creative. Unfortunately, the leader also becomes the team's scapegoat. It's a tough position to be in and very difficult to do successfully. At times, it's almost like conducting a group therapy session. This is why it is important to have a skilled leader who understands the business and the technology, and who knows how to lead people in this type of process. Often, it helps to bring someone in from outside the corporation. You want to do the skunk works just once, and do it right the first time.

After a while people have vented their anger and the inhibitions are gone. Gradually, they learn that there is no one there to tell them they can't do something, and if they want to do it, they can. The way this usually happens is someone lights a spark and the whole team takes off. The realization sinks in that they are in charge, they are the change agents. People loosen up, and the real communication begins. Now anything is possible. They are on their way to becoming what I call architecturists.

EXPLORING THE TECHNOLOGY

It is important that every member of the skunk works understand computer technology. In the early stage, let them explore computer technology in a free-wheeling fashion. Let them talk about the computers the firm currently uses. Let them talk about trends, new products, and new technologies until they are comfortable with them and understand them.

Often, the business people will be asking most of the questions, and the technology people will be doing most of the answering. Let this happen. They may want to discuss artificial intelligence, relational data bases, parallel processing, or local area networks. Let them go into as much detail as they want about designing, creating, and engineering computer systems, until they are thoroughly satisfied.

At this point, the leader or an appointed architecturist will ask, "If you could, how would you do things differently?" It's at this point that you begin learning how to create the new system architecture. Often the questions has to be asked again and again, punctuated with, "Yes, but what if...." But the answers are invaluable.

One thing you learn during this stage is that most of your firm's departments and organizations are islands of automation. Even though they are connected to the central computer, they don't interact very much. You will learn the business technology department is an island, too; there is very little coordination in either data, functions, or ideas, and even less sharing with other departments.

It's important to keep these discussions moving ahead, for in time the team itself will recognize these islands and will want to overcome the isolation. The leader should continue asking questions about what is there and what isn't, probing until they find out what is missing and what is needed. The skunk works is creating the fertile ground in which to begin growing the new system architecture.

This exploration stage generally takes two months. Once completed, it is time for them to begin conceptualizing and designing the new system architecture.

FROM "AS-IS" TO "TO-BE" ARCHITECTURE

The business people start by discussing business practices. They explain the nature of their work and what they want to accomplish. This is a fairly general discussion. For example, they may say they want to capture these or those data, and combine them with something else. They may say they want to automate a particular function or add a graphics workstation.

The technologist ventures opinions on what can or cannot be done. Gradually, the issues begin sorting themselves out. What emerges is an optimistic vision of the future in which a new, simpler, more flexible computer system seems possible. The technologist sees the promise of computers working more efficiently and harmoniously, systems that can be easily changed when necessary. The business people see the possibility of computers that adapt to the way they do their work, that permit growth and changes in the organization, and that serve the firm's missions and goals.

The subject of these early discussions is what I call the "as-is" and the "to-be" architectures: what we have now and what we want to have tomorrow. The reason for discussing the "as-is" architecture is to create a broader understanding of how the business operates today, and to locate the weak points. The "to-be" architecture is developed into a broad schema of what the future could be if technology is appropriately deployed. Now we have an architecture that marries business goals and computer technology.

This is a significant event at the skunk works. People feel they have accomplished something and have come up with a new, promising, viable alternative to the complex, frustrating rat's nest computer system they now have. It is an achievement, and when it's accomplished, the members have indeed become architecturists.

THE NEW ARCHITECTURE

The next stage is to open discussions about the new architecture. The team must keep its focus sharply on how the new architecture will help the company achieve the goals the skunk works addressed. There is a great deal of enthusiasm and interest at this point. The team feels that it has earned its stripes, so to speak, and now they are ready to design the new system.

The work is broken into two phases. The first phase is developing the architectural concepts and then thinking through their various impacts on the organization. Many issues cannot be resolved, but the important thing is to keep the discussion moving toward a new system architecture.

When the team feels they have a preliminary architecture defined, they should prepare a report for senior management. This should explain how the new system architecture will form a solution to the goals with which the team was charged.

In the second place, the team members must turn their ideas into reality. First, they must study senior management's critique and comments, and locate the plan's strengths and weaknesses. They they must revise and refine the plan, over and over if necessary, until they come up with a legitimate, final architecture.

The final stage of the skunk works involves writing a report to senior management that includes the following items:

The system architecture. This explains the strategy for dispersing computer technology, how the functional or organizational applications will perform, and their relationship to other applications and processes.

Organizational impact. This section deals with the functional realignments within the company that are necessary to fulfill the new architecture's mission. It also includes an impact analysis of these changes.

Computer hardware, software, and communications network architecture. The team must explain how to develop the high-level technical architecture that will support the new system. This portion of the report describes where the computer hardware (whether centralized or dispersed) will be located, the interconnections between the hardware and the communications networks, and identifies the implementation policy and standardization requirements.

Computer technology delivery support requirements. This section deals with the organizational aspects of delivering the new system architecture. It covers what should be centralized, what functions should be dispersed, and how these various functions will interact in the future.

Costs and benefits. This section explains, in broad estimates, the costs associated with achieving the new architecture, the benefits the business stands to gain, and how those benefits relate to the original goals the skunk works was charged with.

Migration plan. Here an overall scenario is developed that recommends how to move from the "as-is" to the "to-be" architecture.

The process is neither complex nor new. It combines knowledge and understanding of today's business, corporate goals, and directions with enabling technologies, and gives us the freedom to choose different approaches to achieving tomorrow's business goals. It's the vehicle for identifying the issues and opportunities related to managing today's business and for allowing us to establish future objectives.

System architecture, once developed, becomes the road map to the future. It provides the framework for sound judgment in the development of capital, human, and technical resources, and for the achievement of a more profitable and competitive enterprise.

PART SIX
ENTREPRENEURSHIP,
CAREERS, GLOBAL ECONOMY

EXERCISE 6.1 SO YOU WANT TO BE YOUR OWN BOSS?

The American Dream is to make it big, and certainly one way is to become an entrepreneur.

There are many approaches one can take towards business success and one popular approach to entrepreneurship is franchising. There are many successful franchise operations; McDonald's, Wendy's, The Olive Garden, Godfather's Pizza, Arby's Roast Beef, Midas Transmission, Fantastic Sam's, and scores of others.

For this exercise select a franchise that interests you and make contact with their headquarters. Companies are particularly helpful with student projects.

Name of organization:

Product/Service:

Territory or geographic area policy:

Franchise fee/royalties:

Initial start-up costs:

Financial assistance:

EXERCISE 6.2 FIND YOUR CAREER

One of the most important activities of a business administration student is deciding on a career. Do you want to go into management? Then you should find what a management trainee does and how long is the training period. Are you interested in personnel management? Or to be a computer sales representative? A stock broker?

Obviously, you have some interests or most certainly an interest. But what about the opportunities? Maybe your field of interest is crowded. If that is the case, salaries will be driven down.

1. Visit your university placement office, check through government publications at your library and scrutinize the want ads of a local or regional metropolitan newspaper.

2. Make a list of three positions which appeal to you and list below:
   (a)
   (b)
   (c)

3. By contacting the Human Resources Department of the organizations with the positions you have listed above fill in the following questions:

4. For each position:

Position	(a)	(b)	(c)
Starting salary: Annual salary:	$ $	$ $	$ $
Specific task:			
Length/type of training program:			
Image of the organization as you perceive it:			

5.   Compare and contrast the three positions and their respective organizations.

6.   Assuming the three positions are available, which one would you choose? Why?

Name: _____

Class: _____

Time/Section: _____

EXERCISE 6.3 GOING INTERNATIONAL

American corporations are moving towards more world-wide trade. Even small American firms are going international. This will necessitate changes in the strategic thinking of many managers.

1.   In your opinion which countries offer the greatest opportunities for American goods?

2.   What American-made products, do you think, would have the best chance of success?

3.   Why?

4.   Select three non-English speaking foreign countries and describe three cultural differences from America:

(a)

(b)

(c)

5.   Would you accept a position in a non-English speaking foreign country?

6.   Why or why not?

Sue Thompkins was on the verge of tears as she left Comstock Cannery, Inc. She had just been fired after three years of employment. She slid into her car and started the motor but her mind was on the confrontation with the personnel manager, Craig Bowers.

Craig called her into his office about an hour ago and didn't waste any time as he opened his discussion, "Sue, I'm sorry but we're going to have to let you go."

Sue was dumbfounded, "You're what? What is this? What have I done?"

Craig cleared his throat, "Well it's like this. You're just too bossy. You upset people. You're not a supervisor, but you act like one.

"Wait a minute," Sue interrupted. "I've been here three years and I know what's going on. All I was doing was helping out."

"Sue, you're not a super. You're not a boss! You have no business telling anyone what to do on the line. You've been warned about this a number of times. As a matter of fact,you jumped on an employee the other day to speed up and he got hurt."

"He was too slow. The whole line was getting clogged up."

"But that's not your business, Sue," said Craig, raising his voice. "And look what happened. He jammed his wrist. He was a new employee and...."

"We get piece-work pay and he was cutting into our wages because he was so slow."

"Look Sue," interjected Craig. "You've been let go. We're going to give you two weeks severance pay and a letter of recommendation that you are a loyal, hard-working employee." Sue clenched her teeth, "I don't think you're bein' fair." Craig stood up from behind his desk. "Fair or not. I'm sorry but we're going to have to let you go."

Sue pulled into the freeway and wondered out loud, "What is Tom going to think?"

Later, Tom drove into the garage wondering, "What kind of left overs is Sue warming up. Nuts, I think I'll charcoal some burgers."

Sue was sitting quietly at the kitchen dabbing her eyes as Tom came through the utility room.

Tom looked at her. "Whattsa' matter? My mother coming for a visit?"

"No, Tom. Your old lady is not coming over. I've just been fired."

"What," exclaimed Tom, "Again?"

"Now, wait a minute. I've held this job for three years."

"Yeah, but you've been fired how many times? Three, four..."

"Four," answered Sue. "Look, Tom, I'm not cut out to work for other people. I'm too demanding. Too bossy. I like to get things done."

"O.K. so what are you goin' to do? We need the money. House payments. Jill and Roy are still in school. I need a new pick-up."

"I know, I know," said Sue tearfully. " But I have an Idea."

"What's that?" asked Tom.

"I want to go into business for myself. I know the food business. I think if I open a small bakery I'll make a go out of it. I have all of my grandma's cookie and cake recipes..."

"Wait a minute," interrupted Tom. Where do you think we're goin' to git the bucks for this?"

"From the bank...like everyone else."

"But you can't just go to the bank and borra' money. You havta' have a plan."

Develop a list of items that Sue needs to consider in developing a business plan for a small bakery.

CASE 6.2 IT'S YOUR CAREER, BUDDY

The snow was slowly melting as the sun peeked through a break in the clouds. It was brisk and cold, but a pleasant day as Pete Minnert hurried to the college placement office.

"Eight weeks and I'll be outta' this damn place," he mumbled to himself, "but I gotta find a job."

Pete strolled into the office and asked the secretary for a copy of the Placement Manual, which is a listing of job opportunities offered by various companies who are going to be recruiting on the campus before graduation.

He flipped to the first page and read IBM's job offering for a sales representative. Then he saw Wal Mart's ad for a management trainee. Next, Citibank was looking for finance majors. Pete kept turning the pages and began to think, "I guess I'll send them all a resume and see what happens. But if I have a choice, which company should I go to work for? He reflected a moment on what Dr. Jackson said last week in his Personnel Management class. He lectured on careers and emphasized to graduates to look for interesting and challenging work in a growth industry. Peter recalled the question Alice, his steady girl friend, asked, "How do you decide on a career and how do you pick a company or companies to apply to?"

Dr. Jackson had replied that you must ask yourself what you want to do with your life? What you really want to do? And are you willing to make sacrifices and accept set backs during your career?

1. What recommendations would you make to Pete?
2. How should Pete justify a low beginning salary with a growth company or a high one with a company in a declining industry?
3. From your experiences and knowledge rank in order five companies on the basis of image, employee relations, salaries and growth potential.
4. Justify your first ranking.

The Japanese guide smiled broadly as he talked about the latest electronic technology and how his firm's chips were going to revolutionize computer usage. "Of course," the guide explained, "this could never be accomplished without our hard-working American employees." Will Whitehead thought he detected a smirk rather than a broad smile, but he and the rest of his management class followed the guide as they toured the new Hitachi plant.

A few hours later Will was sitting down for dinner with his parents and young sister after having driven in from the university 126 miles away.

"Dad," he said, "we toured this new Japanese chip plant, and boy what a neat operation it is."

"How so?" asked his dad.

"Well, it's neat and clean. Everybody wears white uniforms. They have a cafeteria with hot food, a day care center for employees' kids, and everybody works hard. Or it appears that way."

"You know Will, sometimes I wonder who won the war! You see Japanese cars, Japanese VCR's, and now they're buying land and buildings."

"What about us, Dad. Are we doing business in Japan?"

His dad laid his fork down and answered, "We're not playing on a level playing field. Our government believes in free trade but they don't. They protect their industries."

"But," interjected Will, "Why do we see so many Japanese cars on the roads?"

1. Answer Will's question, "Are we doing business in Japan?

2. Respond to the comment about not playing on a level playing field.

3. Discuss Will's last question.

MAKING IT ON MAIN STREET

Mark Russell[1]

**From designer clothes to designer foods, it's still a tough sell
when you're keeper of the shop.**

About 12 years ago, Arnold Wilkerson's ambition to make a living as an actor in New York died a slow death. After brief stints with several regional theaters, Wilkerson, who studied at the Royal Academy of Dramatic Arts in London, found himself spending more time waiting tables and washing dishes in restaurants than he did on stage. As the wait between acting jobs grew longer and longer, he had plenty of time to think about doing something else with his life. "Working in restaurants, I was surprised that the quality of desserts wasn't that good," Wilkerson recalls. He also noticed that New Yorkers loved going to specialty shops. Putting two and two together, Wilkerson hit upon an idea. In 1985 he started the Little Pie Company of the Big Apple, and today he is the only baker in New York specializing in apple-based desserts. Wilkerson's decision to leave the stage has paid off big: This year alone, he has grossed $500,000.

SPECIALITY RETAILING TAKES OFF

With the decline in consumer spending and the increasing diversification of the American population, specialization has become the buzzword of the $1.5 trillion U.S. retailing industry. (Specialization involves capturing a market by selling a specific product, from books to teddy bears, to specific consumers; by contrast, general merchandisers, such as Montgomery Ward and J.C. Penny, carry a variety of items.)

Whereas in the 1950s and '60s shoppers flocked to large department stores, today Americans are opting for speciality shops, which offer them convenience, ambience and an in-depth selection of a particular product.

Although the slice of the retailing pie held by black concerns is small when compared with total U.S. retail sales, black retailers have enjoyed substantial growth. According to the U.S. Census Bureau, between 1977 and 1982 (the last year for which figures are available), the number of black-owned retailers grew from 55,428 to 84,053, and their sales increased from $3.35 billion to $4.12 billion.

An increasing number of black entrepreneurs like Wilkerson are riding the wave of specialization to gain a bigger share of the retailing market. *BE* recently interviewed dozens of these specialty retailers to help shed light on the challenges, successes and problems they face and to learn the secrets of their success. They are a diverse lot, ranging in age from 26 to 45. Some ventured into the retailing world with no prior experience, while others were armed with up to 23 years of business savvy. Despite their differences, they all exhibit the dedication, ingenuity and devotion to customers that are necessary ingredients for making it in specialty retailing.

FINDING A NICHE

Arnold Wilkerson, who developed his interest in food while in Europe, started his business in his cramped one-bedroom Manhattan apartment. "It was difficult getting up at 2 a.m. and slicing apples and rolling crust and doing all the baking in one oven that only held four pies at a time," he recalls. In those days Wilkerson would ride his bicycle or take the subway around Manhattan to drop off his pies at a handful of restaurants. Today he services 50 major restaurants and food stores in the city, including such top-of-the-line concerns as Bloomingdale's and Balducci's. Two years ago, the ex-actor moved the business from his apartment into a 750-square-foot space appropriately located in Manhattan's theater district. Wilkerson is hoping to move into an even large space next year in an effort to double his present sales. His long-term goals include developing a mail-order business to distribute his desserts to customers around the country and running a baking school where he can pass on his craft to minorities.

On the opposite coast from Wilkerson, two black entrepreneurs are also making their mark in specialty retailing. It is somewhat surprising that, until recently, Los Angeles, a city that supposedly has everything, did not have a brownie delivery service. A year ago, Gervel S. Jones, 28, and Bambola Allen-Blaine, 26, decided to change that. Today their company, Bambola's Brownies, has successfully elbowed its way into the corporate gift market. With a list of 50 steady clients, including such major corporations as the Southland Corp. and Unocal, an oil company, it has already grossed $50,000 in it's first year.

Blaine started out by baking brownies as a hobby and giving them to physicians at the Sacramento Community Hospital, where her husband was a resident. The brownies were such a hit that everyone urged her to go into business, and some even promised—but didn't deliver—financial backing. Blaine decided to take a chance and start her own company with her longtime friend Gervel Jones, who quit her job as a marketing representative for IBM one month after the founding of the concern.

"We literally made a pan of brownies, gave out samples and decided to start a business," Jones recalls. "And we've never done any advertising. It's all been word of mouth." Of course, it helps that one of the company's first customers was Scott LaFayette, co-owner of a gourmet bakery in West Los Angeles called Mikey's Cookie Jar. LaFayette was so impressed with the duo's brownies that he not only decided to sell their products in his store and advertise them on his marquee, but he also invited them to use his ovens (Bambola's was then renting oven space at $12.00 an hour).

Neither Jones nor Blaine had any previous retailing experience, but, say Jones, "We knew we had a product that was good. We just had to figure out a way to market it. We realized that we couldn't just put the brownies in Saran Wrap and say, 'Here's your corporate gift,'" she adds. Jones and Blaine researched the L.A. corporate gift market to make sure that their Brownie-Gram was a unique concept, and they also investigated different styles of packaging, deciding on an elegant burgundy-and-gold concept that would be appropriate for any holiday or occasion.

As their client list continues to grow, so does their desire to expand the company. With the help of a minority entrepreneurship program at the University of Southern California, Blaine and Jones are working on a business plan to acquire wholesale space next year.

In 1984, after working for 18 years as an advertising buyer for Brown & Williamson Tobacco Corp., in Louisville, Ky., Agnes Sellers Stewart, 40, decided to start her own business distributing custom-imprinted promotional material. To carve out her territory in this crowded arena, Stewart focused on corporate clients. She used contacts from her corporate days to build up her clientele, which now includes General Electric, South Central Bell and the Ford Motor Co., and this year her company, Incentives Inc., grossed $500,000.

Stewart had some lean days in the beginning, however, and she discovered that leaving the corporate umbrella and running her own shop had its surprises. Clients who once responded promptly to her calls no longer returned them when she ventured out on her own. "In all the excitement of changing careers, I never realized that I wouldn't have my phone calls returned," Stewart says.

So far, Stewart's decision to become her own boss has proven to be a wise move, and to ensure that her company continues to grow, she plans to expand services throughout the southeast region and to increase her sales staff from five to eight. She also plans to completely computerize Incentives' financial information system by January.

USING STORES AS A MARKETING TOOL

Unlike big chains, small retailers do not have huge advertising budgets, and they are forced to rely on less costly marketing tools. For the most part, these retailers depend on the location and unique quality of their stores, as well as the special attention they can give customers, to attract and keep a steady clientele.

In the shop that houses Wilkerson's Little Pie Company, the ovens are up front, in full view of the customers. "I wanted to get a sense of audience participation," Wilkerson says, attributing this need to be on stage to his acting background. "I wanted to create a sense that customers were walking into their own kitchen, and I wanted them to enjoy the smell of the bakery."

"If you don't make people feel welcome," he explains, "they won't come back no matter how good your product is."

Wilkerson has also trained his 13 employees to answer any questions customers might have about the pies. Little Pie's speciality is sour cream apple-walnut cake, but customers can choose from a wide selection of all-natural desserts, including apple cupcakes, apple-topped cheesecakes and apple brownies.

To attract the upscale customers who can afford his designer shoes and clothing, Kham Beard decorated his mini-department store in lavish style. Located on the South Side of Chicago, Kham & Nate's Clothing & Shoes has a marble foyer and marble-trimmed windows, and the men's shoe section boasts parquet floors and Oriental rugs. The store employs 17 workers and enjoys annual sales of more than $2 million. "We have to give our customers the same atmosphere that they would find in bigger stores like Neiman-Marcus," explains Beard, who ventured into retailing 16 years ago with a small shoe store in Chicago's inner city.

Walk into DeForest Y. Sessoms' shoe store and you'll be thoroughly pampered. Located in a new shopping strip in an upscale Louisville Suburb, Sessoms' Ltd., which sells shoes priced from $85 to $700, is decorated with exquisite mirrors, lush pastel carpeting, custom woodwork and sumptuous chairs. According to the 45-year-old Sessoms, walking into his shoe store is like entering a salon. "I devote total attention to my customers," he says. "I like romancing the shoes and the person who's buying the shoes."

PLAYING THE FINANCING GAME

Securing financing, either for start-up or expansion, is no easy task for most black entrepreneurs, and prospective specialty retailers are no exception. In addition to traveling the usual avenues in search of capital, such as banks, venture capital firms and the Small Business Administration, these entrepreneurs must often stake their savings on their dreams.

To finance his store, DeForest Sessoms secured a $120,000 bank loan (putting his home up as collateral) and kicked in $40,000 in personal savings.

Kham Beard promised himself that he would not pour substantial amounts of his personal savings into the business, but that has turned out to be a pipe dream. To infuse Kham & Nate's with necessary capital, he has been required to use his personal savings as well as to "mortgage and remortgage" his personal property. "It's impossible to keep a small company going without putting my income back in," Beard notes.

To secure start-up capital for his Little Pie Company, Arnold Wilkerson took advantage of the services offered by New York University's Urban Development Assistant Corp. (UDAC), a program that helps minorities develop small-business proposals for presentation to banks.

Before approaching financial organizations and venture capitalists, Wilkerson, with UDAC's guidance, spent two years developing his business plan. He finally secured a $60,000 loan from the Bowery Saving Bank of New York.

"The difficulty was in persuading the bank to invest in a company with no background," he explains. "But I finally found a banker who believed in the product."

Except for the New York-based Black Retail Action Group Inc. (BRAG), there are few organizations or groups that provide financial counseling or networking opportunities for black specialty retailers. Though its focus is on helping minority trainees and retailing executives make it in retailing corporations, BRAG, which has a chapter in Washington, D.C., also sponsors business and professional development seminars for entrepreneurs.

According to Robert L. Tinnin, director of the Louisville Minority Business Development Center, there is a great need for groups like BRAG. "Why should a young black retailer have to reinvent the wheel when there are successful black retailers who can pass on that knowledge?" he asks.

In Illinois, a program aimed at helping black retailers get financing is taking shape. The Illinois Association of Women Business Owners, which counts about 50 retailers among its 602 paying members, plans to institute a revolving credit facility for its members sometime next year. Audrey L. Davis, executive director of the group, says that members will be able to tap up to $10,000 for start-up or working capital when the program, which will work closely with banks, becomes operational. Guidelines for determining the eligibility of prospective retailers are still being finalized, according to Davis.

SETTING UP SHOP IN THE SUBURBS

While most black retailers remain in black inner-city communities, specialty retailers who deal in upscale items must follow more affluent consumers, including blacks, to suburbs and malls.

Sessoms found the perfect site for his upscale shoe store in a suburban mall in affluent Jefferson County, Ky., where the median family income is nearly $45,000 and $600,000 homes dot the landscape. Beard decided to locate his business near Chicago's relatively prosperous Chatham neighborhood, where the median income is around $20,000. But black retailers have found that doing business in a mall brings its own problems.

A few years ago, Ernie Oden of Oden & Son's Men's Wear envisioned expanding his one store near downtown Atlanta into a chain. Oden wanted to branch out into the malls surrounding Atlanta but found he couldn't meet the high cost of lease-hold improvements, which require a retailer who leases space in a mall to upgrade the store before buying merchandise to stock it. Oden also notes that the rents for retail stores in desirable malls were prohibitive.

"The bargaining power of black retailers usually only reaches to about $100,000," maintains Oden, a retailer for 23 years. "Some of these mall owners will require you to spend at least $100,000 on lease-hold improvements before you can even buy inventory."

COMPETITION AND CONFLICT IN THE CITY

Black retailers who do business in the inner city often face significant problems of their own, however. They must cope with at least two challenges: how to get black consumers to shop at their stores instead of traveling to discount stores in the suburbs, and how to beat the competition from foreign business owners.

GROWTH OF RETAIL BUSINESS

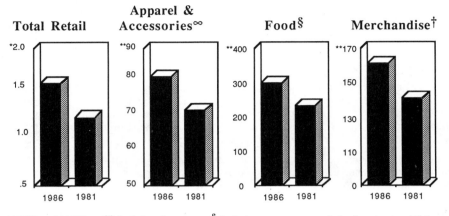

* Trillion ** Billion ∞ Includes shoe store. § Includes grocery stores, bakeries, meat and fish market.
† Includes department and variety stores.
Source: The Dept. of Commerce Bureau of the Census.

The recent influx of Arab, Asian and Oriental retailers into black communities has sparked dissent—sometimes violence—in many major U.S. cities. In New York, Atlanta, Chicago, Detroit, and Washington, D.C., black retailers complain that competition from so-called outsiders often sparks a price war in which discounts flourish and tempers flare, and the problem is spreading to other cities as well.

In Cleveland, for instance, Ahmed Salti, an Arab who emigrated from Jerusalem in the late '60s, and other Middle Eastern immigrants have acquired many businesses in predominantly black neighborhoods. By offering lower prices and using other promotional devices, they have successfully lured customers away from black mom-and-pop stores.

But Salti, who runs a small market called Joe's Square Deal in the Glenville area of Cleveland, bristles at the suggestion that Arab businesses unfairly take profits away from more established black concerns. "Sometimes we lower the price on one or more items, but in most cases we just operate better than [black merchants] do," he insists. Of course, customers have the right to shop wherever they wish, but many black retailers believe blacks should remain loyal to them.

DEALING WITH SUPPLIERS

Black specialty retailers must also deal with suppliers, the bane of many retailers, according to those interviewed for this article. Ernie Oden, for instance, recalls that when he first started his business suppliers often forced him to pay cash for merchandise that was delivered to his clothing store, which grossed about $300,000 last year. "When you have only $50,000 to start a business, that can go pretty quickly," he notes. By paying on time and calling on the same suppliers repeatedly, however, Oden eventually persuaded his suppliers to extend credit to him.

Agnes Sellers Stewart, president of Incentives, Inc., employed a similar strategy. She initially prepaid for supplies and materials for her business and then reordered from the same suppliers, paying within the 30-day credit period. After establishing good relationships with these concerns, she used them as credit references when she needed to approach new suppliers.

"It took about one year to get into a normal pattern in which I would place an order and get billed for it, rather than prepaying or giving cash on delivery for supplies," Stewart recalls. Today suppliers rarely request advance payments from her.

GOING FOR IT!

To be sure, the obstacles to opening one's own retail shop are numerous. The hours are long, profit is uncertain, especially in the early years, and raising capital is always a daunting prospect. In addition, some retailing experts predict that the current wave of specialization may end soon.

However, despite this gloomy forecast, retailing mavens such as J.J. Thomas of BRAG and Audrey Davis of the Illinois Association of Women Business Owners are bullish on the future of black retailers, especially those in the inner cities. "The inner cities of places such as St. Louis, Cleveland and Louisville are starting to rejuvenate themselves, luring back consumers, new vitality and dollars," says Thomas.

"One way to capital self-sufficiency is to own something," Thomas continues. "I've seen more blacks [who were] willing to take a chance [on retailing] in the past ten years than I saw in the previous ten."

Perhaps Arnold Wilkerson's advice to prospective black specialty retailers more dramatically captures the inner passion of that quintessentially American drive to become your own boss: "If you have something you believe in," he says, "go for it!" The current trend toward specialization has given many black entrepreneurs a golden opportunity to do just that.

SO YOU WANT TO OPEN YOUR OWN SHOP

Of course, there are no guaranteed formulas for success in any business venture, but if the desire to open your own shop is too strong to resist, here are some basic ground rules you should keep in mind.

Making it in specialty retailing means finding, developing and defending a niche for your product, defining your customer profile and selecting a good location with lots of customer traffic. That means devoting some of your time to research. You can find statistics on local businesses and consumer markets at the public library, and if there is a minority business development center in your area, you can tap their elaborate network of demographic and income statistics on various regions of the United States.

Visit retailing outlets much like the one you plan to start and talk with the owners, employees and even customers to get a sense of the business.

The biggest hurdle for most retailers is securing start-up capital. Be sure to have a professional business plan ready before setting out to obtain a loan, and, of course, tap all the usual sources, such as banks, venture capital funds, the Small Business Administration, etc.

Unless you can afford to hire skilled professionals to help you run your business, be ready to assume responsibility for all phases of the shop, including displaying the merchandise, selling and, in some cases, cleaning up when the store closes.

A good alliance with suppliers is vital to the smooth operation of any retailing outlet. Unless you have the money to prepay for merchandise or to pay cash on delivery, you will need to establish credit with your suppliers. One way of doing this is to include a detailed credit history with your first order.

Secure enough financing to see you through the long haul. Experts warn that you should not expect to make a profit for at least three years.

Proper pacing, a long-term outlook and the realization that only you control your career are the basis of successful career marketing.

Who controls your career: your company, your parents, the government, your spouse or your peers? Hopefully, you and you alone are in control of your career.

Frequently, people talk about how a difficult boss held them back or how they've never been very good at networking. Such statements only shift the blame for not reaching career goals to others or to "inherent" traits.

In the short run, a person can be the victim of a bad organization or a bad boss. Also, there may be good reasons why a person could not take the proactive step that would help propel his or her career. In the long run, however, there are simply no excuses. You are in control of your career; it does not control you.

Professional speaker Joe Charbonneau says, "Of all the people who will never leave me, I am the only one." This statement means that you will be the only constant factor in all of your career experiences, regardless of where you go, for whom you work, the tasks you undertake, the effort you apply, the hardships you enjoy.

Looked at another way, if you're just going to read this article and say "Yeah, that sounds good," and forget about it, then you are deciding to continue to take no action. On the other hand, if you make a commitment to take action and follow through, you will become living, visible proof that you are the captain of your own ship.

EARLY START

The earlier you set goals, make a commitment and take action, the greater the long-term results. Don't bemoan the fact that you never set goals previously, or you wasted the last three years in a dead-end job. Today is the future we were thinking about six years ago. That time has come and gone. Will your situation in six years be supported by action that you initiated today?

Unfortunately, contemporary society propels us faster and faster toward immediate gratification. Long-term planning, goal setting, sacrifice and patience seem scarce among a generation that wants to "have it all" and "do it all" right now.

The contact you made at your professional association meeting may not yield a job possibility for a few months, and additional time may pass before you are invited for an interview. The groups you called to arrange speaking engagements may not return your call for several weeks or months and may not schedule a date until the middle of next year.

The American Marketing Association's board of directors recently established a new definition of marketing as "the process of planning and executing the conception, pricing,

---

[1] Reprinted by permission, *Management World*, September/October, 1987, pp. 6-7.

promotion and distribution of ideas, goods and services to create exchanges that satisfy individual and organizational objectives."

Applied on an individual level, marketing could be defined as the process of planning and executing how all your ideas and services will be priced, promoted and distributed to create exchanges that satisfy your goals and serve others.

The people you want to reach, whether they're your coworkers, your boss or an organizational president, should be viewed as distinct target audiences that require different approaches and strategies.

LONG HAUL

Few career marketing activities offer immediate payoffs. Successful career marketers realize that careers have a long life. You must balance short-term and long-term activities to handle what must be done today and facilitate what you do tomorrow.

By age 45, most of us have had nearly eight different employers. The number of bosses to whom we report, the number of clients, customers and coworkers with whom we interact and the number of employees we supervise in our careers is staggering. The number of reports, letters and other written materials we are likely to prepare is also overwhelming.

The career professional who views his or her career not simply as what is going to happen today, next week, next month or next year, but as a long, unfolding journey, has an edge over his or her colleagues who don't hold the same view.

Sharon Louise Connelly, Ph.D., in her forthcoming book *"Work Spirit:" Recapturing the Vitality of Work*, observes that "individuals demonstrating work spirit have a sense that everything that they have ever done contributes to what they are doing now, a feeling of doing something of value and making contributions, a sense of connection with people in the universe and a feeling of doing work that they are meant to do."

Preparing for the long haul means assembling the necessary resources, acquiring the proper education or training and making contact with key individuals in your field. Marketing your career takes time. You must develop your skills and contacts with persistence and patience. In most careers, there is a certain amount of "grunt" work that must be done before a person can actually begin moving up in the field.

PROPER PACING

To prepare for the long haul, you must treat and maintain your body like a well-oiled machine. Those who whoop it up until 2:00 a.m. every weekend, burn the candle at both ends and run themselves ragged around the clock may accomplish significant short-term gains, but they will undermine their growth in the long run.

For every man or woman who made it to the top of his or her profession and became a recognized expert or generated great wealth, there are 50 or more equally talented, motivated and ambitious others who lacked the ability to pace themselves. They sought to condense years of studied effort into a short period of manic activity and expected the same return. We have all witnessed the supernova effect, when someone joins the organization, makes awesome strides in a short time and then miscalculates miserably, abruptly leaving the organization or retreating to a quiet corner.

FACING REALITY

The closer we can market our careers in accordance with reality, the greater the return we'll see for our efforts. The great salesman and motivational speaker Earl Nightingale says that "it is easier to adjust ourselves to the hardships of a poor living that it is to adjust ourselves to the hardships of making a better one." This reality applies to individuals, communities, regions or even entire countries. It also helps explain why, when we attempt to move from where we are, we often end up settling for where we started from. How do we justify procrastinating on our own advancement? How do we justify not making the effort to get what we want or achieve what we want to achieve?

Barring outrageous misfortune, for most people, life is a self-fulfilling prophecy. Playing it safe, not taking a risk, not going the extra mile or accepting a poor living becomes our fate. The longer we stay in that mode, the harder it is to get out. The only way out is through action.

In many ways, marketing is like life. It seems that those who get ahead in life are natural born marketers. Elected politicians, your company's president and all those who society respects mastered the ability to successfully and visibly serve a constituency, shareholders or other target market.

Whether you were a marketing major in college or have never read one word on the topic, you can become a successful career marketer. Implementing strategies requires no marketing background, or even an aptitude for it. What you need is the ability to set goals to which you are committed and the desire to vigorously pursue them.

THE INTERNATIONALIZATION OF BUSINESS: ONE COMPANY'S RESPONSE

B. Joseph White[1]

My focus today is on two topics: What the emergence of a global marketplace has meant to Cummins as a manufacturing company and the lessons we have learned in responding to the internationalization of business.

First I need to say a few words about Cummins Engine Company. Cummins is an independent manufacturer of diesel engines and related products and services. Although you probably don't realize it, you have a "passing" acquaintance with Cummins, since we power about 60% of the big trucks on U.S. highways. We are a $2.5 billion company with 22,000 employees worldwide, headquartered in Columbus, Indiana. Our sales mix is 70% U.S. business and 30% international, with the international portion growing steadily. Twenty-eight percent of our people live and work outside the United States, and 21% of our material sourcing in the engine business is done outside the United States as measured by value. In our newer engines, the percentage is much higher—about 50%.

Cummins has had a worldwide presence since World War II, when Cummins-powered trucks—such as Patton's Red Ball Express that rolled across Europe in 1944—supplied the Allied military campaigns around the world. After the war, equipment was left behind for local salvage and reuse of the vehicle or engine and, as a result, we had to establish a parts distribution and service network to serve these customers. Between 1950 and 1975, U.S. domestic demand was explosive and our major international activities were limited to a few countries such as Mexico, Canada, the United Kingdom, and India.

The emergence of the global marketplace as a center-ring business issue occurred for us in the latter part of the 1970s. There were four key reasons for this, which meant new opportunities and new competition for us.

First, we began to look in earnest for major new market opportunities outside the United States. Domestic GNP growth, industrialization, and infrastructure building slowed during that period, and in the developed world we began facing a battle for market share that we were determined to win. But we believed then, and do today, that newly industrializing countries (NICs) are the best long-term bet for engine market growth. Those countries have enormous infrastructure and transportation needs, and with their planned economies they often prefer to select a "partner technologist" in each key industry. With so many of our eggs in the diesel basket, we decided that it is imperative to be on the inside of these controlled markets. As the leading diesel technologist, we've won more than our share: Mexico and China are good examples.

Second, we are constantly seeking high-quality, low-cost sources for forgings, castings, and machined components. This is because product cost reduction is one of our highest priorities. In the past, our supply base was almost exclusively in the United States, the United Kingdom, and more recently, Japan. International sources are more important to us now, especially the NICs.

---

[1] Reprinted by permission, B. Joseph White *Academy of Management Executive*, February, 1988, pp. 29-32.

The NICs will grow in importance as their industrial capacity expands beyond the ability to serve only their domestic manufactures, and they can supply us in the volumes we require.

Third, the worldwide diesel engine industry is rationalizing. This is the process of taking out excess and obsolete capacity, much of which was built in the 1960s and 1970s in anticipation of continued rapid economic growth. Current estimates place worldwide diesel capacity at roughly half the current annual demand and production. Rationalization is a worldwide process, and it is vital for us to emerge as a winner.

Fourth, in the early 1980s, we and our U.S. OEM (Original Equipment Manufacturers) customers felt for the first time the hot breath of foreign competition in "our" market—the U.S. heavy truck and equipment market. The competition came first from the European truck manufacturers like Volvo and Mercedes Benz, then from Japanese manufacturers like Komatsu and Hino, who offered both complete vehicles or pieces of equipment, or loose engines. Whatever the source and the form of the foreign competition, if successful it would mean the same thing for Cummins: The sale of fewer engines and service parts.

These four conditions—new markets, new sources of supply, rationalization, and new competition—thrust upon us the need to manage with a far more global perspective and with much greater international activity than ever before. I want to be specific about what that has meant for us.

BUILDING A DEFENSE

The linchpin in our response to these new conditions has been mounting a successful campaign against the threat to our home market. You have heard the saying, "The best defense is a good offense." Well, we decided that the best offense starts with a good defense. Without a successful defense against the new competition, availing ourselves of the opportunities in the emerging global marketplace would be just a pipe dream. A successful attack on our strong home market position would be the business equivalent of choking off our carotid artery. We had watched with deep concern throughout the 1970s as foreign competition won nearly 100% of the U.S. motorcycle market, 30% of the U.S. auto market, and a big chunk of the domestic steel market, all in about ten years. In our view, by the way, share gains by the new competition were mostly won fair and square, with better products, better quality, better prices, and better responsiveness to the customer. These industries are awfully close to our own. We vowed we wouldn't let it happen to us. So we mounted our defense.

Cummins' defense against the threat of foreign competition has involved working hard on three things: product, price and costs, and performance. In the phrase "foreign competition" we have learned that the more important word by far is "competition." This is a point that is frequently overlooked. Focus on competition evokes the proper response by a company: working to improve the business basics that strengthen the bond with the company's existing customers and enable it to attract new customers anywhere in the world. Focus on the word "foreign" (or even on its more benign cousin, "international") evokes emotional and sometimes ugly responses by those threatened. For example, we have all observed the overwhelming temptation to dive for the escape hatch of protectionism when foreign competition begins to bite. Another example: In the early days of talking to our workforce about the threat of foreign competition, we were happy to see the pride evidenced by the American flag that was hung over the assembly line by people in the plant. But we were not happy to see a few crude and chauvinistic cartoons pinned on bulletin boards around the company. We made it clear that this was not acceptable at Cummins. We also got our response to the new competitive challenge on a constructive footnote by projecting to our people how effective we would be in the global market after we got ourselves in shape to deal with this new challenge.

Getting in shape meant working on the variables of product, prices and costs, and performance. We spent nearly a billion dollars on product development between 1980 and 1985.

This was triple the company's market value in 1980. Our goal was to develop the broadest, freshest, best performing diesel engine line in the world.

Concerning prices and costs, we found that the competition was offering prices as much as 30% lower than ours. We decided to meet world price levels, whatever they were, to maintain and increase market share in advance of our known ability to operate profitably at those levels. We essentially swore off price increases five years ago and we have since swallowed inflation and lowered prices on nearly every engine line.

As for performance, we engaged employees in a campaign called "New Standards of Excellence." We discovered that various new competitors had better quality, lower costs, higher productivity, shorter lead times for new product introduction, and so on. As an industry leader, this was a threat not only to our business: it was also an unacceptable affront to our pride. So we set out to fix it. We put time boundaries around the "New Standards of Excellence" campaign with something called the "Thirty-Month Sprint." We developed specific goals in the areas of quality, cost and delivery, and broke them down and allocated them to work groups throughout the company. Jim Henderson, our president, reported on our progress to all employees in his quarterly videotape message.

Our goals were set after examining our global competition very carefully—up close and personal, as ABC Sports would say. Henderson and many others walked shop floors, technical centers, and offices in Europe and Japan. In Henderson's reports to employees (which were, incidentally, not very welcomed at first), he specified what we needed to do to defend our current businesses. He also pointed out the great opportunities that would be ours in the global marketplace with a premier product line, world competitive prices, and world-class cost, quality, and delivery performance. This was the way in which we all began to recognize that the actions required to mount a strong defense would position us to exploit the opportunities—in new markets, in new supply sources, and in winning out in the worldwide industry rationalization process.

Our response to the competitive threat to our domestic market position was a catalyst for us to exploit these international opportunities. For example, the premier product line developed largely to help us strengthen our domestic position, and world competitive prices established primarily to keep our foreign competition have helped us win a greater share of international business than ever before. This is true in both open markets and in the newly industrializing countries selecting or renewing their partner technologists.

Another example of this catalyst effect is in supply. What has led us to search the world for high-quality, low-cost sources of supply is not an abstraction called "the global market." It is the cost and quality elements of the New Standards of Excellence/Thirty-Month Sprint program through which our Supply people have been assigned specific CQD goals for each component for the engine. These goals, combined with encouragement from top management, have taken them around the world in search of better sources of supply. Important entry points and staging areas in this effort have been our own operations and international affiliate relationships with countries like Brazil, Mexico, India and China.

There is one last example of how the threat of new competition served as a catalyst to exploit international opportunities. We knew we had to improve the way we were managing to achieve the results we needed. So we identified the small number of companies in the world whose operations we most respected and set out to learn as much from them as we could. Several were in the United States, and several were in Japan and Western Europe. I recall well our valuable experience with one Japanese manufacturer with whom we have a long and mutually respectful relationship. As our concern turned to improving the way we operated, our top people talked at length with their top people about operational management and how to improve. We toured their facilities. One hundred of our senior people spent several days in an education session with their top quality person, himself an early student of the renowned Ishikawa. Of course, we reciprocated. There was real learning and a lot of it. Most of what we learned could not be adopted directly—our culture and people are very different—but most of it could be adapted and integrated into our approach to operations improvement. This we have done.

The result of all this is that we have achieved what we intended. We have lost no domestic business to foreign competition. Our domestic market share has grown, as has our success in international markets. The slippage we have experienced is in the schedule of actual accomplishment versus plan. But our plan was exceedingly ambitious.

SOME CONCLUDING OBSERVATIONS

I am concerned at this point that I may have created a picture of a "painless victory." This would be very wrong. First, it is never wise to declare victory in business for it is the game—or war—that can be won but never finished. The toll on short-term profitability associated with new product introductions and price reductions has been substantial. The profit impact bottomed out three quarters ago and we have been recovering. Our people have been stretched, pulled, at times really shaken up in trying to meet all these challenges; facilities have been closed as operations were consolidated and many jobs were lost despite our successful efforts to create new ones. But through it all, the Cummins family pulled together when the chips were down. We have experienced, and managed, a full range of human emotions during these years. They include initial denial of the reality of the threat, anger at the news and its bearers, discouragement at times about our ability to prevail, and hope and encouragement as we made progress. There have been a lot of lows and highs. This process, of course, continues.

I want to conclude by citing some observations from this experience I have described.

First, although our competition in the global market is formidable, U.S. companies can hold their own provided we have the proper strategy, a dedication to operations improvement—which mean major change—and plain old grit and determination. What is also required is a longer-range view of the business on the part of management: An excessive focus on quarter-to-quarter operations can be quite destructive in trying to improve operations. Many foreign competitors have a considerably greater commitment to, and their home countries also place a higher value on, full employment and employment stability than we do. While this can be a burden and a competitive disadvantage, we have found that companies that treat labor as a fixed cost more than we do can be both very creative in how to use it and very aggressive in their pricing to sell products to gain volume and cover those fixed costs.

Second, in addition to a long view and staying power, participation in the world economy requires tolerance and even enjoyment of complex relationships. It is not unusual for a single international business relationship to involve licensing, partnership, one-way or cross-supply agreements, and elements of both cooperation and competition between and among the principals. These relationships also require great flexibility because almost everything in them changes, and does as frequently.

Third, in the global marketplace there is no substitute for getting the business basics right: product, price, and performance. There is also no substitute for soaking up the best ideas, innovations, and practice, both technically and operationally, wherever they are to be found. We have found many, many of those beyond U.S. borders.

Fourth, it is clear that international competition has raised the standards of performance in quality, cost, productivity, product introduction time, and smooth, flowing operations. What is required of managers in the face of these higher standards is not defensiveness or excuses (a normal tendency), but acceptance of the new reality and a resolve to learn better ways and implement them. The underlying attitude that is required is belief in the importance and value of continuous improvement. This is the most powerful change for many of us in American business because if you think you're the best, why bother to improve? However, I can assure you that a company managed in line with the principles of continuous improvement is eventually going to beat out the company that is always confident that it's the best.

Fifth, with respect to business education, I think it is vital to add to the current curriculum new ways of thinking and operating that are necessary to manage effectively in the global marketplace. To get the ball rolling, I suggest (1) whetting students' appetites for the job of operational management (versus financial or advisory services), (2) developing an understanding of continuous improvement, (3) exploring the wide range of business opportunities available in the world economy, and (4) increasing understanding of cultural and human differences.

Regarding the implications of the internationalization of business for human resource management, there are three points I want to make. First, I believe that while the central principles of effective management and people development are universal, their cultural adaptation is exceedingly important. Second, on the much discussed subject of international staffing, we have found few generalizations that work. The most important finding may be that talent and qualification for the job are far more important than nationality. For example, we have an American running our Brazilian operation, joint U.S./Mexican leadership in our Mexican affiliate, a Briton running our U.K. operations, a U.S. national running a major subsidiary in the United Kingdom, a Luxembourg national running our European operations, and an Indian managing our affiliate operation in India. This is an eclectic group, chosen first for their capability and only second for their nationality.

Third, for four years we have had underway a major intervention intended to increase our people's understanding of human diversity and ways to capitalize on it for the benefit of our business. We got into it because of my belief that it is the most positive and constructive foundation for our affirmative action efforts. Interestingly, our people in international operations have really grabbed the program and run with it. It is a very powerful process that can help turn the great diversity of U.S. society and of international business people into a formidable asset for productivity improvement and business effectiveness. It also contributes to the dignity experienced by employees who have been viewed as "different" within the corporation.

In closing, I want to share with you a view I hold strongly about national policy and economic competitiveness. There are two areas that require urgent attention. One is national economic policy and the other is the quality of education. Taking a long view, economic policies that discourage savings and productive investment, encourage excessive borrowing and consumption, and produce enormous budget deficits that are then heavily funded by borrowing from foreign lenders are not supportive of the national goal of restoring our industrial competitiveness. On the matter of education, I firmly believe that the underpinning of a company's, or a nation's, ability to compete is the capability, the knowledge and skills, of its people. Twenty-three million U.S. adults are functionally illiterate. The U.S. literacy rate is 49th of the 158 countries in the United Nations. Our high school dropout rate is a tragedy and a disgrace. The number of required school days, recently raised to 180 in Indiana (which is about the national average), compares with 240 in Japan. This is powerful evidence that our commitment to excellence in education, and therefore to long-term economic development and competitiveness, is inadequate.